ON FREUD'S
"ON BEGINNING THE TREATMENT"

CONTEMPORARY FREUD
Turning Points and Critical Issues

Series Editor: Gennaro Saragnano

IPA Publications Committee

On Freud's "Analysis Terminable and Interminable"
    edited by Joseph Sandler

On Freud's "On Narcissism: An Introduction"
    edited by Joseph Sandler, Ethel Spector Person, Peter Fonagy

On Freud's "Observations on Transference-Love"
    edited by Ethel Spector Person, Aiban Hagelin, Peter Fonagy

On Freud's "Creative Writers and Day-Dreaming"
    edited by Ethel Spector Person, Peter Fonagy, Sérvulo Augusto Figueira

On Freud's "A Child Is Being Beaten"
    edited by Ethel Spector Person

On Freud's "Group Psychology and the Analysis of the Ego"
    edited by Ethel Spector Person

On Freud's "Mourning and Melancholia"
    edited by Leticia Glocer Fiorini, Thierry Bokanowski, Sergio Lewkowicz

On Freud's "The Future of an Illusion"
    edited by Mary Kay O'Neil and Salman Akhtar

On Freud's "Splitting of the Ego in the Process of Defence"
    edited by Thierry Bokanowski and Sergio Lewkowicz

On Freud's "Femininity"
    edited by Leticia Glocer Fiorini and Graciela Abelin-Sas

On Freud's "Constructions in Analysis"
    edited by Thierry Bokanowski and Sergio Lewkowicz

On Freud's "Beyond the Pleasure Principle"
    edited by Salman Akhtar and Mary Kay O'Neil

On Freud's "Negation"
    edited by Mary Kay O'Neil and Salman Akhtar

ON FREUD'S
"ON BEGINNING THE TREATMENT"

Edited by

Christian Seulin & Gennaro Saragnano

Series Editor

Gennaro Saragnano

CONTEMPORARY FREUD
Turning Points and Critical Issues

KARNAC

First published in 2012 by
Karnac Books Ltd
118 Finchley Road
London NW3 5HT

Copyright © 2012 to Christian Seulin and Gennaro Saragnano
for the edited collection, and to the individual authors for their
contributions.

British Library Cataloguing in Publication Data

A C.I.P. for this book is available from the British Library

ISBN 978–1–78049–026–7

Edited, designed and produced by The Studio Publishing Services Ltd
www.publishingservicesuk.co.uk
e-mail: studio@publishingservicesuk.co.uk

Printed in Great Britain

www.karnacbooks.com

CONTENTS

CONTEMPORARY FREUD
 IPA Publications Committee   vii

ACKNOWLEDGEMENTS   ix

EDITORS AND CONTRIBUTORS   xi

Introduction
 Christian Seulin   1

PART I
"On beginning the treatment" (1913c)
 Sigmund Freud   7

PART II
Discussion of "On beginning the treatment"   31

1 "On beginning the treatment": a contemporary view
 Theodore Jacobs   33

2 From past to present: what changes have occurred
     in the acceptance of the conditions for psychoanalytic
     treatment and its setting?
     Marie-France Dispaux   42

3 Transference and associativity, psychoanalysis,
     and its debate with suggestion
     René Roussillon   57

4 The person of the analyst and role of intersubjectivity
     in beginning the treatment
     Lewis Kirshner   77

5 Swimming one's way up to the fundamental rule
     Antonino Ferro   88

6 How Emmy silenced Freud into analytic listening
     Patrick Miller   103

7 The work that leads to interpretation
     Rogelio Sosnik   120

8 Interpretative function:
     two characters in search of meaning
     Alice Becker Lewkowicz & Sergio Lewkowicz   137

9 How to modify the unconscious:
     a transformational–modular approach and its
     implications for psychoanalytic psychotherapy
     Hugo Bleichmar   149

10 Conflicting forces: on the beginning of the treatment
      Norberto C. Marucco   164

REFERENCES   181

INDEX   195

CONTEMPORARY FREUD

IPA Publications Committee

This significant series was founded by Robert Wallerstein and subsequently edited by Joseph Sandler, Ethel Spector Person, Peter Fonagy, and lately by Leticia Glocer Fiorini. Its important contributions have always greatly interested psychoanalysts of different latitudes. It is therefore my great honour, as the new Chair of the Publications Committee of the International Psychoanalytical Association, to continue the tradition of this most successful series.

The objective of this series is to approach Freud's work from a present and contemporary point of view. On the one hand, this means highlighting the fundamental contributions of his work that constitute the axes of psychoanalytic theory and practice. On the other, it implies the possibility of getting to know and spreading the ideas of present psychoanalysts about Freud's *oeuvre*, both where they coincide and where they differ.

This series considers at least two lines of development: a contemporary reading of Freud that reclaims his contributions, and a clarification of the logical and epistemic perspectives from which he is read today.

Freud's theory has branched out, and this has led to a theoretical, technical, and clinical pluralism that has to be worked through. It has therefore become necessary to avoid a snug and uncritical coexistence of concepts in order to consider systems of increasing complexities that take into account both the convergences and the divergences of the categories at play.

Consequently, this project has involved an additional task—that is, gathering psychoanalysts from different geographical regions representing, in addition, different theoretical stances, in order to be able to show their polyphony. This also means an extra effort for the reader that has to do with distinguishing and discriminating, establishing relations or contradictions that each reader will have to eventually work through.

Being able to listen to other theoretical viewpoints is also a way of exercising our listening capacities in the clinical field. This means that the listening should support a space of freedom that would allow us to hear what is new and original.

In this spirit we have brought together authors deeply rooted in the Freudian tradition and others who have developed theories that had not been explicitly taken into account in Freud's work.

"On beginning the treatment" (1913) is one of the most important of Freud's technical articles, a theme he examined between 1904 and 1918. This text, which sets out the basis of the treatment and the conditions of psychoanalysis, still provides a solid reference for the analytic practice. Far from a group of rigid rules, Freud spoke of the technique as an art, thinking always of the singularity of each case, even if the fundamental methods of free association and suspended attention specify the psychoanalytical method that differentiates it from the suggestion.

In this book, ten eminent psychoanalysts, coming from different schools of psychoanalytic thought and from different geographical areas, confront the contemporary technical proposals to the Freudian precepts. The book re-examines, in the light of the latest advances in the analytic practice, such important questions as: the conditions of starting an analysis today; transference and associativity; the play of the person of the analyst and intersubjectivity; the fundamental rule enunciation in contemporary practice; the conditions and functions of the interpretation; and the energetic drives in action during the treatment.

Special thanks are therefore due to the contributors to this volume which enriches the Contemporary Freud series.

Gennaro Saragnano
Series Editor
Chair, IPA Publications Committee

ACKNOWLEDGEMENTS

First of all we wish to thank very much all the distinguished colleagues who have enriched this volume with their most valuable and appreciated contributions. It has been a pleasure to share with them all the efforts for making this book possible. All the members of the Publications Committee of the International Psychoanalytical Association have always given us their support and guidance. We also want to express our gratitude to our assistant at Broomhills, Rhoda Bawdekar, for her irreplaceable work in the editing process, and to Oliver Rathbone of Karnac Books for his continuous helpfulness.

Christian Seulin & Gennaro Saragnano

EDITORS AND CONTRIBUTORS

Alice Becker Lewkowicz is psychiatrist for adults, children, and adolescents, and associate member of the Porto Alegre Psychoanalytic Society (SPPA) where she develops activities with the community, particularly with teachers of small children. She is a professor and supervisor for Psychoanalytic Psychotherapy of Children and Adolescents in the Psychiatry Department at the Medical School of the Federal University of Rio Grande do Sul. Along with Sergio Lewkowicz, she has received the Fabio Leite Lobo prize for the best paper of full members during the Brazilian Congress of Psychoanalysis in 2011.

Hugo Bleichmar, MD, is a member of the Argentine Psychoanalytic Society (IPA) and Director of the Postgraduate Program in Psychoanalytic Psychotherapy (Pontificia Comillas University, Madrid, Spain). He is also the editor of the Journal *Aperturas Psicoanalíticas*. His main interest is to develop a multidimensional model for psychopathology to describe the psychological pathways through which different components combine in a dynamic interaction, serially and in parallel, to generate subtypes of depression, narcissistic disorders, pathological mourning, and affective dysregulation. The implication of this approach is that if there are subtypes of the above mentioned psychopathological conditions, each of them needs to be specifically targeted. Psychoanalytic interventions that are appropriate for a particular case can be iatrogenic for others.

Marie-France Dispaux is a training analyst member of the Belgian Society of Psychoanalysis, and she was President of the Society, President of the Training Committee, and Director of the Belgian Review. Currently, she is European Representative at the IPA Board. She wrote essentially on the processes of transformation in the "difficult cases". She also developed a reflection on the psychoanalytical training, in particular on the supervision.

Antonino Ferro is a training and supervising analyst of the Italian Psychoanalytic Society, and IPA and APsaA member. He has published several books translated in many languages, the last are *Mind Works* and *Avoiding Emotions, Living Emotions* published by Routledge. In 2007 he was selected to be a recipient of the Mary S. Sigourney Award. He also was *Editor for Europe* of the International Journal of Psychoanalysis until September 2008, was elected (2006) member of CAPSA (Analytic Practice and Scientific Activities Committee), member of the EPF Program Committee, and Chair (2007) of Sponsoring Committee for the Turkish Provisional Society of Psychoanalysis.

Theodore Jacobs is clinical professor at the Albert Einstein College of Medicine, training and supervising analyst of the New York Psychoanalytic Institute and the Institute for Psychoanalytic Education, and Past President of the Association for Child Psychoanalysis. He is also the author of *The Use of the Self: Countertransference and Communication in the Analytic Situation*.

Lewis A. Kirshner, MD, is a clinical professor in Psychiatry at Harvard Medical School, Director of Psychodynamic Training in the Harvard South Shore Residency Program, training and supervising analyst of the Boston Psychoanalytic Institute, and was a Fulbright senior research scholar 2010–2011 at the Department of Psychoanalysis and Clinical Consulting, University of Ghent, Belgium.

Sergio Lewkowicz is psychiatrist, training and supervising analyst of the Porto Alegre Psychoanalytic Society (SPPA) where he is currently the Director of Training. He is professor and supervisor of Psycho-analytic Psychotherapy in the Psychiatry Department at the Medical School of the Federal University of Rio Grande do Sul and a member of the Programme Committee of the 43rd Congress of the IPA in New Orleans (2004). He was a former member of the Publications Committee of the IPA (2001–2009) and former Editor of the Psychiatry Journal of Rio Grande do Sul and also former President of the Psychiatry Association of Rio Grande do Sul. He has published and co-edited several papers and books on psychoanalytic technique and theory. Along with Alice Becker Lewkowicz, he has received the Fabio Leite Lobo prize for the best paper of full members during the Brazilian Congress of Psychoanalysis in 2011.

Norberto Marucco is a full member in didactic function of the Argentine Psychoanalytic Association and a professor of the Institute of Psychoanalysis Angel Garma. He was the Scientific Secretary and Past President of APA. He was keynote of the Berlin IPA Congress of 2007 and official Rapporteur in the Latin America Congress in Barcelona in 1997. He was the first editor and chairman of the Editorial Board of the International Latin American Journal. He is currently Chair of the Education Committee of the Latin American Psychoanalytic Federation. He is the author of *Analytic treatment and transference*, published by Amorrortu publishers in 1999 in Buenos Aires, and also author of books published in English, French, Italian, and Spanish. He is currently a member of CAPSA and the ING of IPA and current advisor of the Latin American Psychoanalytic Institute (IPA and FEPAL).

Patrick Miller, MD, is a IPA training and supervising analyst, member of Société Psychanalytique de Recherche et de Formation (SPRF) in Paris, member of C.A.P.S. (Princeton), author of *Le Psychanalyste Pendant La Séance* (PUF, Paris, 2001), and co-author of *Le Travail du Psychanalyste* (PUF, 2003), *La Psychanalyse à l'Epreuve du Malentendu* (PUF, 2006), and *Passé/Présent* (PUF, 2007). He is in private practice in Paris.

René Roussillon is training and supervising analyst of the Paris Psychoanalytical Society and of the Lyon Group of the SPP. He is Professor of Clinical Psychology and Psychopathology at the

University of Lyon 2, where he is Director of the Department of Clinical Psychology. He is also Director of the Research Group on borderline pathology, and Director of the clinical "psycho-hub" of the Rhône-Alpes region in France.

Gennaro Saragnano, MD, is a member and former Secretary of the Italian Psychoanalytical Association, and a psychiatrist and psycho-analyst in private practice in Rome. He was the Editor of the Bulletin of the Italian Psychoanalytical Association from 2000 to 2007. He served the International Psychoanalytical Association as a member of the Website Editorial Board from 2005 to 2009, and he has been a member of the Publications Committee of the International Psycho-analytical Association since 2009. He was appointed Chair of the Publications Committee during the Mexico City IPA Congress in August 2011. He is also currently a member of the Editorial Board of the *International Journal of Psychoanalysis*.

Christian Seulin is training and supervising analyst of the Paris Psychoanalytical Society (SPP), and member of the International Psychoanalytical Association. He is former Secretary of the Training Committee of the Lyon's Institute of the SPP and former Secretary of the Executive Council of the Training Commission of the SPP. Living and practising in Lyon, he is currently President of the Lyon's group of the SPP. He has authored more than fifty articles and book's chapters and one book.

Rogelio Sosnik is training and supervising analyst, Buenos Aires Psychoanalytic Association; training and supervising analyst and faculty, New York Freudian Society; and member of the American Psychoanalytic Association and the IPA. He has published papers in Argentina, Uruguay, Italy, and the US, on the relationship between Ferenczi and Bion, on the British School, and on the work of Bleger. He has written on the Ethical Texture of Psychoanlysis and co-chaired a workshop on the death penalty at the meetings of the American Psychoanalytic Association. For many years he has chaired a discussion group on the Clinical Value of Bion's ideas at the meetings of the American Psychoanalytic Association. He is in private practice in New York City.

ON FREUD'S
"ON BEGINNING THE TREATMENT"

Introduction[1]

Christian Seulin

Freud's paper "On beginning the treatment" (1913c) is without a doubt one of his most significant writings on matters of technique. He wrote several papers on technique between 1904 and 1918, the most important of these dating from 1910 to 1915; the period follow-ing the foundation of the International Psycho-Analytical Association. The development of psychoanalysis, the increase in the number of psychoanalysts, the broadening of its geographic fron-tiers, and the lessons learned from difficulties encountered in some treatments—all of these factors led the inventor of psychoanalysis to establish the fundamental principles of psychoanalytical technique.

Freud did not set down a series of hard and fast rules—quite the contrary: he based his choice on his own experience and saw the practice of psychoanalysis much more as an *art* than as the stereo-typed implementation of precepts. As he himself put it, it was more a matter of "recommendations".

The psychoanalytical method *stricto sensu* dates from the "Rat Man" case, which Freud undertook in 1907; he had learned a great deal from the failure of "Dora's" treatment, in which, as he was later to acknowledge, he had over-emphasised intellectual understand-ing and the systematic analysis of dreams to the detriment of the transference.

In his 1913 paper, the ongoing topicality of what he has to say on beginning treatment—he compares it to learning how to play chess—has in no way been undermined by contemporary clinical practice. The importance of the inviolability of the setting and of the actual conditions under which the treatment is initiated makes it possible for the clinical material to remain comprehensible and for the transference to be grasped *in statu nascendi*.

Freud's idea of a trial period of treatment in order to overcome any uncertainty concerning indications finds an echo in contemporary psychoanalysis not only through the many adjustments made to the setting and the two-stage treatments that had been advocated in the 1970s by Jean Bergeret in borderline cases (Bergeret, 1975), but also through the use for more than fifty years now of various innovative psychoanalytical techniques (psychotherapy with psychotic patients, psychodrama, group analysis, family therapy, mediation therapy). These developments have given rise to technical modifications that are more suitable for patients with whom, initially at least, it is impossible to undertake the classic form of treatment.

As regards the indications for psychoanalysis, in his 1913 paper Freud maintains the position that he had adopted in 1904 in his article "On psychotherapy" (1905a [1904]). I would think it quite legitimate to draw a parallel between these indications, which mainly concern the transference neuroses, the fundamental rule, that he describes in some detail in his 1913 paper, and his conception of the technique of interpretation.

Although most analysts would agree that the fundamental rule is theoretically important, there are significant differences as to when and how it should be introduced. Initially, when it is set out, the fundamental rule is addressed to an analysand whose topographical structure enables connecting thoughts (*einfall*) to be expressed; in such cases, the analysand's psychical apparatus is structured more or less under the aegis of repression. He or she is also assumed to be capable of reflexiveness—the ego is able to observe the course of internal psychical events and to describe them; the metaphor of the passenger travelling by train and describing the countryside to someone else is a good example of how this can be expressed. The fundamental rule has to do with the gap between ego and superego, as Jean-Luc Donnet (1995a) has shown, in its twofold dimension prescriptive/permissive. In that respect, its effectiveness and the issues that it involves will be in some difficulty in the borderline situations (Roussillon, 1991) that occur in psychoanalysis. The expansion of psychoanalytical treatment indications and techniques represents something of a challenge to the fundamental rule; many psychoanalysts no longer make any reference to it, and some go as far as to question its very relevance.

That difficulty with respect to the fundamental rule finds an echo in the analyst's technique of interpretation. In Freud's 1913 paper, interpretation has to do with the lifting of repression and the uncovering of some hidden meaning, which, as Freud implies, is already present. The lifting of repression, of course, is accompanied by the creation of a new meaning, one which until then had remained unheard of, one which in the transference/countertransference encounter both encourages and creates a new kind of meaningfulness. However, when creating meaning prevails over the lifting of repression and when the analyst's psychical work becomes a co-creator of meaning, interpretation as such tends to give way to construction—a topic that Freud explored in his paper on "Constructions in analysis" (1937d). What the analyst says then pertains to what is taking place in the session itself, something that the analysand cannot put into words: in borderline situations, the transference is qualitatively very different from the kind to which Freud was referring in 1913. At that time, he had in mind transference through displacement supported by transference onto verbalisation. In borderline cases, the transference is overwhelming, energetic, and processual, unrecognisable and unacknowledged as such by the analysand, in a here and now dimension that does away with any kind of temporality. The past is acted out with the analyst and is not understood as belonging to the past. Winnicott's work on regression in the psychoanalytical situation (1958a) and on the use of the object (1971) is a major contribution to our understanding of these issues in contemporary psychoanalysis. It is only through the analyst's work on, and processing of, the countertransference that temporality can be brought to life or re-established in the course of the treatment. This kind of interpretative technique is no longer a matter of putting the final touches to the analysand's becoming aware of something; through projection, the analyst as a person is involved. These processes can be understood in terms of projective identification and of constructions based upon a "selected fact"

(Bion, 1962). In this case, however, the risk that suggestion might again infiltrate the technique of psychoanalysis—Freud was always wary of that—must be taken into consideration.

These developments in the indications for psychoanalytical treatment have strengthened the emphasis placed on the analyst's evenly suspended attention, no doubt as a means of avoiding the threat of suggestion; Freud had recommended that technique in his paper, "Recommendations to physicians practising psycho-analysis" (1912e), written the year before "On beginning the treatment". The fundamental rule has as its aim the setting up of free association; its implementation, together with the analyst's evenly suspended attention, lies at the very heart of the psychoanalytical method. Nowadays, however, greater emphasis is placed on the analyst's free-floating attention, with its implicit corollary, the analysis of the countertransference. When transference on to verbalisation is in great difficulty, the signs of what cannot be put into words in the transference will be looked for in the analyst's internal state that is assumed to be ideally available and free of any *a priori* impressions.

This brings us to the meaning that can be given to the analysand's silence once the fundamental rule is announced. Freud saw in this a form of resistance: female patients expressing their anxiety about sexual attack, while male patients are anxious about their powerful homosexual tendencies. Basically, Freud was tempted in this case to interpret the content, leaving aside the economic aspects of the mental processes that are at work. Has it to do with the sudden emergence of a massive transference that overwhelms the psychical apparatus, with the refusal to give up thing-presentations when the movement towards word-presentations is under way? Perhaps expressing the fundamental rule had such a traumatic impact on the analysand that it became impossible to take it on board. When Freud suggested to the patient who remained silent that he or she must have thoughts about the setting, the room, the objects in it, or the analyst, this bears witness to the fact that he felt intuitively that there was a need to have recourse to perception, given that representation was not functioning in any appropriate manner. Can we really argue that this clinical pattern is a kind of resistance?

That fairly extreme example shows that the real issue in some forms of treatment is that of encouraging free association—which, in these cases, is less the means of treatment than its very aim and objective. Here, the idea is not so much to unearth an unconscious conflict, but rather to restore, in the analysand, some degree of topographical functioning. The aim is to set up a sufficiently flexible interplay between primary and secondary processes—henceforth brought back into play whereas, before, they had been disjointed or merged together. Green (1995) has very appositely written of tertiary processes in the analyst, which can bring about some degree of restoration of the functional pairing between primary and secondary processes. The analysand's silence, of course, is not the only way in which problems with free association can be expressed; what also should be considered is the quality of the symbolic efficiency of language, the capacity to give meaning to the strength of the drives, and the ego's ability to make itself heard when splitting and denial mask meaningfulness or when discharge takes over once working-through proves to be inadequate.

In his paper on beginning treatment, the picture that Freud gives of psychoanalytical treatment is ideally suited to the transference neuroses, in which the work of interpretation focuses on the analysis of resistance; the dynamics of the method employed unfold, as it were, quite naturally. Freud compared that process to pregnancy. The analyst initiates a process just as the male partner triggers an impregnation that will run its course until its natural termination. The order in which conflicts will be addressed and the derivatives of what has been repressed lie outside of the analyst's control. The main emphasis of the analysand's role is that of working-through—this is much more than a mere intellectual understanding; it implies the facilitation of communication between the Cs, Pcs, and Ucs areas of the topography of the mind.

The analyst's "sympathetic understanding" and "neutrality" mean that he or she will be the object of a positive transference, the driving force behind the treatment; this will link up with the analysand's thirst for self-knowledge, and ensure that the process will be successful.

The image of pregnancy as suggested by Freud—leaving aside the idea of its natural course—introduces a third-party element within the analytical couple. That element has its own momentum; it is neither just the one nor the other, but the fruit of the encounter, in the context of the analytical setting, between both participants in the treatment. That image of a fruitful and creative encounter has, in contemporary psychoanalysis, lent itself to many developments concerning how the dynamics of psychoanalytical treatment have come to be understood.

Given the analyst's specific role, the encounter between patient and analyst creates in the patient a shock that to some extent at least is traumatic; this does not imply, however, that a process will automatically begin. Our present experience tends rather to highlight processual discontinuity or chaos (as Green (2002a) has pointed out in his work on borderline states). The more difficult the clinical pattern and fragile the patient's topographical structure, the greater the threat of defects in the development of a process or of its involution. Freud's 1913 paper has to be read in context—it was written before the turning-point of the 1920s, when it became clear that it was necessary also to take into account the stumbling-block of the compulsion to repeat, the havoc wrought by the negative therapeutic reaction, and the diabolical nature of moral masochism.

Here, in the pages that follow Freud's paper "On beginning the treatment", the principal points that he made in it are examined in some depth in the light of the clinical patterns that we encounter in contemporary psychoanalysis. In addition, some of the ideas that I have outlined in this brief Introduction are explored more fully.

Note

1. Translated by David Alcorn.

PART I

"On beginning the treatment" (1913c)

Sigmund Freud

ON BEGINNING THE TREATMENT[1]
(FURTHER RECOMMENDATIONS ON THE TECHNIQUE OF PSYCHO-ANALYSIS I)

ANYONE who hopes to learn the noble game of chess from books will soon discover that only the openings and end-games admit of an exhaustive systematic presentation and that the infinite variety of moves which develop after the opening defy any such description. This gap in instruction can only be filled by a diligent study of games fought out by masters. The rules which can be laid down for the practice of psycho-analytic treatment are subject to similar limitations.

In what follows I shall endeavour to collect together for the use of practising analysts some of the rules for the beginning of the treatment. Among them there are some which may seem to be petty details, as, indeed, they are. Their justification is that they are simply rules of the game which acquire their importance from their relation to the general plan of the game. I think I am well-advised, however, to call these rules 'recommendations' and not to claim any unconditional acceptance for them. The extraordinary diversity of the psychical constellations concerned, the plasticity of all mental processes and the wealth of determining factors oppose any mechanization of the technique; and they bring it about that a course of action that is as a rule justified may at times prove ineffective, whilst one that is usually mistaken may once in a while lead to the desired end. These circumstances, however, do not prevent us from laying down a procedure for the physician which is effective on the average.

Some years ago I set out the most important indications for selecting patients[2] and I shall therefore not repeat them here. They have in the meantime been approved by other psychoanalysts. But I may add that since then I have made it my

---

[1] [In the first edition only, the following footnote appeared at this point: 'Continuation of a series of papers which were published in the *Zentralblatt für Psychoanalyse*, 2 (3, 4 and 9). ("The Handling of Dream-Interpretation in Psycho-Analysis", "The Dynamics of Transference", and "Recommendations to Physicians Practising Psycho-Analysis".)']

[2] 'On Psychotherapy' (1905a).

123

habit, when I know little about a patient, only to take him on at first provisionally, for a period of one to two weeks. If one breaks off within this period one spares the patient the distressing impression of an attempted cure having failed. One has only been undertaking a 'sounding' in order to get to know the case and to decide whether it is a suitable one for psychoanalysis. No other kind of preliminary examination but this procedure is at our disposal; the most lengthy discussions and questionings in ordinary consultations would offer no substitute. This preliminary experiment, however, is itself the beginning of a psycho-analysis and must conform to its rules. There may perhaps be this distinction made, that in it one lets the patient do nearly all the talking and explains nothing more than what is absolutely necessary to get him to go on with what he is saying.

There are also diagnostic reasons for beginning the treatment with a trial period of this sort lasting for one or two weeks. Often enough, when one sees a neurosis with hysterical or obsessional symptoms, which is not excessively marked and has not been in existence for long—just the type of case, that is, that one would regard as suitable for treatment—one has to reckon with the possibility that it may be a preliminary stage of what is known as dementia praecox ('schizophrenia', in Bleuler's terminology; 'paraphrenia', as I have proposed to call it[1]), and that sooner or later it will show a well-marked picture of that affection. I do not agree that it is always possible to make the distinction so easily. I am aware that there are psychiatrists who hesitate less often in their differential diagnosis, but I have become convinced that just as often they make mistakes. To make a mistake, moreover, is of far greater moment for the psycho-analyst than it is for the clinical psychiatrist, as he is called. For the latter is not attempting to do anything that will be of use, whichever kind of case it may be. He merely runs the risk of making a theoretical mistake, and his diagnosis is of no more than academic interest. Where the psycho-analyst is concerned, however, if the case is unfavourable he has committed a practical error; he has been responsible for wasted expenditure and has discredited his method of treatment. He cannot fulfil his promise of cure if the patient is suffering, not from hysteria or obsessional neurosis, but from paraphrenia, and he therefore has particularly strong

[1] [See above, footnote 1, p. 76.]

motives for avoiding mistakes in diagnosis. In an experimental treatment of a few weeks he will often observe suspicious signs which may determine him not to pursue the attempt any further. Unfortunately I cannot assert that an attempt of this kind always enables us to arrive at a certain decision; it is only one wise precaution the more.[1]

Lengthy preliminary discussions before the beginning of the analytic treatment, previous treatment by another method and also previous acquaintance between the doctor and the patient who is to be analysed, have special disadvantageous consequences for which one must be prepared. They result in the patient's meeting the doctor with a transference attitude which is already established and which the doctor must first slowly uncover instead of having the opportunity to observe the growth and development of the transference from the outset. In this way the patient gains a temporary start upon us which we do not willingly grant him in the treatment.

One must mistrust all prospective patients who want to make a delay before beginning their treatment. Experience shows that when the time agreed upon has arrived they fail to put in an appearance, even though the motive for the delay—i.e. their rationalization of their intention—seems to the uninitiated to be above suspicion.

Special difficulties arise when the analyst and his new patient or their families are on terms of friendship or have social ties with one another. The psycho-analyst who is asked to undertake the treatment of the wife or child of a friend must be prepared for it to cost him that friendship, no matter what the outcome of the treatment may be: nevertheless he must make the sacrifice if he cannot find a trustworthy substitute.

Both lay public and doctors—still ready to confuse psycho-analysis with treatment by suggestion—are inclined to attribute

[1] There is a great deal to be said about this uncertainty in diagnosis, about the prospects of success in analysing mild forms of paraphrenia and about the reasons for the similarity between the two disorders; but I cannot enlarge on these subjects in the present context. I should be glad to follow Jung in contrasting hysteria and obsessional neurosis as 'transference neuroses' with the paraphrenic affections as 'introversion neuroses', if it were not that such a usage would deprive the concept of 'introversion' (of the libido) of its sole legitimate meaning. [Cf. footnote 1, p. 102.]

great importance to the expectations which the patient brings to the new treatment. They often believe in the case of one patient that he will not give much trouble, because he has great confidence in psycho-analysis and is fully convinced of its truth and efficacy; whereas in the case of another, they think that he will undoubtedly prove more difficult, because he has a sceptical outlook and will not believe anything until he has experienced its successful results on his own person. Actually, however, this attitude on the part of the patient has very little importance. His initial trust or distrust is almost negligible compared with the internal resistances which hold the neurosis firmly in place. It is true that the patient's happy trustfulness makes our earliest relationship with him a very pleasant one; we are grateful to him for that, but we warn him that his favourable prepossession will be shattered by the first difficulty that arises in the analysis. To the sceptic we say that the analysis requires no faith, that he may be as critical and suspicious as he pleases and that we do not regard his attitude as the effect of his judgement at all, for he is not in a position to form a reliable judgement on these matters; his distrust is only a symptom like his other symptoms and it will not be an interference, provided he conscientiously carries out what the rule of the treatment requires of him.

No one who is familiar with the nature of neurosis will be astonished to hear that even a man who is very well able to carry out an analysis on other people can behave like any other mortal and be capable of producing the most intense resistances as soon as he himself becomes the object of analytic investigation. When this happens we are once again reminded of the dimension of depth in the mind, and it does not surprise us to find that the neurosis has its roots in psychical strata to which an intellectual knowledge of analysis has not penetrated.

Points of importance at the beginning of the analysis are arrangements about *time* and *money*.

In regard to time, I adhere strictly to the principle of leasing a definite hour. Each patient is allotted a particular hour of my available working day; it belongs to him and he is liable for it, even if he does not make use of it. This arrangement, which is taken as a matter of course for teachers of music or languages in good society, may perhaps seem too rigorous in a doctor, or even unworthy of his profession. There will be an inclination to point to the many accidents which may prevent the patient from attending every day at the same hour and it will be expected that some allowance shall be made for the numerous intercurrent ailments which may occur in the course of a longish analytic treatment. But my answer is: no other way is practicable. Under a less stringent régime the 'occasional' non-attendances increase so greatly that the doctor finds his material existence threatened; whereas when the arrangement is adhered to, it turns out that accidental hindrances do not occur at all and intercurrent illnesses only very seldom. The analyst is hardly ever put in the position of enjoying a leisure hour which he is paid for and would be ashamed of; and he can continue his work without interruptions, and is spared the distressing and bewildering experience of finding that a break for which he cannot blame himself is always bound to happen just when the work promises to be especially important and rich in content. Nothing brings home to one so strongly the significance of the psychogenic factor in the daily life of men, the frequency of malingering and the non-existence of chance, as a few years' practice of psycho-analysis on the strict principle of leasing by the hour. In cases of undoubted organic illnesses, which, after all, cannot be excluded by the patient's having a psychical interest in attending, I break off the treatment, consider myself entitled to dispose elsewhere of the hour which becomes free, and take the patient back again as soon as he has recovered and I have another hour vacant.

I work with my patients every day except on Sundays and public holidays—that is, as a rule, six days a week. For slight cases or the continuation of a treatment which is already well advanced, three days a week will be enough. Any restrictions of time beyond this bring no advantage either to the doctor or the patient; and at the beginning of an analysis they are quite out of the question. Even short interruptions have a slightly obscuring effect on the work. We used to speak jokingly of the 'Monday crust' when we began work again after the rest on Sunday. When the hours of work are less frequent, there is a risk of not being able to keep pace with the patient's real life and of the treatment losing contact with the present and being forced into by-paths. Occasionally, too, one comes across patients to whom one must give more than the average time of one hour a day, because the best part of an hour is gone before they begin to open up and to become communicative at all.

An unwelcome question which the patient asks the doctor at the outset is: 'How long will the treatment take? How much time will you need to relieve me of my trouble?' If one has proposed a trial treatment of a few weeks one can avoid giving a direct answer to this question by promising to make a more reliable pronouncement at the end of the trial period. Our answer is like the answer given by the Philosopher to the Wayfarer in Aesop's fable. When the Wayfarer asked how long a journey lay ahead, the Philosopher merely answered 'Walk!' and afterwards explained his apparently unhelpful reply on the ground that he must know the length of the Wayfarer's stride before he could tell how long his journey would take.[1] This expedient helps one over the first difficulties; but the comparison is not a good one, for the neurotic can easily alter his pace and may at times make only very slow progress. In point of fact, the question as to the probable duration of a treatment is almost unanswerable.

As the combined result of lack of insight on the part of patients and disingenuousness on the part of doctors, analysis finds itself expected to fulfil the most boundless demands, and that in the shortest time. Let me, as an example, give some details from a letter which I received a few days ago from a lady in Russia. She is 53[2] years old, her illness began twenty-three years ago and for the last ten years she has no longer been able to do any continuous work. 'Treatment in a number of institutions for nervous cases' have not succeeded in making an 'active life' possible for her. She hopes to be completely cured by psycho-analysis, which she has read about, but her illness has already cost her family so much money that she cannot manage to come to Vienna for longer than six weeks or two months. Another added difficulty is that she wishes from the very start to 'explain' herself in writing only, since any discussion of her complexes would cause an explosion of feeling in her or 'render her temporarily unable to speak'.—No one would expect a man to lift a heavy table with two fingers as if it were a light stool, or to build a large house in the time it

---

[1] [This sentence has been slightly expanded in translation for the sake of clarity.]

[2] [In the editions before 1925 this read '33'.]

would take to put up a wooden hut; but as soon as it becomes a question of the neuroses—which do not seem so far to have found a proper place in human thought—even intelligent people forget that a necessary proportion must be observed between time, work and success. This, incidentally, is an understandable result of the deep ignorance which prevails about the aetiology of the neuroses. Thanks to this ignorance, neurosis is looked on as a kind of 'maiden from afar'.[1] 'None knew whence she came'; so they expected that one day she would vanish.

Doctors lend support to these fond hopes. Even the informed among them often fail to estimate properly the severity of nervous disorders. A friend and colleague of mine, to whose great credit I account it that after several decades of scientific work on other principles he became converted to the merits of psycho-analysis, once wrote to me: 'What we need is a short, convenient, out-patient treatment for obsessional neurosis.' I could not supply him with it and felt ashamed; so I tried to excuse myself with the remark that specialists in internal diseases, too, would probably be very glad of a treatment for tuberculosis or carcinoma which combined these advantages.

To speak more plainly, psycho-analysis is always a matter of long periods of time, of half a year or whole years—of longer periods than the patient expects. It is therefore our duty to tell the patient this before he finally decides upon the treatment. I consider it altogether more honourable, and also more expedient, to draw his attention—without trying to frighten him off, but at the very beginning—to the difficulties and sacrifices which analytic treatment involves, and in this way to deprive him of any right to say later on that he has been inveigled into a treatment whose extent and implications he did not realize. A patient who lets himself be dissuaded by this information would in any case have shown himself unsuitable later on. It is a good thing to institute a selection of this kind before the beginning of the treatment. With the progress of understanding among patients the number of those who success-fully meet this first test increases.

I do not bind patients to continue the treatment for a certain length of time; I allow each one to break off whenever he likes. But I do not hide it from him that if the treatment is stopped after only a small amount of work has been done it will not be

[1] [An allusion to Schiller's poem 'Das Mädchen aus der Fremde'.]

successful and may easily, like an unfinished operation, leave him in an unsatisfactory state. In the early years of my psycho-analytic practice I used to have the greatest difficulty in prevailing on my patients to continue their analysis. This difficulty has long since been shifted, and I now have to take the greatest pains to induce them to give it up.

To shorten analytic treatment is a justifiable wish, and its fulfilment, as we shall learn, is being attempted along various lines. Unfortunately, it is opposed by a very important factor, namely, the slowness with which deep-going changes in the mind are accomplished—in the last resort, no doubt, the 'timelessness' of our unconscious processes.[1] When patients are faced with the difficulty of the great expenditure of time required for analysis they not infrequently manage to propose a way out of it. They divide up their ailments and describe some as unbearable, and others as secondary, and then say: 'If only you will relieve me from this one (for instance, a headache or a particular fear) I can deal with the other one on my own in my ordinary life.' In doing this, however, they over-estimate the selective power of analysis. The analyst is certainly able to do a great deal, but he cannot determine beforehand exactly what results he will effect. He sets in motion a process, that of the resolving of existing repressions. He can supervise this process, further it, remove obstacles in its way, and he can undoubtedly vitiate much of it. But on the whole, once begun, it goes its own way and does not allow either the direction it takes or the order in which it picks up its points to be prescribed for it. The analyst's power over the symptoms of the disease may thus be compared to male sexual potency. A man can, it is true, beget a whole child, but even the strongest man cannot create in the female organism a head alone or an arm or a leg; he cannot even prescribe the child's sex. He, too, only sets in motion a highly complicated process, determined by events in the remote past, which ends with the severance of the child from its mother. A neurosis as well has the character of an organism. Its component manifestations are not independent of one another; they condition one another and give one another mutual support. A person suffers from one neurosis only, never from several which have accidentally met together in a single individual. The patient freed, according to his wish, from his

[1] [Cf. 'The Unconscious' (1915e), *Standard Ed.*, **14**, 187 and footnote.]

one unendurable symptom might easily find that a symptom which had previously been negligible had now increased and grown unendurable. The analyst who wishes the treatment to owe its success as little as possible to its elements of suggestion (i.e. to the transference) will do well to refrain from making use of even the trace of selective influence upon the results of the therapy which may perhaps be open to him. The patients who are bound to be most welcome to him are those who ask him to give them complete health, in so far as that is attainable, and who place as much time at his disposal as is necessary for the process of recovery. Such favourable conditions as these are, of course, to be looked for in only a few cases.

The next point that must be decided at the beginning of the treatment is the one of money, of the doctor's fee. An analyst does not dispute that money is to be regarded in the first instance as a medium for self-preservation and for obtaining power; but he maintains that, besides this, powerful sexual factors are involved in the value set upon it. He can point out that money matters are treated by civilized people in the same way as sexual matters—with the same inconsistency, prudishness and hypocrisy. The analyst is therefore determined from the first not to fall in with this attitude, but, in his dealings with his patients, to treat of money matters with the same matter-of-course frankness to which he wishes to educate them in things relating to sexual life. He shows them that he himself has cast off false shame on these topics, by voluntarily telling them the price at which he values his time. Ordinary good sense cautions him, furthermore, not to allow large sums of money to accumulate, but to ask for payment at fairly short regular intervals—monthly, perhaps. (It is a familiar fact that the value of the treatment is not enhanced in the patient's eyes if a very low fee is asked.) This is, of course, not the usual practice of nerve specialists or other physicians in our European society. But the psycho-analyst may put himself in the position of a surgeon, who is frank and expensive because he has at his disposal methods of treatment which can be of use. It seems to me more respectable and ethically less objectionable to acknowledge one's actual claims and needs rather than, as is still the practice among physicians, to act the part of the disinterested philanthropist—a position which one is not, in fact, able to fill, with the result that one is secretly aggrieved, or complains aloud, at the lack of consideration and the desire for exploitation evinced by one's patients. In fixing his fee the analyst must also allow for the fact that, hard as he may work, he can never earn as much as other medical specialists.

For the same reason he should also refrain from giving treatment free, and make no exceptions to this in favour of his colleagues or their families. This last recommendation will seem to offend against professional amenities. It must be remembered, however, that a gratuitous treatment means much more to a psycho-analyst than to any other medical man; it means the sacrifice of a considerable portion—an eighth or a seventh part, perhaps—of the working time available to him for earning his living, over a period of many months. A second free treatment carried on at the same time would already deprive him of a quarter or a third of his earning capacity, and this would be comparable to the damage inflicted by a severe accident.

The question then arises whether the advantage gained by the patient would not to some extent counterbalance the sacrifice made by the physician. I may venture to form a judgement about this, since for ten years or so I set aside one hour a day, and sometimes two, for gratuitous treatments, because I wanted, in order to find my way about in the neuroses, to work in the face of as little resistance as possible. The advantages I sought by this means were not forthcoming. Free treatment enormously increases some of a neurotic's resistances—in young women, for instance, the temptation which is inherent in their transference-relation, and in young men, their opposition to an obligation to feel grateful, an opposition which arises from their father-complex and which presents one of the most troublesome hindrances to the acceptance of medical help. The absence of the regulating effect offered by the payment of a fee to the doctor makes itself very painfully felt; the whole relationship is removed from the real world, and the patient is deprived of a strong motive for endeavouring to bring the treatment to an end.

One may be very far from the ascetic view of money as a curse and yet regret that analytic therapy is almost inaccessible to poor people, both for external and internal reasons. Little can be done to remedy this. Perhaps there is truth in the widespread belief that those who are forced by necessity to a life of hard toil are less easily overtaken by neurosis. But on the other hand experience shows without a doubt that when once a poor man has produced a neurosis it is only with difficulty that he lets it be taken from him. It renders him too good a service in the struggle for existence; the secondary gain from illness[1] which it brings him is much too important. He now claims by right of his neurosis the pity which the world has refused to his material distress, and he can now absolve himself from the obligation of combating his poverty by working. Anyone therefore who tries to deal with the neurosis of a poor person by psychotherapy usually discovers that what is here required of him is a practical therapy of a very different kind—the kind which, according to our local tradition, used to be dispensed by the Emperor Joseph II. Naturally, one does occasionally come across deserving people who are helpless from no fault of their own, in whom unpaid treatment does not meet with any of the obstacles that I have mentioned and in whom it leads to excellent results.

As far as the middle classes are concerned, the expense involved in psycho-analysis is excessive only in appearance. Quite apart from the fact that no comparison is possible between restored health and efficiency on the one hand and a moderate financial outlay on the other, when we add up the unceasing costs of nursing-homes and medical treatment and contrast them with the increase of efficiency and earning capacity which results from a successfully completed analysis, we are entitled to say that the patients have made a good bargain. Nothing in life is so expensive as illness—and stupidity.

Before I wind up these remarks on beginning analytic treatment, I must say a word about a certain ceremonial which concerns the position in which the treatment is carried out. I hold to the plan of getting the patient to lie on a sofa while I sit behind him out of his sight. This arrangement has a historical basis; it is the remnant of the hypnotic method out of which psycho-analysis was evolved. But it deserves to be maintained

[1] [The idea of a 'secondary gain from illness' occurs in Section B of the paper on hysterical attacks (1909a), though the actual phrase seems to be used for the first time here. For a fuller discussion see a footnote added by Freud in 1923 to the 'Dora' case history (1905e), *Standard Ed.*, 7, 43.]

for many reasons. The first is a personal motive, but one which others may share with me. I cannot put up with being stared at by other people for eight hours a day (or more). Since, while I am listening to the patient, I, too, give myself over to the current of my unconscious thoughts, I do not wish my expressions of face to give the patient material for interpretations or to influence him in what he tells me. The patient usually regards being made to adopt this position as a hardship and rebels against it, especially if the instinct for looking (scopophilia) plays an important part in his neurosis. I insist on this procedure, however, for its purpose and result are to prevent the transference from mingling with the patient's associations imperceptibly, to isolate the transference and to allow it to come forward in due course sharply defined as a resistance. I know that many analysts work in a different way, but I do not know whether this deviation is due more to a craving for doing things differently or to some advantage which they find they gain by it. [See also below, p. 139.]

The conditions of treatment having been regulated in this manner, the question arises at what point and with what material is the treatment to begin?

What the material is with which one starts the treatment is on the whole a matter of indifference—whether it is the patient's life-history or the history of his illness or his recollections of childhood. But in any case the patient must be left to do the talking and must be free to choose at what point he shall begin. We therefore say to him: 'Before I can say anything to you I must know a great deal about you; please tell me what you know about yourself.'

The only exception to this is in regard to the fundamental rule of psycho-analytic technique[1] which the patient has to observe. This must be imparted to him at the very beginning: 'One more thing before you start. What you tell me must differ in one respect from an ordinary conversation. Ordinarily you rightly try to keep a connecting thread running through your remarks and you exclude any intrusive ideas that may occur to you and any side-issues, so as not to wander too far from the point. But in this case you must proceed differently. You will

[1] [See footnote 2, p. 107.]

notice that as you relate things various thoughts will occur to you which you would like to put aside on the ground of certain criticisms and objections. You will be tempted to say to yourself that this or that is irrelevant here, or is quite unimportant, or nonsensical, so that there is no need to say it. You must never give in to these criticisms, but must say it in spite of them—indeed, you must say it precisely *because* you feel an aversion to doing so. Later on you will find out and learn to understand the reason for this injunction, which is really the only one you have to follow. So say whatever goes through your mind. Act as though, for instance, you were a traveller sitting next to the window of a railway carriage and describing to someone inside the carriage the changing views which you see outside. Finally, never forget that you have promised to be absolutely honest, and never leave anything out because, for some reason or other, it is unpleasant to tell it.'[1]

[1] Much might be said about our experiences with the fundamental rule of psycho-analysis. One occasionally comes across people who behave as if they had made this rule for themselves. Others offend against it from the very beginning. It is indispensable, and also advantageous, to lay down the rule in the first stages of the treatment. Later, under the dominance of the resistances, obedience to it weakens, and there comes a time in every analysis when the patient disregards it. We must remember from our own self-analysis how irresistible the temptation is to yield to these pretexts put forward by critical judgement for rejecting certain ideas. How small is the effect of such agreements as one makes with the patient in laying down the fundamental rule is regularly demonstrated when something intimate about a third person comes up in his mind for the first time. He knows that he is supposed to say everything, but he turns discretion about other people into a new obstacle. 'Must I really say everything? I thought that only applied to things that concern myself.' It is naturally impossible to carry out analysis if the patient's relations with other people and his thoughts about them are excluded. *Pour faire une omelette il faut casser des oeufs.* An honourable man readily forgets such of the private affairs of strangers as do not seem to him important to know. Nor can an exception be made in the case of names. Otherwise the patient's narratives became a little shadowy, like the scenes in Goethe's play *Die natürliche Tochter* [*The Natural Daughter*], and do not lodge in the doctor's memory. Moreover, the names that are withheld screen the approach to all sorts of important connections. But one may perhaps allow names to be left on one side until the patient has become more familiar with the doctor and the procedure of analysis. It is very remarkable how the whole task becomes impossible if a reservation is allowed at any single place. But we have only to reflect what would happen if the right of asylum existed at any one point in a town;

Patients who date their illness from a particular moment usually concentrate upon its precipitating cause. Others, who themselves recognize the connection between their neurosis and their childhood, often begin with an account of their whole life-history. A systematic narrative should never be expected and nothing should be done to encourage it. Every detail of the story will have to be told afresh later on, and it is only with these repetitions that additional material will appear which will supply the important connections that are unknown to the patient.

There are patients who from the very first hours carefully prepare what they are going to communicate, ostensibly so as to be sure of making better use of the time devoted to the treatment. What is thus disguising itself as eagerness is resistance. Any preparation of this sort should be disrecommended, for it is only employed to guard against unwelcome thoughts cropping up.[1] However genuinely the patient may believe in his excellent intentions, the resistance will play its part in this deliberate method of preparation and will see to it that the most valuable material escapes communication. One will soon find that the patient devises yet other means by which what is required may be withheld from the treatment. He may talk over the treatment every day with some intimate friend, and bring into this discussion all the thoughts which should come forward in the presence of the doctor. The treatment thus has a leak which lets through precisely what is most valuable. When this happens, the patient must, without much delay, be advised to treat his analysis as a matter between himself and his doctor and to exclude everyone else from sharing in the knowledge of it, no matter how close to him they may be, or how inquisitive. In later stages of the treatment the patient is usually not subjected to temptations of this sort.

Certain patients want their treatment to be kept secret, often because they have kept their neurosis secret; and I put no

how long would it be before all the riff-raff of the town had collected there? I once treated a high official who was bound by his oath of office not to communicate certain things because they were state secrets, and the analysis came to grief as a consequence of this restriction. Psychoanalytic treatment must have no regard for any consideration, because the neurosis and its resistances are themselves without any such regard.

[1] Exceptions may be made only for such data as family relationships, times and places of residence, operations, and so on.

obstacle in their way. That in consequence the world hears nothing of some of the most successful cures is, of course, a consideration that cannot be taken into account. It is obvious that a patient's decision in favour of secrecy already reveals a feature of his secret history.

In advising the patient at the beginning of the treatment to tell as few people as possible about it, we also protect him to some extent from the many hostile influences that will seek to entice him away from analysis. Such influences may be very mischievous at the outset of the treatment; later, they are usually immaterial, or even useful in bringing to the fore resistances which are trying to conceal themselves.

If during the course of the analysis the patient should temporarily need some other medical or specialist treatment, it is far wiser to call in a non-analytic colleague than to give this other treatment oneself.[1] Combined treatments for neurotic disorders which have a powerful organic basis are nearly always impracticable. The patients withdraw their interest from analysis as soon as they are shown more than one path that promises to lead them to health. The best plan is to postpone the organic treatment until the psychical treatment is finished; if the former were tried first it would in most cases meet with no success.

To return to the beginning of the treatment. Patients are occasionally met with who start the treatment by assuring us that they cannot think of anything to say, although the whole field of their life-history and the story of their illness is open to them to choose from.[2] Their request that we should tell them what to talk about must not be granted on this first occasion any more than on any later one. We must bear in mind what is involved here. A strong resistance has come to the front in order to defend the neurosis; we must take up the challenge then and there and come to grips with it. Energetic and repeated assurances to the patient that it is impossible for no ideas at all to occur to him at the beginning, and that what is in

[1] [Compare this with Freud's own experiences in his very earliest cases as described in *Studies on Hysteria* (1895*d*), e.g. *Standard Ed.*, **2**, 50 and 138.]

[2] [This technical problem is already discussed by Freud in the last pages of his contribution to *Studies on Hysteria*, ibid., 301–4.]

question is a resistance against the analysis, soon oblige him to make the expected admissions or to uncover a first piece of his complexes. It is a bad sign if he has to confess that while he was listening to the fundamental rule of analysis he made a mental reservation that he would nevertheless keep this or that to himself; it is not so serious if all he has to tell us is how mistrustful he is of analysis or the horrifying things he has heard about it. If he denies these and similar possibilities when they are put before him, he can be driven by our insistence to acknowledge that he has nevertheless overlooked certain thoughts which were occupying his mind. He had thought of the treatment itself, though nothing definite about it, or he had been occupied with the picture of the room in which he was, or he could not help thinking of the objects in the consulting room and of the fact that he was lying here on a sofa—all of which he has replaced by the word 'nothing'. These indications are intelligible enough: everything connected with the present situation represents a transference to the doctor, which proves suitable to serve as a first resistance.[1] We are thus obliged to begin by uncovering this transference; and a path from it will give rapid access to the patient's pathogenic material. Women who are prepared by events in their past history to be subjected to sexual aggression and men with over-strong repressed homosexuality are the most apt thus to withhold the ideas that occur to them at the outset of their analysis.

The patient's first symptoms or chance actions, like his first resistance, may possess a special interest and may betray a complex which governs his neurosis. A clever young philosopher with exquisite aesthetic sensibilities will hasten to put the creases of his trousers straight before lying down for his first hour; he is revealing himself as a former coprophilic of the highest refinement—which was to be expected from the later aesthete. A young girl will at the same juncture hurriedly pull the hem of her skirt over her exposed ankles; in doing this she is giving away the gist of what her analysis will uncover later: her narcissistic pride in her physical beauty and her inclinations to exhibitionism.

[1] [Cf. 'The Dynamics of Transference', p. 101 f. above.—In a footnote to Chapter X of *Group Psychology* (1921c), *Standard Ed.*, **18**, 126, Freud draws attention to the similarity between this situation and certain hypnotic techniques.]

A particularly large number of patients object to being asked to lie down, while the doctor sits out of sight behind them.[1] They ask to be allowed to go through the treatment in some other position, for the most part because they are anxious not to be deprived of a view of the doctor. Permission is regularly refused, but one cannot prevent them from contriving to say a few sentences before the beginning of the actual 'session' or after one has signified that it is finished and they have got up from the sofa. In this way they divide the treatment in their own view into an official portion, in which they mostly behave in a very inhibited manner, and an informal 'friendly' portion, in which they speak really freely and say all sorts of things which they themselves do not regard as being part of the treatment. The doctor does not accept this division for long. He takes note of what is said before or after the session and he brings it forward at the first opportunity, thus pulling down the partition which the patient has tried to erect. This partition, once again, will have been put together from the material of a transference-resistance.

So long as the patient's communications and ideas run on without any obstruction, the theme of transference should be left untouched. One must wait until the transference, which is the most delicate of all procedures, has become a resistance.

The next question with which we are faced raises a matter of principle. It is this: When are we to begin making our communications to the patient? When is the moment for disclosing to him the hidden meaning of the ideas that occur to him, and for initiating him into the postulates and technical procedures of analysis?

The answer to this can only be: Not until an effective transference has been established in the patient, a proper *rapport* with him. It remains the first aim of the treatment to attach him to it and to the person of the doctor. To ensure this, nothing need be done but to give him time. If one exhibits a serious interest in him, carefully clears away the resistances that crop up at the beginning and avoids making certain mistakes, he will of himself form such an attachment and link the doctor up with one of the imagos of the people by whom he was accustomed

[1] [Cf. above, p. 133 f.]

to be treated with affection. It is certainly possible to forfeit this first success if from the start one takes up any standpoint other than one of sympathetic understanding, such as a moralizing one, or if one behaves like a representative or advocate of some contending party—of the other member of a married couple, for instance.[1]

This answer of course involves a condemnation of any line of behaviour which would lead us to give the patient a translation of his symptoms as soon as we have guessed it ourselves, or would even lead us to regard it as a special triumph to fling these 'solutions' in his face at the first interview. It is not difficult for a skilled analyst to read the patient's secret wishes plainly between the lines of his complaints and the story of his illness; but what a measure of self-complacency and thoughtlessness must be possessed by anyone who can, on the shortest acquaintance, inform a stranger who is entirely ignorant of all the tenets of analysis that he is attached to his mother by incestuous ties, that he harbours wishes for the death of his wife whom he appears to love, that he conceals an intention of betraying his superior, and so on![2] I have heard that there are analysts who plume themselves upon these kinds of lightning diagnoses and 'express' treatments, but I must warn everyone against following such examples. Behaviour of this sort will completely discredit oneself and the treatment in the patient's eyes and will arouse the most violent opposition in him, whether one's guess has been true or not; indeed, the truer the guess the more violent will be the resistance. As a rule the therapeutic effect will be nil; but the deterring of the patient from analysis will be final. Even in the later stages of analysis one must be careful not to give a patient the solution of a symptom or the translation of a wish until he is already so close to it that he has only one short step more to make in order to get hold of the explanation for himself. In former years I often had occasion to find that the premature communication of a solution brought the treatment to an untimely end, on account not only of the

---

[1] [In the first edition only, the latter part of this sentence read: '. . . if one behaves like a representative or advocate of some contending party with whom the patient is engaged in a conflict—of his parents, for instance, or the other member of a married couple.']

[2] [Cf. the detailed example of this which Freud had already given in his paper on ' "Wild" Psycho-Analysis' (1910k).]

resistances which it thus suddenly awakened but also of the relief which the solution brought with it.

But at this point an objection will be raised. Is it, then, our task to lengthen the treatment and not, rather, to bring it to an end as rapidly as possible? Are not the patient's ailments due to his lack of knowledge and understanding and is it not a duty to enlighten him as soon as possible—that is, as soon as the doctor himself knows the explanations? The answer to this question calls for a short digression on the meaning of knowledge and the mechanism of cure in analysis.

It is true that in the earliest days of analytic technique we took an intellectualist view of the situation. We set a high value on the patient's knowledge of what he had forgotten, and in this we made hardly any distinction between our knowledge of it and his. We thought it a special piece of good luck if we were able to obtain information about the forgotten childhood trauma from other sources—for instance, from parents or nurses or the seducer himself—as in some cases it was possible to do; and we hastened to convey the information and the proofs of its correctness to the patient, in the certain expectation of thus bringing the neurosis and the treatment to a rapid end. It was a severe disappointment when the expected success was not forthcoming. How could it be that the patient, who now knew about his traumatic experience, nevertheless still behaved as if he knew no more about it than before? Indeed, telling and describing his repressed trauma to him did not even result in any recollection of it coming into his mind.

In one particular case the mother of a hysterical girl had confided to me the homosexual experience which had greatly contributed to the fixation of the girl's attacks. The mother had herself surprised the scene; but the patient had completely forgotten it, though it had occurred when she was already approaching puberty. I was now able to make a most instructive observation. Every time I repeated her mother's story to the girl she reacted with a hysterical attack, and after this she forgot the story once more. There is no doubt that the patient was expressing a violent resistance against the knowledge that was being forced upon her. Finally she simulated feeble-mindedness and a complete loss of memory in order to protect herself against what I had told her. After this, there was no choice but to cease attributing to the fact of knowing, in itself, the importance that had previously been given to it and to place the emphasis on the resistances which had in the past brought about the state of not knowing and which were still ready to defend that state. Conscious knowledge, even if it was not subsequently driven out again, was powerless against those resistances.[1]

The strange behaviour of patients, in being able to combine a conscious knowing with not knowing, remains inexplicable by what is called normal psychology. But to psycho-analysis, which recognizes the existence of the unconscious, it presents no difficulty. The phenomenon we have described, moreover, provides some of the best support for a view which approaches mental processes from the angle of topographical differentiation. The patients now know of the repressed experience in their conscious thought, but this thought lacks any connection with the place where the repressed recollection is in some way or other contained. No change is possible until the conscious thought-process has penetrated to that place and has overcome the resistances of repression there. It is just as though a decree were promulgated by the Ministry of Justice to the effect that juvenile delinquencies should be dealt with in a certain lenient manner. As long as this decree has not come to the knowledge of the local magistrates, or in the event of their not intending to obey it but preferring to administer justice by their own lights, no change can occur in the treatment of particular youthful delinquents. For the sake of complete accuracy, however, it should be added that the communication of repressed material to the patient's consciousness is nevertheless not without effect. It does not produce the hoped-for result of putting an end to the symptoms; but it has other consequences. At first it arouses resistances, but then, when these have been overcome, it sets up a process of thought in the course of which the expected influencing of the unconscious recollection eventually takes place.[2]

It is now time for us to take a survey of the play of forces

---

[1] [The very different views on this subject held by Freud during the Breuer period are clearly shown in the account he gives of a similar case in *Studies on Hysteria* (1895*d*), *Standard Ed.*, 2, 274–5.]

[2] [The topographical picture of the distinction between unconscious

which is set in motion by the treatment. The primary motive force in the therapy is the patient's suffering and the wish to be cured that arises from it. The strength of this motive force is subtracted from by various factors—which are not discovered till the analysis is in progress—above all, by what we have called the 'secondary gain from illness';[1] but it must be maintained till the end of the treatment. Every improvement effects a diminution of it. By itself, however, this motive force is not sufficient to get rid of the illness. Two things are lacking in it for this: it does not know what paths to follow to reach this end; and it does not possess the necessary quota of energy with which to oppose the resistances. The analytic treatment helps to remedy both these deficiencies. It supplies the amounts of energy that are needed for overcoming the resistances by making mobile the energies which lie ready for the transference; and, by giving the patient information at the right time, it shows him the paths along which he should direct those energies. Often enough the transference is able to remove the symptoms of the disease by itself, but only for a while—only for as long as it itself lasts. In this case the treatment is a treatment by suggestion, and not a psycho-analysis at all. It only deserves the latter name if the intensity of the transference has been utilized for the overcoming of resistances. Only then has being ill become impossible, even when the transference has once more been dissolved, which is its destined end.

In the course of the treatment yet another helpful factor is aroused. This is the patient's intellectual interest and understanding. But this alone hardly comes into consideration in comparison with the other forces that are engaged in the struggle; for it is always in danger of losing its value, as a result of the clouding of judgement that arises from the resistances. Thus the new sources of strength for which the patient is indebted to his analyst are reducible to transference and instruction

and conscious ideas had been discussed by Freud already in the case history of 'Little Hans' (1909b), *Standard Ed.*, **10**, 120-1, and he had referred to it again by implication in his paper on 'wild' analysis (1910k), *Standard Ed.*, **11**, 225. The difficulties and insufficiencies of the picture were pointed out some two years after the publication of the present work in Sections II and VII of the metapsychological paper on 'The Unconscious' (1915e), where a more deep-going account of the distinction was propounded.]

[1] [See footnote above, p. 133.]

(through the communications made to him). The patient, however, only makes use of the instruction in so far as he is induced
to do so by the transference; and it is for this reason that our
first communication should be withheld until a strong transference has been established. And this, we may add, holds good
of every subsequent communication. In each case we must
wait until the disturbance of the transference by the successive
emergence of transference-resistances has been removed.[1]

[1] [The whole question of the mechanism of psycho-analytic therapy
and in particular of the transference was discussed at greater length in
Lectures XXVII and XXVIII of the *Introductory Lectures* (1916–17).—
Freud makes some interesting comments on the difficulty of carrying out
the 'fundamental rule of psycho-analysis' (p. 134 ff. above) in Chapter
VI of *Inhibitions, Symptoms and Anxiety* (1926d).]

PART II

Discussion of
"On beginning the treatment"

1

"On beginning the treatment": a contemporary view

Theodore Jacobs

Like his other papers on technique, Freud's 1913 essay on beginning an analysis had an enduring influence on psychoanalysts for generations to come. Although he took pains to make clear that the precepts that he set down were meant not as rules to be slavishly followed, but as recommendations that in individual cases might need to be modified or dispensed with altogether, the authoritative manner in which he stated his positions, combined with his role as the father of psychoanalysis and fount of ultimate knowledge in our field, has caused his followers to view his recommendations in precisely the way that he cautioned them not to. That is, as rules of technique that defined the attitudes to be taken and the methods used by practitioners when beginning a new treatment.

It took many years, a great deal more clinical experience, and the waning of the influence of the émigré analysts, many of whom were close to Freud, for his contributions to be assessed and re-evaluated. Contemporary ideas concerning the beginning phase of treatment reaffirm a number of Freud's ideas while augmenting, modifying, and correcting others. I am speaking here from the perspective of analysts working in the traditional or Freudian model. As an analyst trained in a classical institute and who utilises an approach that has been termed modern conflict theory, I will be writing from what is essentially a traditional Freudian point as modified by newer findings with regard to the influence of countertransference, enactments, nonverbal behaviour, and the interactive dimension of the psychoanalytic situation.

My approach in this chapter will be to take up in sequence the major issues that Freud discusses in his paper, "On beginning the treatment" and comment on them from the viewpoint of contemporary theory and practice. I will also make some comments about some relevant issues that Freud does not discuss.

Freud begins his paper by emphasising the necessity, with new patients, of undertaking a trial period of analysis of one or two week's duration. This is necessary, he states, in order to rule out conditions such as covert schizophrenia—Freud often used the term, paraphrenia, to indicate a psychosis of this kind that may not be detectable in face-to-face interviews. Such a trial period can also be useful, he states, to aid the analyst in assessing a potential patient's suitability for analysis; that is, whether he or she takes to, and can utilise, the analytic process. Freud indicates that a short trial of analysis presents no particular problems. If the patient turns out not to be a suitable case, neither patient nor analyst has made a commitment to analysis and, presumably, the patient can, without difficulty, be referred for a different type of treatment.

Until quite recently, most modern day analysts rejected the idea of a trial of analysis as not particularly informative and as potentially harmful to patients. The experience for a patient of being on trial, as it were, would, they claimed, so alter and distort the analytic process that no valuable information could be obtained from such a procedure. Moreover, there was general agreement that if a patient proved unsuitable for analysis and the trial had to be stopped, that individual could suffer a severe narcissistic blow; one that could, in fact, inflict a good deal of longstanding damage.

In recent years some analysts, notably Rothstein (1995), have championed the idea of a trial analysis. Contending that our current notions of, and methods for, assessing analysability are seriously flawed, Rothstein has suggested that most individuals who seek our help deserve a trial of analysis. Since, in his view, analysis is the very best treatment available for all but frankly psychotic or psychopathic individuals, our patients deserve such a trial. And in contrast to many of his colleagues, Rothstein holds that if the trial does not work out, the damage is minimal as the patient can usually be switched to a form of psychotherapy that not only better meets her needs, but that is often welcomed by individuals for whom analysis has proven to be unsuitable. Rothstein's influence has been considerable in the US, and a number of American analysts have begun to adopt his views.

Freud then goes on to say that it is inadvisable for patients seeking analysis to have been in prior psychiatric treatment. Moreover, he contends, it is best that the patient not have had any prior contact with the analyst. Although he does not spell out the reason for these recommendations, it is clear that Freud was concerned that the transference could be contaminated by a prior treatment experience. Prior treatment, in other words, could result in transferences carried over from the previous therapist. This would distort the analytic transference. He also believed that prior contact with one's analyst was inadvisable as such contact could lead to the initiation of transferences that did not arise in the analytic setting. In his view, it was only those transferences that developed in the analytic process itself that yielded valuable insights.

Until approximately the mid-1970s, traditional analysts held to the idea that prior therapy, especially with the treating analyst, was inadvisable as it could interfere with the development of an analytic process. In fact, it was standard practice to refer one's psychotherapy patients to another analyst should a switch to analysis be indicated. Students treating psychotherapy patients were prohibited from converting these patients into analytic cases. Analysis with the person doing the prior psychotherapy was not considered feasible, as being in psychotherapy would both ruin an individual's ability to enter into an analytic process and would lead to the development of unanalysable transferences.

Today that situation is totally reversed. Most analytic cases are developed from the analyst's psychotherapy practice. Being in psychotherapy with an analyst is no longer viewed as a barrier to an effective analytic experience with the same analyst at a later time. In fact, in some cases the prior psychotherapy is viewed as a necessary preparation for analysis.

The primary reason for this shift, however, has been the decline in the popularity of analysis in the last two decades. For most practitioners, analytic cases are difficult to come by. Very few individuals today seek out analysis directly. The great majority of patients wish to have therapy on a once or twice a week basis. And in many cases it is only after a patient has been in psychotherapy for some time—sometimes a number of years—that he becomes interested in, and is prepared to undertake, a more intensive treatment. This change, a worldwide phenomenon, illustrates the fact that, often, it has been a practical necessity, the result of shifting economic conditions and changes in societal values, rather than fundamental theoretical differences with traditional views, that have been responsible for this alteration in analytic practice.

Two areas in which most analysts have adhered to Freud's recommendations concern the matter of charging for missed sessions and adopting a direct and frank attitude toward money.

In the strongest terms, Freud advised his colleagues to adopt his policy of leasing a specific hour to each patient who would then be responsible for that time. His reason for insisting on this arrangement was twofold; to protect the analyst's income and to reduce those resistances in the patient that took the form of finding reasons to miss sessions. Most traditional analysts accept Freud's reasoning and his practice of both charging for all sessions and being direct and forthright in discussing financial matters. However, a minority of our colleagues feel that Freud's attitude was extensively authoritarian and inflexible and that it failed to take into account the patient's needs or emotional condition. Hence these practitioners modify the usual arrangements in a number of ways; by not charging for appointments that are filled, or if sufficient notice of an absence is given; or by allowing several weeks vacation time if the patient is unable to coordinate her vacation with the dates that the analyst is away. Certain realities in today's world have also led to modifications of Freud's policy. The fact that in the US the hourly fee for analysis may be two hundred dollars or more has made it difficult for analysts to charge that much money due to illness or other unavoidable circumstances. In addition, certain patients, feeling that the traditional arrangement is grossly unfair, simply refuse to go along with it and will not enter treatment with an analyst who is unwilling to modify this practice.

The situation with regard to the frequency of sessions is quite different today as compared to Freud's time. His recommendation that all new patients be seen six days a week is no longer feasible. It is interesting that the reason Freud gave for the recommendation was that this degree of frequency was necessary for the analyst to be able to keep up with the patient's real life circumstances. He did not speak of the need to maintain an open channel to the unconscious, although this is implied in his reference to the Monday crust, which quickly forms when there is a missed session.

The debate about frequency, carried on at an international level, has been one of the most contentious in modern times. Traditional analysts in America, England, and parts of Europe, and South America have maintained that analysis cannot be carried out in a satisfactory way with a frequency of less than four sessions per week. Colleagues elsewhere, particularly in France and parts of South America, have insisted that a frequency of three sessions per week is sufficient. Until recently the standard for training analysis in the International Psychoanalytic Association has been four times a week. In order to effect a compromise between the different positions, the IPA now endorses three models of training, one of which, the French model, allows for training analysis on a three times a week basis.

The dispute over frequency has revolved, not such much about theoretical matters—although there has been some disagreement on this score—but practical ones. Economic realities in some countries have made four times a week analysis virtually impossible. Patients will not come at this frequency. As a result, analysis, including the training analysis, has had to be conducted on a three times a week schedule. While Freud maintained that almost daily sessions were necessary at the beginning of an analysis, he believed that at a later time, or in the case of a re-analysis, three appointments per week were adequate. While the debate over the optimal frequency for analysis continues, increasingly practical considerations have influenced practice so that all over the world the number of patients in three times a week analysis has increased markedly. Many informed colleagues predict that this will become the new standard for psychoanalytic treatment.

As is well known, the average duration of analysis at the time that Freud wrote his paper on beginning the treatment was anywhere from six months to a year. The aim was, as far as possible, to lift repression, which, in Freud's view, was chiefly responsible for creating the internal conditions that led to the patient's symptoms. It was through the lifting of repression, a task largely accomplished through the analysis of resistance, chiefly transference resistance, that the patient could gain relief from his distress.

Today the emphasis is not primarily on symptoms but on the analysis of character problems and the maladaptive compromise formations that give rise to them. Hence the opening phase of treatment, which for Freud was a matter of a month or two, is now measured in years. It is not unusual for a colleague reporting on a case in treatment for two or three years to speak of the patient as still in the opening phase.

Where current practice has remained in accord with Freud's 1913 views is in the importance of analysing resistance and on the centrality of the transference in analytic work.

For many contemporary analysts, analysis consists very largely in the stepwise analysis of resistances, particularly transference resistances as they arise in treatment. Where differences chiefly arise is in the question of how and when to deal with the transference. Freud advised not interpreting with the positive transference, which in his view, fostered the patient's ability to speak freely and to open up in analysis, until it became a resistance. Then interpretation of it was essential for progress to continue.

Today many analysts, following Gill's (1982) lead, believe that early interpretation of the patient's experience of the analyst is essential as resistances based on these perceptions often act to inhibit patients and block the analytic process. Other analysts, however, hold that the current trend toward seeking out and interpreting the transference distorts the listening process and creates an artificial, intrinsically induced emphasis on transference material.

As of today, this debate goes on in many quarters and has not been resolved. Each analyst's view of this issue will dictate his or her way of dealing with the opening phase. Those who favour Freud's view—endorsed by Heinz Kohut as an integral part of the Self-Psychology approach—will allow the analysis to unfold and reserve transference interpretations to a time when resistances centring around transference perceptions block further progress. Those who follow Gill (1982), and also Melanie Klein (1952), will focus on transference issues and interpret the patients' perceptions of, and response to, the analyst early on. As yet there is no hard evidence that one of these approaches has proven to be more effective, and has yielded better results, than the other.

In his 1913 paper, Freud put a good deal of emphasis on the value of free association and on the use of the couch as an aid to fostering this process. He also made it clear that the patient needed to be instructed, not only to say everything that came to mind, but, quite explicitly, to avoid the temptation to withhold any thoughts, no matter how distressing or embarrassing. Freud, in other words, sought out and encouraged the patient's conscious cooperation with the analytic endeavour. He did not, as analysts today are inclined to do, view the ability to free associate as the result of, rather than a condition for, entering into an analytic process. In other words, Freud seemed to believe that the resistances to free association could be largely overcome by means of instruction and suggestion, whereas, today, analysts understand that resistance to free association is to be expected and that it is only through interpretation of the underlying anxieties that feed this resistance that a patient can allow himself to begin to speak freely and to enter into a process of free association.

Perhaps the greatest difference between Freud's approach to beginning an analysis and contemporary views of this phase of treatment lies in the roles of countertransference, nonverbal behaviour, including enactments, and, more generally, the interactive dimension of analysis.

In his 1913 paper, Freud does not mention countertransference. He emphasises the importance of the patient's developing rapport with the analyst but believes that this will naturally develop if the analyst displays the proper empathy and understanding. The role that countertransference plays in the analytic process was not an issue that Freud discussed very much in his writings. Although he was well aware of the potential problems that stem from countertransference feelings that are acted on—he was concerned about some of the excesses of his colleagues—his contributions to understanding the psychology of the analyst at work are meagre. Certainly in 1913, when he was preoccupied with understanding the dynamic forces at play in the minds of his patients, the issue of countertransference and the interactive dimension of analysis were not matters to which he paid much attention.

Things are very different today. From his very first contact with the prospective patient, the contemporary analyst is attuned not only to transferences issues that may be developing, but to his own reactions to the voice, appearance, and personality of the new patient.

In the US this quality of self-awareness, as well as awareness of the other, is an aspect of analytic technique that has been emphasised in the training of candidates since the mid to late 1970s when the writings of Heimann (1950), Little (1951), Klein (1952), Racker (1968), and the British object relations theorists became important influences, and the older idea of the objective analyst was replaced by a view of him as inevitably contending with his own subjectivity.

The view of analysis as a two-person psychology, with the analytic material influenced not only by the patient's wishes, fantasies, and defences, but also by the interplay of transference and countertransference was given impetus by the writings of Gill (1982), Loewald (1960), Stolorow, Brandchaft, & Atwood (1983) and the relationists such as Greenberg and Mitchell (1983), as well as by the British object relations school. This perspective has altered our view of the opening phase of analysis from one which focuses exclusively on understanding the psychology of the patient to one which views what transpires in this phase as being the product of the dynamic interaction of two psychologies, each influencing and being influenced by the other.

Due in part to the contribution of contemporary research on mother–infant interaction, modern analysts today are aware of unconscious transmissions of affect and fantasy between patient and analyst from their very first contact. At their initial meeting patient and analyst gain impressions of one another from their physical appearance, dress, facial expression, and tone of voice that can have an enduring impact on their psyches and can help determine the extent to which they feel well matched (Kantrowitz, 2002).

This initial contact stimulates transference and countertransference responses that can, and often do, colour the ongoing treatment. The modern analyst is aware of these forces and, when appropriate, will interpret resistances that arise from this interplay of transferences.

The strong impact of first impressions in analysis can be illustrated by a story that I have related elsewhere (Jacobs, 1991). It concerns an analyst who was quite small of stature. He was about five foot two in height and weighed perhaps 120 pounds. One day the analyst received a phone call from a man who requested an appointment. At the time of the agreed upon appointment, the patient arrived and took a seat in the waiting room. The analyst then emerged from his office to greet his new patient. There in front of him was an individual who was six foot eight in height, weighed 280 pounds, and was wearing cowboy boots and a ten-gallon hat.

For a moment, the diminutive analyst just stared at the patient. Then shrugging his shoulders, he smiled, offered a greeting, and gestured toward his office. "Come on in anyway," he said.

Like Freud in 1913, the contemporary analyst views the beginning of an analysis as a crucial time; one that sets the tone for all that is to come. And, like Freud, he believes that the development of rapport, or a working alliance, is essential to progress in the analysis. And he also believes, with Freud, that such rapport is largely the product of the patient's positive transference feelings. But while Freud believed that proper technique on the part of the analyst will ensure the development of rapport and a good start to the analysis, the modern analyst is aware from his initial contact with the patient, not only of the interplay of transference and countertransference, but of the effect of unconscious, and, especially, nonverbal, communication in affecting the nature of the analytic relationship and the ongoing analytic process.

These changes, which have enforced and enriched our analytic work, are the result of both a century of clinical experience and of research, especially in the area of infant–mother interaction, that was unavailable to Freud. It was he, however, who by means of his remarkable insight and intuition provided us with ground rules for beginning analytic treatment that, in large measure, remain valid today. As Freud stated, his recommendations were not to be taken as rules, but as suggestions that would be subject to change as the field progressed. The advances that have taken place have, indeed, led to modifications, as well as additions, to Freud's early ideas. But although nearly a century old, his recommendations have retained their value for us, as they have provided us with the building blocks, the foundation, upon which we have built our current understanding of how best to initiate analytic treatment.

2

From past to present: what changes have occurred in the acceptance of the conditions for psychoanalytic treatment and its setting?[1]

Marie-France Dispaux

Any careful reading of Freud's paper "On beginning the treatment" (1913c) cannot but prove once again how astonishingly modern some of his ideas were. The clinical aspects of that paper are particularly striking; it begins with the well-known metaphor about "the noble game of chess" (p. 123), which reminds us of the difficulties encountered whenever an analysis is being envisaged.

My present task is to explore the ways in which, in contemporary psychoanalytic practice, the ability of the patients who seek our help to accept the conditions and setting of the treatment has changed over time. There are several levels on which we could investigate this matter. First of all, we must ask ourselves if we have become aware of significant changes in the initial stages of psychoanalytic treatment and, if so, attempt to discover the underlying reasons for these. Have these changes to do with modifications in the pathology of the patients who seek our help? What impact have changes in society had on the possibility of accepting the conditions for psychoanalytic treatment? Why, and in what way, does that question seem more of an issue today than it was before? I shall try to answer these questions.

Freud began by issuing a warning.

The extraordinary diversity of the psychical constellations concerned, the plasticity of all mental processes and the wealth of determining factors oppose any mechanization of the technique; and they bring it about that a course of action that is as a rule justified may at times prove ineffective, whilst one that is usually mistaken may once in a while lead to the desired end. (1913c, p. 123)

We must therefore bear in mind the idea that no two beginnings of treatment are the same. I think it important to emphasise the fact that, while he was writing the paper on beginning treatment, Freud was also working on *Totem and Taboo* (1912–1913), and studying narcissism in depth in preparation for the paper that would be published the following year, "On narcissism: an introduction" (1914c). I have identified three lines of enquiry in Freud's attempt to mark out what happens when treatment is proposed: (i) the indications for analysis and what Freud called "a trial period [of] one or two weeks" (1913c, p. 124); (ii) the establishment of the setting, specifying the time and length of sessions, payment, and the couch-armchair arrangement; and (iii) the assessment of the analysand's potential for free association linked to his or her cathexis of verbal expression and past history. For each of these elements, I shall say a few words about Freud's thinking before exploring the changes that we sometimes encounter in present-day practice; I shall base these comments both on my own experience and on questions that have arisen in the course of supervisions. For some years now, in my own work as a psychoanalyst as well as in discussions with colleagues and in supervision, issues concerning the beginning of treatment have often to be thought about, so as to prepare patients who consult us for undertaking some form of psychoanalytic treatment or even psychoanalysis in the classic sense of the word.

I shall begin by emphasising one important element. In my view, if our way of working has indeed changed somewhat, this should not necessarily be seen as something negative. I do think that we are now much more ready to propose a kind of setting that is really suitable for each patient. This does not mean, all the same—and here I shall quote the title of Raymond Cahn's book, which, by the way, I find very interesting—that this is "the end of the couch" (Cahn, 2002). I personally always have in mind the idea that, whenever it seems preferable for the patient, I should suggest psychoanalysis; in some situations, I keep that idea in the back of my mind for as long as may be necessary before sharing it with the patient.

Indications for psychoanalysis and "a trial period"

After reminding the reader of the indications that he had set out in an earlier paper ("On psychotherapy", 1905a [1904]), Freud explains that he would usually suggest a "trial period". He does nevertheless point out that

> [this] preliminary experiment, however, is itself the beginning of a psycho-analysis and must conform to its rules. There may perhaps be this distinction made, that in it one lets the patient do nearly all the talking and explains nothing more than what is absolutely necessary to get him to go on with what he is saying. (1913c, p. 124)

I was very interested to see expressed in this way a modification that our training committee had introduced with respect to the length of supervisions; that modification is totally in keeping with what Freud says in that extract.

It was some seven years ago now that we made that important change as regards supervisions carried out in the context of the training programme. In many of our discussions, we came to realise that candidates were finding it more and more difficult to suggest that their patients have psychoanalysis. I would draw a distinction here between, on the one hand, the fact that young analysts usually find it to some extent difficult to make use themselves of the treatment that we call psychoanalysis and, on the other, difficulties that are specific to the patients themselves. In my own work—and my colleagues also have found this to be the case—patients need time to prepare themselves for undertaking proper psychoanalytic work, given the constraints as to time and setting that are an integral part of an analysis. This preparatory phase has proved to be very important and, in our view, is very much part of the analysis—in fact, at times, it appears to be a precondition for any such work to be undertaken. We therefore decided to add one year onto the minimum time required for supervision in the case of the training programme, so that enough time could be allotted to that important part of the work whenever it was deemed necessary, before beginning analysis in the classical sense. The minimum supervision period was henceforth to be three years instead of two; the time required by that initial phase, with analyst and patient sitting opposite each other, would be included in the overall supervision period, as long as the two-year minimum supervision of analysis with the patient on the couch was adhered to. That new arrangement enabled candidates not to search anxiously and at all costs for a patient suited to the training programme—inevitably, that would lead them sometimes to "pre-empt" the decision, not only to their own detriment but also to that of the patient. Some situations are extremely complex, as for example when the opposite movement arises—when the couch is brought into the consultation setting, some surprising changes can occur in the kind of material that the patient develops. It is as though that new element suddenly reveals a whole chapter of the mind that had been kept in the background until then—and that transformation might stimulate the wish for psychoanalysis *stricto sensu*. Incidentally, this goes to show how important psychoanalytic training is for this kind of psychotherapeutic and psychoanalytic treatment, with patient and analyst sitting facing each other.

It is important to emphasise what makes this phase a truly psychoanalytic one, what makes it—to use Freud's term—"the beginning of a psychoanalysis". It is essential that, from the outset, the analyst should be in a position of attentive listening as similar as possible to that of the psychoanalytic situation—due regard must be paid to benevolent neutrality, evenly suspended attention, and the kind of silent listening that opens up for the patient the possibility of associating freely. The setting must be defined—more flexible, perhaps, than that of psychoanalysis, but one that lets the patient feel and experience the validity and containing aspect of consistency.

I was able to propose that kind of set-up to a patient of mine whom I shall call Mr B. A man in his forties, he had already undergone many different kinds of treatment and had been hospitalised on several occasions. A highly intelligent person, he had begun working in research, but, on his return from the US, he began to feel more and more depressed. In his life there were many features typical of the problem situations so prevalent in contemporary society: the difficulty in facing up to life's demands—this came to the fore when he began working, but it had long been simmering, hidden beneath what he and other people saw as his success at school and university level. In short, his problem had to do with narcissism, and in the initial phase of our work together the central themes involved subjectivation and dependence. The kind of distress that nowadays most frequently underlies any request for help has less to do with the neurotic dimension and intrapsychic conflict; most of the time, the suffering that patients express has to do with narcissistic conflicts of self-identity, with kinds of pathology that involve enactments, soma-tisation, and addictive behaviour. Depression is palpable, even though it may not be experienced directly. The overall feeling of discomfort is often vague and ill-defined.

In his paper, Freud thought of the indications for psychoanalysis above all in terms of nosographic factors; the classic form of treat-ment was intended for transference neuroses, even though he was already thinking that some cases of near-psychosis could also be improved thanks to psychoanalysis. I think that there is quite a clear link between his discussion of the indications for analysis and his thoughts on narcissism, which were developing more or less at the same time as he was writing his paper on beginning treatment. I would not go as far as to say that diagnosis is no longer of any impor-tance to us. We do, however, look at the question of indications more in terms of the individual's mental functioning; in other words, we focus more on the element of analysability. In the case of Mr B, for example, I felt that he would benefit from a stable setting; however, the urgency of his request for help, his fear of dependence, and his difficulty in tolerating separation meant that some preliminary work had to be carried out first. The initial difficulty that we may come up against in this kind of situation has to do with dependence, linked to the patient's difficulty in committing him- or herself to the work involved. In fact, all the treatments that Mr B had undertaken since coming back from the US had promised him quick results focused on the relevant symptom—but he had given up these treatments just as quickly. Primary dependence is a normal process for each of us, but many of our patients nowadays are afraid of it. I would go so far as to say that the fact that individualism and independence are extolled as being the very models of relationship is the social expression of this state of affairs. Why is the necessary and normal dependence on the object so frightening? Why do so many people prefer to have recourse to a relationship short-circuit that leads to an illusory quest for breaking free of dependence, either through remaining in a narcissistic capsule—"I don't need anybody"—or through becoming dependent on some addictive substance or other? In other words, dependence lies at the heart of all human relationships (true love without dependence cannot exist) be they family-based, between partners, friendship, or love; yet so many people strive as hard as they can to avoid it—to the point, sometimes, of rushing headlong into substance dependence in order to fight against what I would call "true" dependence.

From the "Project" (1950a [1895]) all the way through to his final papers, Freud laid particular emphasis on primary dependence and the helplessness [*Hilflosigkeit*] that goes with it. With patients like Mr B, it is quite clear that, in every situation in which the ego feels over-whelmed or about to be overwhelmed, distress and infantile depen-dence are reawakened, as well, of course, as the deep anxiety that is part of them. Freud emphasised the idea of being overwhelmed—in other words, he stressed the element of psychical economy in every situation that is potentially traumatic. From a clinical point of view, we can quite easily understand the feeling of urgency that some patients describe when that kind of distress overtakes them; it is as though they felt some kind of pressing need to break free of it. They see that need more or less in terms of a short-circuit device—a fuse or trip-switch that breaks the circuit before it explodes. Even in the preliminary interviews we can see that the depressive position has never been adequately processed. Patients who have problems with dependence remain fixated on external objects; they are extremely dependent on these while at the same time they reject them. This makes introjection quite a problem for them.

In talking about these patients who are caught between anxiety about being trapped inside and by the object, and their fear of being abandoned and left all alone, I feel sure that you all have similar clin-ical examples. One of my female patients said: "I can't stay all by myself, but whenever I'm with anybody, I want to run away . . ." Mr B is another example: he lives with his mother, but never takes any of his meals with her.

This cannot but make us think of one of Winnicott's (1958b) famous paradoxes: the capacity to be alone in presence of the object. This is one of the most important indications of the maturity of an individual's emotional development, a major element as regards the kind of treatment that can be proposed. In its most developed form, the capacity to be alone is based on the ability to face up to the feelings aroused by the primal scene; this implies the maturity of erotic development, genital capacity, and acceptance of femininity. At the outset, however, being alone in the presence of someone else can come about only if the self's immaturity is compensated for by the support that the mother gives it naturally; her attentive presence and the support that she gives to her infant will be internalised, thereby making it possible for the child to be alone without the need for the mother's actual presence. It is only when he or she is alone—in the presence of someone—that the infant can discover his or her existence as a person. If there is too much absence or, conversely, an over-exciting presence (absence leaves the infant in the grip of his or her own excitation), something like a false existence constructed on the basis of excitation will, at least potentially, be set up. When the capacity to be alone is integrated, the child, or the adult, reaches a state of relaxation in which it becomes possible simply to *be*. That is when true drive-related experiences can begin. It is the prerequisite for the infant's experiences to be felt as real and as owned by the self and for those experiences to be accompanied by a feeling of going on being (Winnicott, 1956, p. 303). This experience is qualitatively very different from that of infants who excite themselves in a compulsive manner without ever reaching a state of relaxation; in such cases, they have the impression that what they experience is not real, leaving them with a feeling of pointlessness and of something missing. They tend to seek out all kinds of excitation, the more the better. Self-soothing procedures are set up, rather than any true and integrated form of auto-eroticism.

As regards the always-sensitive evaluation of analysability, I would like to say a word or two about one element that links dependence to the world of the drives—passivity. As we know, the active/passive pairing is one of the three great dimensions that dominate mental life: pleasure/unpleasure, active/passive, and self/other. The active/passive pairing is an integral part of sexuality; passivity in men and in women has to do with the feminine dimension, with receptiveness. For passivity to be experienced as something pleasant, the drive has to be bound and the ego already well-established. On this point, Green (1999a) draws a helpful distinction between passivity/pleasure and passivity/distress: he suggests that we call this latter feeling "passivation". If passivity opens on to pleasure, dependence on the drive-related dimension will be experienced in a pleasant way. On the other hand, if passivity is experienced in terms of dependence and distress, passivation will be felt as a kind of annihilation giving rise to nameless dread and/or to a disruptive form of excitation. This is an important factor to take into account when we are trying to decide whether a given patient will be able to tolerate lying down on the couch, without the support of seeing the analyst; it is in the initial stages of the work that we have to try to make that assessment.

Establishing the setting: constructing the analytic site

Freud went on to describe in detail the features of the setting which best enable the transference neurosis to unfold: payment for and times of the sessions, the use of the couch by the patient with the analyst sitting in the background. He emphasised the importance of the patient paying for any missed sessions, the regularity of the sessions and their frequency in order to avoid the "Monday crust" (1913c, p. 127)—elements that are still very much part of contemporary practice. These different aspects of the setting are still firmly upheld by psychoanalysts today and are indeed one of the ways in which they are recognised as belonging to the IPA. Even though there may be variations, depending on which country we find ourselves in, as to the number of weekly sessions, establishing the setting correctly remains a guarantee of genuine psychoanalytic practice. Nonetheless, for many patients, this kind of setting is not self-evident. With his idea of the "analytic site", Donnet (1995b) has widened the scope of the setting:

> The analytic site should be looked upon first of all from the point of view of the landscape that it presents to us as more or less attractive or convenient . . . That "geography" is also a factor in the "indication", lending support to the assessment of the potential adequacy between the site and the patient and by anticipating what adjustments may be necessary. In short, it prepares the way for deciding how to "establish" the setting, a decision which, in a random kind of way, has to be taken. . . . The geography of the site, however, is theoretical. Analytic practice demands that out of the encounter between the individual—together with his or her

project of "psychical" survival and expansion—and the site where
this will be set up there arises a history marked by *après-coup*
[deferred retroactive impact]. The "local elements" of the site will
reach consistency in their existence only thanks to the *use* that the
patient discovers he or she is able to make of it. (pp. 9–47)

In *The Analysing Situation*, Donnet (2005) draws a more precise
distinction between the analytic site and the analysing situation. The
idea of "site" acknowledged the need for putting in place an initial
set-up for psychoanalysis, but one that would not have the inflexibil-
ity of a setting that would lend more importance to bearing witness
to the analyst's formal identity as such than to helping the patient.
He emphasises the need for the patient to self-appropriate the site.
Donnet realised that his fellow analysts who made use of the idea of
the analytic site were referring from the outset to the construction of
the site; he agreed with me (Dispaux, 2002) that we cannot properly
talk of a site without taking into account how it is explored between
patient and analyst in the course of their initial encounters.

Freud took into consideration only the form of treatment that we
would nowadays call the classic one, and he saw the indications for
psychoanalysis in terms of that choice. Although in his view the classic form of treatment was limited to transference neuroses, we can
say today that many of his patients were more like those whom we
treat nowadays than is generally thought, that is, patients presenting
narcissistic problems. We have, over the years, given its rightful place
to what I call the work of psychoanalysis. I mean by that the settings
and arrangements that are more adapted to this kind of psychological structure, in an alloy of pure gold and copper (cf. Freud 1919a
[1918], p. 168). (Some earlier translations, for example into French,
spoke of gold and lead, which do not combine together, thereby
initially throwing discredit on the whole idea.) We could say—this, of
course, is just a rough outline—that patients make use of three main
forms of expression and representation in what they want to
communicate to us: representation and its well-tempered work,
motility through enacting, and the perceptual dimension as a
defence and a representation of what could not otherwise be thought
about and represented. The difficulty lies in offering them a setting,
a *modus operandi* that will enable their preferred form of expression
to be accepted and allowed to unfold, even though we might find it
difficult to fall in with it and allow ourselves to be put off balance

when we let go of our usual landmarks. I am thinking here, for example, of a patient whose manner of speaking was very much in secondary-process mode, giving the impression that his preferred means of communication was through verbal expression and representation; in fact, he made use of these as an enormous counter-cathexis when faced with what he saw as being on the edge of a precipice. The main part of what he communicated to me was expressed through the perceptual and visual modes. The risk of seeing the dykes collapse—as it was, they could barely hold up—had, in my view, to be avoided at all costs. We were on a mountain ridge and he was constantly in danger either of falling into a blank and bottomless depression or of exploding whenever his underlying violence began to surface. Also, at the end of each of our meetings, his separation anxiety was intense—and at the same time, his anxiety about being intruded upon was just as acute. Suggesting that he lie down on the couch might well have caused him to lose his bearings, which were already extremely fragile, and given rise to a constant fight against regression experienced not as opening on to something but as threatening him with a potential breakdown. The support that looking/seeing offered, proof as it were of attentiveness, and the analyst's presence seemed to me to be something that he could lean on so as to enable some form of psychic envelope to be built up or rebuilt around him. There was another factor that led me to offer him just two sessions per week in a face-to-face situation: he was at a very unsettled point in his life—he had only recently arrived in the country and was unsure of how long he would be staying. I shall say a few words later about this kind of problem that is specific to some of the ways in which people live nowadays.

On the other hand, with a patient who was regressed and in a comparably serious pathological state, I had no hesitation in proposing four sessions per week with the patient lying on the couch. With that patient, I was sure that, in spite of the difficulties that I could imagine lay in the future, it was the only way of enabling him to make any fundamental change in his life. His family and professional environment were, all the same, much more stable and we both of us felt that it was possible and desirable to undertake the treatment without any limitation as to its length.

There remain two issues involving the setting that can be proposed: money and time. Freud spoke of the necessary sacrifices that have to be made when undertaking an analysis, both as regards the time that has to be devoted to it and as to the financial aspect. In his view, money was a lever and an absolutely necessary reality-factor in the treatment—free treatment could in fact harm the process itself. It was, however, a matter for regret for him that, given the financial aspect, analysis would be possible only for the better-off. What is the situation today? My own view is that the real "luxury" nowadays is that of time. I would not deny, of course, that an analysis costs a lot of money, but I would tend to agree with what Freud, not without humour, wrote:

> . . . the expense involved in psycho-analysis is excessive only in appearance. Quite apart from the fact that no comparison is possible between restored health and efficiency on the one hand and a moderate financial outlay on the other, when we add up the unceasing costs of nursing-homes and medical treatment and contrast them with the increase of efficiency and earning capacity which results from a successfully completed analysis, we are entitled to say that the patients have made a good bargain. Nothing in life is so expensive as illness—and stupidity. (1913c, p. 133)

Time is a much more important issue nowadays. Reading two interviews with J.-L. Donnet (Donnet & Gougoulis, 2006; Donnet & Minazio, 2005) on the subject of how requests for help addressed to the Jean Favreau Centre in Paris have developed over time, I was struck by the fact that, even when treatment is free to the end-user— no financial issue is, therefore, directly involved—patients hesitate to commit themselves to an analysis with several sessions per week, just as we find in private practice.

> The consultant's perplexity is very often commensurate with the gap between the quality of the preliminary interview—very processual and meaningful—and the obstacles that arise whenever the patient has to think about long-term treatment. This is all the more striking since the treatment itself will be free. Concretely, these obstacles are often related to factors that have to do with external reality—but we would be mistaken were we to see in them nothing but resistance: the unsettled nature of their situation in life, their availability for undertaking a training course or accepting a vacancy far from where they live, their lack of job security and the fear of asking their employer to agree to their appointments, etc. (Donnet & Gougoulis, 2006, p. 1028)

I have come to realise that a similar kind of situation exists with analysands who work in hospitals or mental health centres; that kind of employment could be thought of as being more open to arranging working hours so as to make it easier for those concerned to undertake analysis or even supervision—this was indeed the case until about ten or so years ago, but it is more difficult now, because the idea of "productivity" seems to be more important than the carer's training and personal development. Social and cultural factors have a considerable impact on the requests for help that are addressed to us. Financial insecurity and employment problems are social constraints, as is productivity in the work setting. There is a risk that analysis could be seen as a cocoon, a protected space in which people take refuge in order to avoid having to face up to the real world. The outside world seems to be more and more problematic, with little heed being paid to the needs of human beings. Work-related pathology is becoming more and more frequent and is now being studied in some depth. It is no longer the case that we can attribute these difficulties simply to resistance on the patient's part. One example of that kind of situation is becoming more and more frequent in Belgium (and probably in many capital cities across Europe)—that of the "expatriates", or "expats" as they call themselves, using the English word.[2] The term refers to employees of the various European Union bodies and business executives whose appointment in this country will last for a few years, although, generally speaking, no definite time-span is decided upon at the outset. They settle here with their spouse and children—who, more often than not, have not wanted to move but who are doing their best to adapt to their new circumstances. These families go on to develop a particular kind of pathology that has to do with being uprooted, losing their home country, their familiar environment, their family and friends—and, for the spouse who did not actually choose to leave all this but followed his or her partner—their job. Added to this is the idea that they may be leaving again at short notice, so that they find it impossible to settle down properly in their new country. I have seen people who have come back to this country from abroad; the problems that they encounter are all the more difficult in that they were expecting to find themselves in the same kind of situation as "before"—their disappointment is therefore even greater. It is not difficult to understand why so many of our patients nowadays have a kind of backcloth of depressive symptoms. Depression—what Fédida (2001) so rightly called the "human" illness—lies at the heart of the kind of problem that patients present nowadays, very often in stark contrast to the values of performance and action that are those of society. There is a kind of obligation to *be stronger, better, quicker* . . . the slogan that the outside world seems to impose on people. The internal world, all the same, needs presence and time for it to be built up.

A few words on cathecting verbal expression and the past

Freud pointed out that we must let patients say what they want to say: ". . . Please tell me what you know about yourself" (1913c, p. 134). He seemed to think that it was obvious that the patient would immediately begin talking and telling him about his or her life. I would like to say a few words about an important aspect of indications for psychoanalysis, one that has to do with the patient cathecting his or her own verbal expression and life history. By "verbal expression", I am not referring to the number of words pronounced but to what André Green has called indexation (Green, 2002a), that is, the reflexive/reflective way in which patients look upon what they say in the preliminary interviews. Patients who talk all the time and make your head spin, without seeming to take into account the fact that you are present too, are demonstrating that they use speech in order to evacuate something and to protect themselves from entering into contact with the analyst. A quite different situation occurs when a patient says: "Oh, what I just said there is something of a surprise; I hadn't made that connection before talking to you". Such patients show that they are able to think about themselves and to cathect this space for thinking that the analyst is offering them. There is a link between, on the one hand, this capacity to cathect the analyst and verbal expression, and, on the other, the idea of time, memory and subjective life-history. Repressed memories—Freud was always on the lookout for these—will return for example in the patient's dreams thanks to something that is related, however remotely, to the initial event, or perhaps through a sudden flush of the senses, as in Proust's memory of the madeleine. Some memories that have been recorded simply as traces that were not then meaningful will return in a more compulsive, hallucinatory, or bodily mode, with no possibility of those traces being rediscovered as memories. In the pathological states that we encounter nowadays, it is that kind of memory which is more and more at the forefront. This raises issues concerning the impact on the analytical encounter of failures in *après-coup*.

In conclusion

The patient whom I spoke about earlier, Mr B, had begun several courses of treatment, all of which seemed to offer speedy solutions to his problems. After a few months' work together, Mr B said to me:

> I know this will take some time. The further I go, the more I realise that everything has to be looked at again, that I haven't built myself up on any solid foundation, that I'm always wobbling. It's strange when I think about that. I tried to talk to my father about it—but all he said was "What! With your intelligence and the diplomas you have, it's just not possible!" But I know that it is possible, even though it's not easy to accept the fact.

Mr B was beginning to understand that, in wanting to do things quickly, in fact he had wasted a lot of time.

One final thought about the issues that I raised earlier, as regards the idea as to whether we have seen any significant changes in the way treatment begins nowadays. Have these to do with changes in the pathologies of the patients who come to us? What impact do changes in society have on the possibility of agreeing to the preconditions of psychoanalytic treatment? Why and in what ways does that kind of question appear on the agenda more often nowadays than in the past? I do indeed think that the idea of agreeing to analysis, with the constraints that it implies, has changed. There are new openings both as regards psychopathology and in terms of sociocultural changes, even though patients themselves may have changed less than we sometimes think. If we look at Freud's patients, for example, it would be difficult to see them as purely neurotic! There are, all the same, many factors nowadays that have a significant impact on mental functioning: the increased tempo of modern life, the need to be independent too quickly with its demand for everything at once and as quickly as possible; enactments seem to be more important than thinking, appearances preferred to relationships, everything that glitters is better than going beneath the surface, confusion between genitality and sex . . . Yet in my view the tools that we have are still useful—perhaps even more so than before, as long as we manage to use them to open up new avenues. As Freud suggested—but not for the same reasons—a time for, what shall I call it, taming or learning seems to be necessary more and more. That time will help the patient to make the most of our particular tools—attentive listening, the setting, and interpretation. That phase can be flexible, focusing on psychoanalytic consultations or, as in the example I described earlier, interviews followed by a fairly strict face-to-face setting with the idea of moving toward psychoanalysis *stricto sensu* at a later date. In that initial phase, our neutrality will often be severely put to the test. I see that neutrality as an internal space linked to our psychoanalytic way of listening; it acts as a barometer and as a guarantee of the analyst's freedom to associate—the mark of genuine psychoanalytic work, as Freud saw it, from the very beginning of the treatment.

Notes

1. Translated by David Alcorn
2. To the ears of those who are not native English-speakers, the word has a somewhat barbaric note to it.

3

Transference and associativity, psychoanalysis, and its debate with suggestion

René Roussillon

"On beginning the treatment" (Freud, 1913c) is one of three papers that Freud wrote on the technique of psychoanalysis between 1913 and 1915, the other two being "Observations on transference love" (1915a [1914]) and "Remembering, repeating and working-through" (1914g). Taken together, they are the most effective of Freud's attempts to define the essence of the psychoanalytic situation and the work of psychoanalysis.

By 1913, he already had sufficient experience of the practice of psychoanalysis to be able to take stock of its strategy and essential characteristics. He was refining his conception of narcissism in a way that would open up a new chapter in the exploration of the mind and its workings,[1] laying the foundations for what, in 1921, would be the analysis of the ego without falling into the trap of mere self-reference. As he was working on his theory of narcissism and the way in which this would help to identify narcissistic patterns, he undertook a series of reflexive and reflective reappraisals not only of the history of psychoanalysis (Freud, 1914d) but also of its practical and theoretical aspects; this led him to envisage undertaking the colossal task of writing the fifteen papers on metapsychology that would provide an overall view of psychoanalysis and of its underlying theory.

The years 1913 to 1915 thus represent the first turning point in the development of his thinking, probably indeed the first great reflexive/reflective moment of it. The three papers on psychoanalytic practice that I mentioned above are the technical side of this reappraisal; in them, Freud sums up the overall development of psychoanalysis and highlights the essential features of what that experience had taught him. The paper on remembering[2] and that on transference love highlight some specific issues in psychoanalytic treatment and what the psychoanalyst must do when these particular problems arise in the course of an analysis. The issues raised in the paper on which I am at present focusing—that on beginning treatment—are different: the overall framework and central theme of that paper involve the general strategy that underlies the psychoanalytic method and the conditions under which it can be implemented.

The fundamental feature of the psychoanalytic method involves two closely linked aspects: the reference to the transference, a precondition for any attempt at interpretation according to Freud, and the associativity of mental functioning as evidenced in the rule of free association.

Analysis of the transference and the conditions under which this becomes possible

The first fundamental concept is that of the transference. The work of psychoanalysis is based on transference. It is this and what it brings into the here-and-now situation of a given session that give weight to the process as a whole and ensure that the analysis will not be superficial—that it will not be an intellectual form of analysis, but will call upon affects and drive-related experiences, the necessary conditions for genuine change and transformation to take place thanks to the analysis.

> When are we to begin making our communications to the patient? . . . The answer to this can only be: Not until an effective transference has been established in the patient, a proper *rapport* with him. (Freud, 1913c, p. 139)

There is also Freud's famous remark according to which "it is impossible to destroy anyone *in absentia* or *in effigie*" (Freud, 1912b, p. 108);

this makes it plain that, for any genuine transformation to occur, a given problem situation must be brought into the here-and-now of the transference.

The transference is therefore a precondition for the work of analysis. Its presence, its manifestations, and its subsequent analysis, draw the line between medical psychotherapies based on suggestion and psychoanalytic psychotherapy[3] based on the analysis of the effects of suggestion linked to the impact of the transference on the way in which the analyst's comments are received and integrated. That was also why Freud remained sceptical of any preliminary remark about what was going to take place in the course of an analysis—for example, what as yet inexperienced psychoanalysts may say about a transference love that is still to come. Freud did of course point out in his paper on transference love (1915a [1914]) that this is a product of the psychoanalytic situation—indeed, this is the very condition for its being interpreted. For it to be interpreted, as Freud himself pointed out, it must appear to be spontaneous. The psycho-analytic process takes place within this kind of paradoxical context; these paradoxes must be taken on board by both analyst and analysand if the persuasive effect of the work of the analysis is to be in any way convincing, thereby enabling the anticipated in-depth changes to take place.

This allows me to make a brief comment on Freud's famous idea according to which cure or recovery comes as a bonus, a remark that, in my opinion, has often been misunderstood. That declaration is sometimes—mistakenly—attributed to Lacan; Freud did not mean by it that psychoanalysis is not a kind of psychotherapy or that its aim has nothing to do with a therapeutic outcome—quite the contrary, in fact. He meant that going on with an analysis, without looking for any immediate relief from symptoms of the kind that suggestion aims to bring about, is the best way of treating the analysand's distress—it is the best kind of psychotherapy for this. Freud did not contrast psychotherapy with psychoanalysis, as is often the case nowadays; he drew a distinction between a flawed or superficial form of psychotherapy and a good-quality one that, through its in-depth work, can bring about lasting change. He explained that very appo-sitely in his metaphor of the dog-race in which a sausage was thrown onto the track (1915a [1914], p. 169)—with the result that the dogs threw themselves upon it so as to have immediate satisfaction rather than focus on the much more enlarged satisfaction awaiting the winner of the race: a whole garland of sausages. Nevertheless, as I shall make clear later, when treatment is being set up, there are aspects of the psychoanalytic situation that have to be imposed from the outset; these have the unavoidable effect of "fatherly suggestion", as Ferenczi put it (Groddeck, 1923, pp. 266–267). In such situations, suggestion would seem to be unavoidable; one major aspect of the treatment will be to make it possible to go beyond that thanks to the work of the analysis. The initial suggestion will then be seen as an "advance" that enabled the analysis to take place, a necessary suggestion that facilitated the subsequent possibility to go beyond suggestion.

Transference, however, is not exclusive to the psychoanalytic situation. As Freud pointed out as early as 1912, it develops in the great majority of treatment situations. The capacity to set up a transference represents a general process of mental functioning and is one form of the "compulsion to repeat" (Freud, 1914g). Nor is transference neurosis specific to psychoanalysis; each time that a transference is set up with respect to some institution or other (Freud spoke of the Church and the Army; we could probably add the family and any kind of treatment situation), a transference neurosis is or can be set up too.

What is specific to psychoanalysis is that it makes it possible to *analyse* the transference neurosis—it creates the conditions not only for that neurosis to be set up, but also for it to be analysed. That was Freud's most fundamental response to the threat of suggestion that hangs over—and will never stop hanging over—psychoanalysis. The transference represents a fundamental threat to the veracity of the psychoanalytic process insofar as it is a factor of influence and suggestion. To counteract influence and suggestion, it is not enough simply to avoid giving advice or to refrain from making use of the suggestion impact common to "medical" psychotherapies (to use Freud's term)—that would simply be a matter of intentional self-control and willpower. That alone, however, would not do away with unconscious influencing and suggesting, since it applies only to the deliberate and intentional aspect of these. Suggestion and influence can have an impact that has nothing to do with the analyst's intentional decisions—they involve the manner in which the analyst's comments and responses are understood by the analysand; in other words, they involve the unconscious transference. That kind of suggestion, influence, or even seduction cannot be countered simply by deciding to abstain intentionally from so responding; in order to go beyond the effect that it may have, the unconscious motives that underlie it have to be explored. This is one of the crucial issues at stake in the analysis of the transference—and that is why analysis of the transference is such an essential part of the definition of psychoanalysis when compared to other forms of psychotherapy based on suggestion; it is the dividing line between psychoanalytic psychotherapy and medical psychotherapy. The fundamental issue is therefore that of the conditions that make analysis of the transference possible.

One set of conditions concerns what we might call the transference arena—the early manifestations of the transference, those that, in the preliminary interviews, tend to focus initially on the setting and on the concrete rules that govern the treatment. This led Freud to explore how, in setting up the psychoanalytic situation, these early manifestations of the transference could be overcome—those that focus on the situation itself and take the initial stages of the analysis as their chosen medium. Freud was always drawing attention to the question of how those elements that tended to take the psychoanalytic setting itself as a locus for the transference or its manifestation could be moved away from that particular dimension and brought, as far as possible, into the transference onto the analyst. However, when the treatment is being set up, it is with respect to the setting itself that the transference and resistances tend initially to be manifested. The strategy behind beginning the treatment—the "general plan of the game" (Freud, 1913c, p. 123), as it were— consists in not allowing the transference to focus on that particular aspect. But how is this to be brought about, given that transference— and, more specifically, transference on to the analyst—is the very condition that determines the possibility of the analyst's interventions being in any way effective? Freud's idea was to combine two modes of intervention. On the one hand, certain specific aspects of the setting have quite simply to be imposed, the hope being that, with the evolution of the analytical process, that initial enforcement will be transformed into something more convincing, based on the analysand's ongoing experience of the analysis. Some things cannot be justified in advance (for example, matters concerning payment of the sessions: "My answer is: that's just the way it is"); they will become meaningful only through the treatment process itself and be felt to be valid thanks to an experience which, at that particular point, is still to come. This echoes what I said earlier about the "advance" that has to be granted initially to the analysis. At other times, Freud explained the essential reasons for such a setting, and the limitations placed on the analyst's prior knowledge. He did this, for example, with reference to Aesop's fable concerning the length of the Wayfarer's stride (1913c, p. 128) as an illustration of matters that have to do with the length of treatment in general. He did not, there-fore, immediately interpret this kind of "resistance", because the necessary conditions for such an interpretation to be effective were not yet in place. He imposed what could not be explained and explained what at that point could be—he made use both of coercion and of meaningfulness.

It was also for the analysis of the transference that he recom-mended that the analysand lie on the couch. His argument—which he did not share with his analysands—seemed initially to be a matter of personal comfort: he could not bear being looked at all day long by his patients. However, when he did get round to explaining why, it became clear that the real reason had to do with the analysis of the transference: on his face, in his gestures and movements, the analysand could "read" his reactions to what he or she was saying, and therefore adapt what was being said to the visible "responses" of the analyst. Whole chapters of associativity and transference pro-cesses might therefore be buried and prevented from being expres-sed. Here too, the actual setting is an attempt to offset any threat of unconscious or involuntary influence or suggestion coming from the analyst.

It was also so that transference feelings could be brought to the fore that Freud limited as much possible what we now call lateral transference. This represents a source of potential loss to the analy-sis of a whole aspect of the transference that is attempting to find another stage on which it can be played out. It should be pointed out that what Freud meant by lateral transference was much more restrictive than the manner in which some contemporary psychoan-alysts use the concept. For Freud, lateral transference was not just anything; it applied only to situations in which the analysand spoke about his or her analysis to some other person, reporting the sessions or duplicating, as it were, the analytical sessions with other "sessions" carried out with someone in his or her emotional environment.

At this point, it may well be worthwhile reminding the reader that Freud's definition of the transference was not limited to what transpired with the analyst and the psychoanalytic situation. This is also too often forgotten by contemporary psychoanalysts for whom the concept of the transference applies only to what transpires with the analyst. In "Remembering, repeating and working-through", Freud wrote: ". . . the transference is itself only a piece of repetition, and . . . the repetition is a transference of the forgotten past not only on to the doctor but also on to all the other aspects of the current situation" (1914g, p. 151).

Summarising the conditions under which the transference can be interpreted leads us naturally enough to evoke the rule of free association and, beyond that, associativity in general.

In the first place, the logic behind the fundamental rule is that of making it possible to interpret the transference; it therefore has to be expressed in words. How could we interpret what is *not* expressed (the transference and its historical sources) other than by means of what *is* expressed (its displacement and therefore its transference onto the present situation)? This implies the lifting of the various levels of censorship that apply to what can be expressed in words.

In addition—and this element was present from the very beginning in Freud's conception of the situation—there is an intrinsic and fundamental link between transference and associativity. In *The Interpretation of Dreams* (1900a), Freud points out that transference can be inferred whenever associativity breaks down or when resistance brings displacement and shifts in it. In that book, for example, Freud has this to say:

> We learn . . . that an unconscious idea is as such quite incapable of entering the preconscious and that it can only exercise any effect there by establishing a connection with an idea which already belongs to the preconscious, by transferring its intensity on to it and by getting itself 'covered' by it. Here we have the fact of "transference", which provides an explanation of so many striking phenomena in the mental life of neurotics. The preconscious idea, which thus acquires an undeserved degree of intensity, may either be left unaltered by the transference, or it may have a modification forced upon it, derived from the content of the idea which effects the transference. (pp. 562–563)

In the papers that he wrote between 1913 and 1915, Freud added to this central premise; he commented on several occasions that every breakdown in free associations should be seen as the result of some censorship being applied to the chain of associations or to some thought involving the analyst or the psychoanalytic situation. Transference and associativity are therefore linked closely together; the rule concerning free association is also a necessary condition for the interpretation of the transference, one of the ways in which the potential influence of the analyst can be circumvented. The idea of associativity opens up many more avenues for thinking, avenues that are to a large extent ignored by contemporary analysts for whom associativity is so well known that it need no longer be the subject of any exploration. Recalling the historical background to these issues may well be of some use, because, after all, that background is an essential feature of psychoanalysis—one that perhaps is not well enough known. It is essential in that it illustrates Freud's ongoing attempts to liberate psychoanalysis from the effects of suggestion that are part of the method itself. Free association and associativity are not prescribed by the analyst—or at least not only and not fundamentally by the analyst; they are above all modalities in which the mind itself functions. Their recommendation in psychoanalytic methodology aims simply to encourage free expression in the face of everything that in the past or in the present situation might obstruct its deployment; the objective is to free the analysand from the effect of past influences that might have had an impact on it.

The fundamental rule and associativity

When we examine in detail what Freud had to say about the origins, as he saw them, of the method that he invented, our attention is drawn to a short paper he wrote in 1920, "A note on the prehistory of the technique of analysis" (1920b). In that paper, he mentions the fact that, as a teenager, he had read the works of Ludwig Börne, a German writer of the Romantic Movement, and that this brought the idea of free association to his attention. In an essay entitled "The art of becoming an original writer in three days", Börne says that the "free association" method of writing is the key to what he does. In fact, that method was invented by the followers of Mesmer and early spiritists of the clinic of the Chevalier de Barberin situated on the Croix Rousse hill in Lyons. The method was invented by two "artificial somnambulists" (called G. Rochette and The Unknown Agent) of that clinic, then brought via Masonic lodges to Strasbourg (Roussillon, 1992), which at that time (the beginning of the nineteenth century) was the hub for everything that concerned Germany and the German Romantic Movement.

As to the history of the link between associativity and clinical matters, it is in Freud's *On Aphasia* (1891b) that we first come across it. In that book, Freud's theory of psychical representation is based on his work on aphasia—a set of perceptual elements that are associated or connected together. The model that he presents is, it must be said, astonishingly modern and "neuroscientific"—it comes close, for example, to the model of interconnected networks of representation, and to that of groupings of neurones (Braitenberg & Schüz 1998; Hebb, 1949).

In his famous "Project for a scientific psychology", Freud (1950a [1895]) continued his attempt to devise a model of the associative workings of the mind. In that paper, he refers explicitly to conditioned reflexes as a way of conceiving of how symptoms are generated—the "false connections" that lie at the heart of reminiscences come about through association by simultaneity or contiguity. Here again, his model is a very modern one when we compare it, for example, with that of LeDoux (1996), in which conditioned reflexes are a fundamentally important feature of brain functioning, especially with respect to the emotions.

In that same paper, in his attempt to show how the ego functions, Freud again made use of associative functioning: the ego is a set of associated connections, of groupings that are themselves associative. He went on to say that some associations may be inhibited or hampered when primary defences ("fending off" (Freud 1950a (1895), p. 321)) are mobilised; this tends to block the associative movement between different parts of the ego. The ego is a set of complex interrelated elements, a set of associative groups or networks. It is important to realise that this model applies both to basic mental functioning and to pathological mental states: certain life events may fortuitously fixate a set of associated elements (by simultaneity or contiguity); some elements may be associated for reasons that are no more than circumstantial. The primary defence fixates the associative flow of life and prevents the recombining that is necessary for adapting to present circumstances, which are determined by that primary defence. That is why, when the free association method is indeed freed up, it improves that situation; it restores the free movement of the flow of associations, liberates the mind from its "fixation-points", its *idées fixes* (Janet), its harmful historical impact.

In *Studies on Hysteria* (1895d [1893–1895]), Freud gave a more precise description of the first version of the psychoanalytic method both as to its technical aspects and as regards its implementation. Initially, this involved the pressure of the analyst's hand on the patient's forehead; when the hand was removed, an idea emerged— the first idea that came to mind was the best one, the one that was awaited expectantly. The technique was to be repeated as often as necessary. By 1900 and *The Interpretation of Dreams*, that technique had already undergone some development. Henceforth, it was not simply the first idea that was seen to be relevant for the analysis but also those that were associated with that idea; in other words, the method aimed at uncovering a whole sequence of ideas. As a leftover from the suggestion method, the psychoanalyst breaks the dream down into its separate elements, each of which is the starting point of a sequence, a crop of associations that are focalised on a given element. The psychoanalyst, who thereby "keeps his hands on" the treatment, then brings together the associative groupings that emerge and puts forward an interpretation of the whole sequence— a synthesis, as it were. Freud's own dream of Irma's injection is analysed following that model, as the step-by-step description makes clear; this is the case also of Dora's dreams (Freud, 1905e [1901]). It was not until the "Rat Man" analysis that Freud (1909d) announced that the psychoanalytic method was henceforth to be based on the rule of free association, without any attempt at inducing associations.

The *Minutes of the Vienna Psycho-Analytic Society* (Nunberg & Federn, 1962) report that, in one of the two scientific meetings devoted to that case in October–November 1907, Freud said: "The technique of psycho-analysis has changed to the extent that the psycho-analyst no longer seeks to elicit material in which he is interested, but permits the patient to follow his natural and spontaneous trains of thought".

The meaning of these technical developments is quite clear: any remaining elements of influence and suggestion that derive from hypnosis have to be removed. They must be deconstructed so that, as far as possible, the analysand can function in a free and spontaneous manner that lends itself to analysis. Psychoanalysis depends on the gradual deconstruction of the backcloth of suggestion that is part of all kinds of psychotherapy; it is possible—and tolerable—to do this only as a result of developing its theoretical foundations. After 1907, the analysand chooses the associative theme of the session and follows his or her natural and spontaneous trains of thought—and this because Freud had come to the conclusion that so-called "free" associations are in fact constrained by the existence of unconscious associative networks that determine what path these associations follow. There is no need to be afraid of losing one's way because some internal cohesion secretly governs the flow of associations; there is no need to regulate this from outside, because it has its own internal logic and it is on this that the psychoanalyst must concentrate.

The psychoanalyst's careful listening to associativity and the transference

The method and the technique by which it is implemented depended on how Freud conceived of the workings of the mind and on his firm belief in its fundamental cohesion. The fundamental rule was meaningful because Freud had by then developed an associative theory of mental functioning and was convinced of the cohesion of the mind over and beyond any apparently psychopathological aspects; in his view, associativity depended both on conscious and on unconscious networks.

In his chapter on "The psychotherapy of hysteria" (1895d [1893–1895]), he pointed out that hysterical patients are perfectly capable of giving coherent associations; if these do not appear to be coherent, this implies that one link in the chain remains obscure, hidden, or unconscious. "For we may make the same demands for logical connection and sufficient motivation in a train of thought, even if it extends into the unconscious, from a hysterical patient as we should from a normal individual. It is not within the power of a neurosis to relax these relations" (p. 293).

He became more and more convinced of this as the years went by. He was then exploring in depth how associative links came secretly to be organised and combined together, and discovering the logic behind associative networks and other products of the unconscious.

This gradually led him to think that what was "fundamental" was not really the actual "rule", because this simply expressed how the natural associativity of the mind should be listened to and made that work easier. What is fundamental is that the psychoanalytic method enables the lifting of the censorship that surrounds the free expression of ideas. What is fundamental is the rule that applies to how the psychoanalyst attends to the material. Associations should be listened to with the idea that they are coherent; this implies that, if any two elements are brought together, there must be some kind of link between them. If that link is manifest, if it is obvious, conscious, expressed as such, and coherent, there is no difficulty; the problem begins when the link is not manifest, not obvious, not expressed as such, and not conscious. It is at that point that the specific nature of psychoanalytic attentiveness comes to the fore in the clinical sphere. The analyst must listen to those associations with the idea that there is some kind of implicit and unconscious link between them; hypotheses have to be made as regards that link, and the analyst must try to reconstruct it and reconstruct the logic that underpins the sequence of associations.

Two kinds of cohesion and unconscious logic emerge from Freud's perspective at that time. On the one hand, cohesion may be circumstantial and related to the specific events in the individual's ongoing history. In this case, links are set up according to the conditioned reflex pattern that I mentioned above; they are conditioned by elements that may be fortuitous, and they come into play only because of their proximity, contiguity, or simultaneity with respect to the mentally significant event.

On the other hand, cohesion may be structural, as Freud came to understand only gradually. In this case, it is related to the important issues, conflicts, and problems that occur in the life of human beings—especially with respect to emotions and sexuality (the father complex, followed by the Oedipus complex). Since most of the time these issues are in stark contrast to ordinary social life (which to a considerable degree is desexualised), they are often repressed. Freud would go on to show that they are "drawn" to the structures that organise the life of the unconscious; these unconscious concepts or "products of the unconscious" (Freud, 1917c, p. 128)[4] took on an almost structural quality in his thinking.

It is on this minimal theory of mental functioning that Freud developed his view of psychoanalytic listening; it forms a latent part of this attentiveness and structures the forms that this will take. For a more detailed view of the relationship between transference and associativity, we must look again at Freud's paper on beginning the treatment (1913c) and take into account another element concerning the fundamental rule and the interplay of transformations that it implies.

Freud stated that, in describing to his analysands the fundamental rule, he used the metaphor of a train journey: "Act as though, for instance, you were a traveller sitting next to the window of a railway carriage and describing to someone inside the carriage the changing views which you see outside" (1913c, p. 135). That metaphor implies a double transfer, a twofold transformation: transferring something from the motor/sensorimotor sphere—the train must pass through the countryside—to the visual one; the idea is to describe the countryside, then transfer that visual impression into the apparatus for verbal language. It emphasises the fact that the psychoanalytic method implies that the individual is able to carry out this twofold transfer/transformation. The transfer into speech and the transference tend therefore to become superimposed one on the other or at least linked together. In this method, both sensorimotor and visual spheres are transferred into speech and the apparatus for verbalisation. Listening to what is said in the course of a session—the transference listening to its vocal vector—can be a good way of trying to identify not only the conditions required for listening attentively, but also what is conveyed about both of these spheres; that is, what is produced when something is transferred into vocal expression. The body lends support to the voice and to what is said, and at the same time the voice conveys something of what is physically experienced— it carries with it the person's body as it conveys something of what he or she wants to say. The analysis of the transference is therefore not something "intellectual"; it is the analysis of what is actually taking place in the session, of what is expressed through the here-and-now act of speaking. This is all the more the case when the sensorimotor and visual spheres are effectively transferred into the verbal apparatus. That apparatus will take on board both the metaphorical aspect (a visual image transferred into words) and the pragmatic and rhetorical effects (the effect of motor acts on language, which becomes an action on the other person, a force for influence and suggestion). In psychoanalysis, words are not simply representations; they have an impact and they actualise something—they are a "represent-action". When this double transferring occurs, the analyst is the one who is subjected to the seductive aspect of the transference; it is on the analyst that the impact of suggestion and hypnosis falls. That is why the analysis of the transference and that of the countertransference have to be brought into a dialectical relationship—more precisely, that part of the countertransference which, in a *lapsus calami*, I once referred to as the "showing-transference".[5]

What happens when this process fails or encounters significant resistance? When the individual cannot transfer his or her primary feelings into the apparatus for language? When sensorimotor experiences have not been organised in such a way as to enable them to be transferred into speech? It is not enough simply to listen attentively to what is actually expressed in words—Freud himself pointed this out on several occasions (1913c, and in his papers written in 1914 and 1915).

Listening to associativity is not restricted to what the analysand says; it pertains to the transference as a whole, which is not simply a way of enacting through or by means of words, as if it were some kind of verbal enactment or other. The transference can be manifested in all kinds of expressiveness and through non-verbal language. In order for it to play its full part in the analysis of the transference, listening to associativity must therefore be able to integrate pre-verbal and non-verbal language; it must integrate and take into account not only sequences of verbal associations but also those pertaining to primary forms of expression that are conveyed through the body and through actions. These are to be seen as primary forms of language because they contain within themselves aspects that are of great importance for the analysis of the transference whenever it has more to do with enacting than with remembering.

That kind of careful listening to associativity was present from the very beginning of Freud's work. My feeling is that not enough attention has been paid to it; I would therefore like to add a few comments of my own.

In *Studies on Hysteria* (1895d [1893–1895]), and in particular in the chapter on the psychotherapy of hysteria, Freud describes his understanding of how the associative method is employed. It is quite clear that he included in this various physical manifestations, in particular those that had to do with symptoms of conversion hysteria, which he saw as "joining in the conversation" (p. 296). He brought into his own manner of attentive listening everything that had to do with facial expressions, gestures, and postures—these too have something to say. It is important to note that, for Freud, symptoms and bodily manifestations were a means of expressing truth; he saw in them a kind of compass. This implies that he was already seeing the transference as an important feature of what was being actualised in the course of the session. If a patient stated that he or she had nothing more to say, yet the symptoms were still present, Freud followed the indications offered by those symptoms, sure in his own mind that something had been left unsaid. It was only once the physical symptom had been eliminated that Freud would consider the associative network linked to it as having been expressed in its entirety; the elimination of the symptom implied that what was being played out in the transference had found other means of expression, so that the patient was no longer under the unconscious influence of what he or she was expressing by means of enactment.

> Further, her painful legs began to "join in the conversation" during our analyses. . . . As a rule the patient was free from pain when we started work. If, then, by a question or by pressure upon her head I called up a memory, a sensation of pain would make its first appearance . . . it would reach its climax when she was in the act of telling me the essential and decisive part of what she had to communicate . . . I came in time to use such pains as a compass to guide me; if she stopped talking but admitted that she still had a pain, I knew that she had not told me everything. . . . (1895d [1893–1895], p. 148).

In 1913, in a paper devoted to the scientific interest of psychoanalysis (1913j), Freud makes it clear what "speech" means in psychoanalysis. He points out (p. 176) the fact that " 'speech' must be understood not merely to mean the expression of thought in words but to include the speech of gesture and every other method . . . by which mental activity can be expressed." That comment is the culmination of a series of ideas that can be found in several papers in which he explored neurotic symptomatology.

In his paper on "Obsessive actions and religious practices" (1907b), he wrote of the girl who was under the compulsion to rinse round her wash-basin several times after washing. It was only then that she could throw out the water. Freud's analysis of that compulsive ritual shows that "obsessive actions are perfectly significant in every detail [and] they serve important interests of the personality" (p. 120). In addition, they are a representation, direct or symbolic, of something that has been experienced—they must therefore be interpreted either in terms of a given event in the individual's past or symbolically. In the example of the wash-basin, the analysis revealed that it was a warning addressed to the patient's sister who was thinking of leaving her husband—she should not throw away the dirty water of her present husband before finding the clean water of someone to replace him. It is important to note here that, for Freud, that ritual was meaningful not only as regards the relationship of the patient to her own self, the intra-psychic meaning; it involved also her relationship with her sister in so far as it was a message addressed to that person. Compulsive actions are meaningful; they tell a story, a history that, in addition, is addressed to someone else. In that sense, they are transferred towards some other person in the form of a message—in this particular case, a "warning", as Freud put it, addressed to the patient's sister.

The action and the transference understood in terms of an action, an enacting, illustrate a thought or a fantasy; they tell of a particular moment in time. They are shown to or spoken to someone else who plays a meaningful role in the individual's life; they are addressed to that person, even though their actual content may not be taken fully on board or if the thought that underlies them is hidden behind the means of expression itself. An enactment "shows" something, it does not "speak" about it. It tells a story, but hidden behind a mask; it forgets its own primary historical origin and displaces or reverses the original scene, which is transferred onto the here-and-now situation. In this way, it disguises the significance of what was originally experienced.

In 1909, Freud further developed his thoughts about hysteria and the show that this can put on, following what he had already set out in 1892 in his paper, written in collaboration with Breuer, "On the theory of hysterical attacks" (1940d [1892]). In "Some general remarks on hysterical attacks" (1909a [1908]) he emphasised the fact that in hysterical attacks, fantasies are "translated into the motor sphere" and "projected onto motility" (p. 229). Hysterical attacks and the "pantomimic portrayal" that they display are the outcome of the condensation of several fantasies (in particular relating to bisexuality) or of the acts of several characters in a traumatic scenario from the past. For example, what appeared to be an incoherent restlessness in one woman, as if she were playing out a meaningless pantomime, began to be meaningful once the overall movement could be broken down into its component parts—it could then be seen as a rape. One part of the scene, in which the woman tore off her clothes with one hand, represented the rapist's attack on her, while the second part of her movements, in which she pressed her clothes to her body, represented an attempt at protecting herself from being attacked.

In that example, an apparently meaningless pantomime that, on a manifest level, seemed to be uncoordinated restlessness could be shown to have meaning once it was analysed and broken down into the various components that secretly structured the overall pattern. What initially seemed to be simply a "discharge" then revealed the complexity of meaning that was in fact part of it, although hidden away. Hysteria "speaks" through the body; it "shows" what the person cannot put into words and hides that aspect. In hysterical processes, actions can be interpreted in terms of affect representatives; they are a kind of language, more of an acting-language than an acting-out. They transfer language into the body and the modes of expression that are specific to it. They are also addressed to someone, to the self—a way of saying something to oneself—and to another person; there is perhaps the expectation that the other person may be able to understand the message and reflect back on the speaker what he or she said without realising it, without actually putting it into words. In *An Outline of Psycho-Analysis*, Freud (1940a [1938], p. 202) remarks on the importance, in all of the scenarios that are reported and played out, of the person whom he called the detached spectator. The scenario is addressed to that spectator, who is also an externalised representative of the self, a double; it tells something to that spectator and once again is a message addressed to someone else, who is required to bear witness to what, in the past, had not been witnessed. Here, then, new forms of the transference are implicitly at work.

All the examples that I have taken from Freud's writings concern the neuroses. They have to do with the anal or phallic economic dimension and are part of the universe marked by the apparatus of verbal language. Surrounded by verbal language, that universe is structured by metaphor. The body "speaks", plays out, what the individual cannot express in words—although the potentiality for this is present; the body metaphorises the scene. The structure of the action and of its playing out is that of a narrative, as Freud makes clear. The scenes that are played out narrate a scenario, a story, the story of a chapter in the person's life that he or she cannot take on board. That narrative is part of the world of language and of its symbolisation modalities, even though it is the body that actually talks and shows. Although there is an attempt to tell it to the person him- or herself, it is also, and perhaps above all, a narrative addressed to some other person in his or her own right.

In the section of his paper devoted to the psychological interest of psychoanalysis (Freud, 1913j), Freud expressed his belief that actions—including the stereotyped gestures that can be observed in *dementia praecox* (schizophrenia)—are not meaningless. Even in that extreme case they are "the remains of perfectly significant mimetic actions" which belong to the person's past (p. 174). He adds that, into "[the] craziest speeches and the queerest poses and attitudes [where] hitherto nothing but the most freakish capriciousness has seemed to prevail, psycho-analytic research has introduced law, order and connection, or has at least allowed us to suspect their presence where its work is still incomplete." (ibid.)

These ideas would be added to all through his life; they are at their most complete in his writings of 1937–1938, which put the finishing touches to these theoretical concepts.

It is clear, then, that although the fundamental rule of free association concerns verbal language as such and attempts to channel associativity along that path, the psychoanalyst's attentive listening cannot be restricted to that domain alone. This is particularly true when the analyst's attentiveness is dependent on the analysis of the transference and on what attempts to be enacted in that transference. In the psychoanalytic situation, suggesting and influencing are not confined to verbal speech; every kind of expression and all forms of language contribute to transferring the forgotten situation onto the present one.

Freud took all these issues into account when, partly influenced by Ferenczi, he wrote his paper on "Lines of advance in psychoanalytic therapy" (1919a [1918]) and when he explored compliant dreams in 1923. In such cases, the analyst is faced with an alternative. On the one hand, there is an attempt to force all other modes of expression to adopt verbal language and thus make interpretation possible. That was the attitude adopted by Ferenczi at the beginning of the 1920s: increase abstinence, prohibit any other means of expression—that's the way it's going to be—and have recourse to a "forceful" modality, the suggestion and influence effects of which cannot be ignored; indeed, these are potentially a paradoxical form of superego seduction. The other possibility, Ferenczi later tried this way of proceeding, is to adopt techniques that would increase the receptiveness of language and of the analysand to the sensorimotor sphere. This would develop the effects of cathartic trance (Ferenczi, 1930) in the psychoanalytic situation. In order to do this, some kind of intervention based on psychodrama or with a psychodramatic aim to it could be adopted; here, all the same, the threat of another kind of influencing and suggesting appears; this time more narcissistic.

It was only after a slow process of development of psychoanalytic theory that lasted until 1936–1938 that Freud again took up the question. It could then be expressed in terms of other problem situations concerning psychoanalytic technique, and developed in his final papers on the subject: "Constructions in analysis" (1937d) and "Analysis terminable and interminable" (1937c).

Notes

1. In 1915 and 1916, he wrote two fundamental papers on the analysis of the impasses and paradoxes of narcissism—"Mourning and melancholia" (1917e [1915]) and "Some character types met with in psychoanalytic work" (1916d), which represent a significant contribution to the analysis of various kinds of narcissistic pathology.

2. For an analysis of that paper, see Roussillon (2010).

3. It is perhaps worthwhile reminding the reader that, for Freud, psychoanalysis did not stand in opposition to psychotherapy; in his view, psychoanalysis was a "psychoanalytic psychotherapy". The real difference, for him, was between psychotherapy based on analysis—and more specifically on the analysis of the transference—and those forms of psychotherapy that made use of suggestion as their principal means of treatment. Some degree of suggestion

is unavoidable in psychoanalysis, all the more so in that it is linked to the transference and to the position in which transference phenomena place the psychoanalyst.

4. I prefer the idea of products or concepts to that of primal fantasies. For Freud, these had a structural value for mental experiences. In 1917, with reference to the penis as a "detachable part of the body" (1917c, p. 133) and castration, he put forward the idea of unconscious conceptions as organisers of part of the mental associativity that enables different signifiers to navigate amongst its various components.

5. In French, countertransference is *contre-transfert*; in his slip of the pen, the author wrote *montre-transfert*, "show" the transference. (Translator's note)

4

The person of the analyst and role of intersubjectivity in beginning the treatment

Lewis Kirshner

> Among the factors which influence the prospects of analytic treatment and add to its difficulties in the same manner as the resistances, must be reckoned not only the nature of the patient's ego but the individuality of the analyst.
>
> Freud, 1937

"Say as little as possible to the patient at the beginning of the treatment. Do not interfere with the patient's thoughts. Let it unfold." Probably no candidate today would receive this advice, as I did thirty years ago, to refrain from participating actively in the analytic process. My training followed Freud's comment in "On beginning the treatment" that "one lets the patient do nearly all the talking and explains nothing more than what is absolutely necessary to get him to go on with what he is saying" (Freud, 1913c, p. 124). Since that time, however, the psychoanalytic situation has changed enormously. More than the familiar set up and enduring rituals of clinical practice might suggest, the notion of a standard technique applied by a well-analysed expert to an ill patient has given way to a more interactive conception of psychoanalytic treatment. In particular, our ways of understanding the nature of the analyst's participation in the process and our notions of what is therapeutic about it have shifted toward a more shared and co-constructed model. In this chapter, I focus on two aspects of this conceptual change: the presence of the analyst as a "real person" and the influence of the perspective of intersubjectivity on the treatment relationship.

Freud's principal concern in "On beginning the treatment" is to set the conditions for a successful analysis while patiently waiting to discover whether he will be able to utilise them appropriately. Of course, he was not unaware of the analyst's personal limitations, as the opening quotation shows, as well as his commitment to preferred methods and theories that inevitably impact the nature of the work. Today, we would emphasise even more strongly that the analyst's way of working with his patient influences what ensues between them, so that in beginning an analysis he is prone to rediscover what he already knows and expects. Freud addressed this personal equation by insisting on "the analyst's obligation to make himself capable, by a deep-going analysis of his own, of the unprejudiced reception of the analytic material" (1926e, p. 219). Yet his confidence in the effectiveness of the analyst's own analysis is qualified by one of his final statements in which he referred to what he recognised as a blind spot in some analysts, who convey "an atmosphere which is not favourable to objective investigation" (1937d, p. 248). From this observation, Freud made the utopian suggestion of a return to analysis every five years, apparently in the hope of maintaining the superior state of "mental normality and correctness" (1937d, p. 247) that he regarded as desirable. His palpable wish to preserve the scientific objectivity of the analytic process independent of the uniqueness of its two participants and their interwoven transference and countertransferences seems clear. The contemporary turn toward examining the contributions of the analyst and accepting the intersubjective nature of the process represents another way of dealing with the problem.

The analyst as a "real person"

Over the years, analysts have attempted to parse out their different roles and functions in the treatment from the early ideal of an objective, minimally self-revealing transference object. Beginning with

Freud, the various types of transferences and even the "individuality of the analyst" were widely recognised as playing a part in the treatment. Ferenczi is often cited as the first to draw serious attention to the personal equation in treatment (Szecsödy, 2009), but the theme has been addressed by many other important analysts including Anna Freud. In commenting upon the widely read paper by Leo Stone (1961) on the widening scope of psychoanalysis, she emphasised the different ways analysts behave with different patients and even used the expression "real relationship", which she differentiated from countertransference (A. Freud, 1954). The American psychoanalyst Ralph Greenson shared and expanded her observations and, perhaps because of his detailed description of the nontransferential aspects of treatment in his influential textbook of psychoanalysis (Greenson, 1967), mention of these began to appear increasingly in the literature (see review by Couch, 1999).

In an important article written with Milton Wexler (Greenson and Wexler, 1969), Greenson characterised the analytic interaction as partaking of three major elements: transference, working alliance, and real relationship, the latter being seen as the "core" of the alliance. As is commonly the case, their effort to define these terms is a mixture of truisms and assumptions that immediately create suspicion of a too-ready acceptance of a prevalent cultural model. They defined the working alliance as "the non-neurotic, rational, reasonable rapport which the patient has with his analyst and which enables him to work purposefully in the analytic situation despite his transference impulses" (p. 28). The real relationship appears associated with the patient's correct perception of features of the analyst's personality.

Words like rational, reasonable, and real, of course, may conceal more than they attempt to assert—namely ideals of normality, successful adaptation, and health. The article also contains a partial review of the relevant literature, perhaps most notably Esther Menaker's 1942 unvarnished endorsement of the real relationship, which she described as "a direct human relationship between patient and analyst, . . . independent of the transference," (p. 172). For their part, the authors mainly rely on clinical examples to explain their ideas, and these vignettes have not lost their richness, demonstrating how the three components of the analytic relationship set forth by Greenson are intertwined.

Greenson's proposals were also controversial. In 1979, Brenner commented that he saw little justification for them, while Curtis found his conceptions useful, especially for patients outside the neurotic range (Brenner, 1979; Curtis, 1979). Abend (2000) summarised the prevalent criticism, arguing that the notion of a working alliance failed to address the specific fantasies stimulated in patients by clinical transactions supporting a therapeutic alliance and by expressions of a "real" relationship. It would take us far afield to document all the details, but the reason for this debate and controversy is obvious: the persistent fear of losing the specificity of psychoanalysis by blurring its boundaries with unscientific methods and ordinary human influences in "real life". The same explanation applies to the frequently voiced concerns about providing encouragement and support, using suggestion, or sharing personal experiences, all parts of "real," everyday relationships and many nonanalytic therapies. Until recently, these kinds of personal interactions have either been viewed as inevitable, but marginal aspects of psychoanalysis, as Freud seemed to imply, or, at best, demarcated as an important, but distinct area of technique (Lipton, 1977). The splitting-off of alliance and relationship as special techniques may in part have represented a reaction to an artificial and impersonal style of psychoanalysis as practiced in an earlier period, which had to be offset by these newer concepts.

What may still be at stake in the on-going debates about the so-called real relationship and the subjectivity of the analyst is a contested conception of the analyst's role and of the specifics of therapeutic action. In particular, the notion of an infantile transference neurosis largely independent of the analyst's participation that can be reconstructed and interpreted is linked to a conception of etiology and a medical–scientific view of psychopathology. The concern is to preserve a basic medical model of the treatment situation in which a patient seeks help for his or her neurotic illness through a scientific method. From this perspective, it makes sense to cordon off an area of analytic objectivity and technique from the fuzzier terrain of relationship and alliance.

Although it seems incontrovertible that the analyst relates as a person with a life and history of his own that impact everything he does, he also applies a non-directive model based on conceptions of the unconscious, the importance of free verbal expression, and transference (used here in its widest sense of representing a wish or purpose directed to the analyst that is to some degree unknown and desired by the patient). Likewise, he is taught the necessity of attaining a certain degree of mastery over his countertransference, as Freud (1913a) insisted. Finally, regardless of adherence to a theory, all analysts, even the most non-traditional, modulate their personal presence and self-expression in ways that create myriad versions of the familiar analyst–patient dyad. The debate about technique within psychoanalysis, then, seems to reduce itself to one about the limits of these different versions. How much countertransference, personal expression, and ideology enters into the analyst's work?

With this set of issues in mind, we may raise the question of the value of holding onto the tripartite distinction of Greenson. Why not simply acknowledge that analysis involves a relationship containing many elements, like every relationship (as Greenson implied), and give up the fruitless attempt to delineate what is real, objective, and rational in psychoanalysis from transference, neurosis, or sheer fantasy? It seems more accurate to accept that each case represents a unique amalgam of these elements (along with countertransference) and that these boundaries need to be sorted out as best they can by the participants as part of their work together. Perhaps this very amalgam is itself the best definition of transference in contemporary psychoanalysis, namely, the unique mix and shape of feelings and expectations that emerges in the interactive field of the analysis (Baranger & Baranger, 2008).

In terms of the therapeutic alliance (and its closely related sibling the working alliance), the variables that researchers have studied are obviously difficult to separate from a wider view of the transference. This, in fact, seems to be the conclusion of current research that emphasises the specificity of each therapeutic dyad. According to Blatt, Zuroff, Quinlan, and Pilkonis (1996) available data suggests that,

> . . . treatment outcome is facilitated by the patient's feeling that the therapist is empathic, caring, open, and sincere. But the particular dimensions of therapists' activities that achieve this goal seem to vary depending on the needs of individual patients. . . . The quality of this alliance is not determined by the procedures of the treatment protocol but by the relationship the therapist is able to establish with the patient.

From his review of the research, Strupp (2001) concluded similarly that each patient–therapist dyad is unique. Likewise, Baranger and Baranger (2008) proposed that the structure of the analytic relationship "is something created between the two, within the unit that they form in the moment of the session, something radically different from what each of them is separately," (p. 806).

In reading the analytic literature on beginning the treatment, it is hard to escape the impression of highly intelligent and experienced clinicians expressing reasoned assertions of their own views, without recourse to any systematic attempt to document them. Until relatively recently, questions that might be resolved empirically have not been subjected to rigorous research investigation. The therapeutic alliance variable is one that has been the object of considerable work, however, both within and outside psychoanalysis. The influential review of these studies by Martin, Garske, and Davis (2000), in line with Blatt's work, describes three themes in common: (a) the collaborative nature of the relationship, (b) the affective bond between patient and therapist, and (c) the patient's and therapist's ability to agree on treatment goals and tasks (p. 438). It is easy to recognise that, at the very least, these items are closely related to transference and countertransference. In this regard, it is of interest in terms of beginning the treatment that the authors found that patients tend to view the alliance (as measured by different scales) as more consistent throughout the course of the work than do clinicians or researchers. Patients are more likely to evaluate the alliance as positive at termination if their initial assessment was positive. Moreover, research shows that outcomes of treatment are significantly associated with the same measures of the therapeutic alliance, as well as with so-called supportive relationship variables (see the comprehensive review of studies of psychoanalysis and psychoanalytic psychotherapy by Shedler, 2010; also the discussions by Ablon and Jones, 1998, 1999; Castonguay, Goldfried, Wiser, Raue, and Hayes, 1996; Strupp, 2001; and Wallerstein, 2000). Levy and Inderbitzen (2000, p. 748) argue that "the analyst, to get the treatment started, relies heavily on suggestive influence." The widely cited Menninger study, (Wallerstein, 2000) concluded that even the fundamental distinction between expressive and supportive psychotherapy, "while it may define two broad directions of therapeutic activity, has in actual practice often given way to complexly interacting and varying admixtures of approaches, with an equally broad blurring in the interface zone" (p. 687).

In this vein, research has confirmed Freud's impression of the very poor ability of analysts to make accurate initial assessments of patients, predict outcomes, or even to choose the most appropriate patients (Bachrach, Weber, & Solomon, 1985; Caligor, et al., 2009; Kantrowitz, 1993). A common explanation given by researchers and clinicians for this result is that each dyad represents a unique expression of psychoanalytic principles, a singular way of making analysis work. Ablon (1994, p. 315) observed that "the analyst has his or her own dance style but has to learn the steps of the new partner." In fact, this emphasis on a jointly evolved process is the conclusion of several empirical researchers of psychoanalysis (Ablon, 2005; Blatt, 2001; Kantrowitz, 1993, 1995, 1997; Strupp, 2001).

If "each analytic relationship has qualities that reflect the uniqueness of the relationship and that make it different from any other analytic relationship" (Viederman, 1991) and is one in which so-called real, collaborative, and transferential processes are in practice inseparable, what consequences does this hold for beginning treatment? Perhaps most important is that analysts need to be less concerned about contaminating a sterile field of potential transference by displaying personal reactions and affective responses. Adler (1980, p. 253), from a Self Psychology perspective, asserted that borderline and narcissistic patients "often require an awareness of the person and personality of the analyst as someone appropriately interested, caring, warm, and wishing to be helpful at the beginning of treatment". But it seems likely that his statement applies to most patients, especially since it is becoming increasingly frequent for analysis to begin after a preparatory psychotherapy (Caligor et al., 2003). Dickes, in his review, (1967, p. 512) criticised a "point of view in which the analyst is considered as essentially objectless or nonhuman". He quotes Stone's earlier book in which a colleague had asserted that his patient would have developed the same intense transference "to a brass monkey". In this regard, Caligor and colleagues (2003, p. 202) observe that "there has been an attenuation of the belief that it is necessary to hide the person of the analyst in order to promote the emergence of transference".

It is much easier to critique a false separation of person from transference and the artificial technique that flows from making this distinction than to prescribe a better technique. Especially if each case and dyad creates a singular situation, it does seem that the analyst must, after all, actually work towards relearning the art anew with every patient. Perhaps the most thoughtful commentator in this regard is Viederman (1991, 2000), who advocates implementing an actively involved relationship that he regards as "real", although his conception of this process seems closer to the integrative emphasis I am advocating. He underlines the quality of the analyst's *presence*, a term with a long history in the literature (Balint, 1960; Blum, 1998; Green, 1999b; Kohut, 1968; Nacht, 1961; and many others):

> The affective presence of the analyst, namely his self-expression with feeling and conviction . . . acts as a stimulus for an affective interchange and the development of transference which has a different quality from transference evoked by an analyst who insists on absolute abstinence and interpretation as the only vehicle for communication . . . Many analyses become sterile by virtue of the apparent detachment of the analyst . . . and sink into a comfortable but distant and non-productive modus vivendi that not infrequently characterizes some particularly long analyses. (Viederman, 2000, p. 453)

Whether or not Viederman is being unduly harsh on the profession, the important point that successful analyses involve affective intensity (one that fits the "match") seems confirmed by both the research on "alliance" and relationship, and clinical experience. Perhaps the shared affect is the glue that enables the amalgam to cohere. For this reason, the analyst would be better served attending to presence, rather than absence in beginning the treatment, as he was formerly advised.

Intersubjectivity

The term intersubjectivity has appeared with increasing frequency in psychoanalytic writings in recent years. In a survey of the PEP archives, there were two citations from the years 1940 to 1960; 17 between 1960 and 1980; 974 from 1980 to 2000; and 1193 in the last ten years! Although its usage has been especially significant within the relational school, intersubjectivity has been adopted by a many other theoreticians. Originating in the field of phenomenology as a concept addressing the complexities of interaction between two persons, intersubjectivity was first applied to psychoanalytic practice by Jacques Lacan in his early seminars, only to be put aside later (see 1953a, 1953–1954). His emphasis was on the nature of psychoanalysis as a relation between two speaking subjects, not one of an objectification of the patient. The corollary hypotheses to this axiom are the possibilities of unconscious communication, the mutual influences of the partners on each other, and the intertwining of transference and countertransference. The problem Lacan saw relates to how we define the subject, and here, of course, we run into a thicket of conflicting and diverse conceptions.

It is remarkable that references to intersubjectivity abound not only in the writings of analysts who emphasise the relational dimension of treatment, but in classically oriented practitioners, Self Psychologists, infant researchers, and object relations theorists. For this reason, Beebe, Rustin, Sorter, & Knoblauch (2003) have suggested the term "forms of intersubjectivity". What they all have in common is the so-called two person model, but their responses to Lacan's hypotheses vary widely. Most would concur with the conclusion of M. Baranger (1993) that "the conscious and unconscious work of the analyst is performed within an intersubjective relationship in which each participant is defined by the other". A major concern is the impact of the person of the analyst on the shape of the specific intersubjective construction, sometimes called the analytic third (Ogden, 1994a) or the co-pensée (Widlöcher, 1996), which tends to be addressed primarily in the here and now interaction, in the use of the analyst's own thoughts and feelings, and in his or her receptivity to transference. Whether and how to employ self-disclosure is a related issue. This constellation of questions about what is going on between analyst and patient apart from the interpretation of deeply rooted infantile fantasies emerging in the transference represents a paradigm shift in analytic thought, but one that is far from accomplished.

Although we can see by the published record that the intersubjective perspective is on a crescendo in contemporary psychoanalysis, we cannot yet draw firm conclusions about its impact on technique. What role could it have in beginning the treatment, for example? Careful attention by the analyst to his or her subjective responses to the patient, while always important, must be moderated

by the knowledge discussed above of the unreliability of such perceptions. On the other hand, since beginnings tend to set the tone,
perhaps a closer examination of these initial responses could provide
an overview of the presence of specific conflicts and experiences, as
well as the obscurity of other areas, notably the analyst's own resistances or blind spots. If this state of affairs is likely to be crucial for
the future unfolding of the treatment, it is wise to be looking for indications of the kinds of collusions and engagements between
analysand and analyst from the very onset. It is here that the literal
or figurative presence of a referential "third" (whether a supervisor,
a set of theories, or peer colleagues) is essential. In fact, we should
anticipate these unconscious processes at work in every case. Here,
the analyst does well to attend closely from their initial contact to the
patient's perceptions of him, which may respond to aspects of his
personality, unconscious communications, or countertransference
attitudes and wishes of which he is unaware.

A second point concerns diagnosis. Although gross diagnostic
features probably are worth discerning, despite the documented
inaccuracy of the process, on a more fine-tuned level it probably does
not make sense to construct an elaborate formulation, as candidates
are sometimes asked to do. As we have seen, the conclusions drawn
are unreliable, but, more importantly, the effort to gather data and
complete a presenting portrait may damage or significantly inflect
the developing amalgam of alliance, relationship, and transference/
countertransference that has already begun to form. It suggests to
the patient that the conclusions of the anamnesis will bring definite
answers to his or her problems and perpetuates a relationship to
authority that may impede progress. These two aspects of the
analytic relation are likely to be present in any event in the transference without the analyst seeming to validate and grant reality to
them. In this regard, conveying the message of authoritative knowledge by taking an evaluative approach to a new patient remains a
pitfall of current practice.

Conclusions

In this paper, I have focused on the person of the analyst and the intersubjective relation that is installed at the beginning of an analysis.

I suggest that separating the "real relationship", therapeutic alliance, and transference as distinct elements had historical reasons that derived from the desire to maintain a scientific, etiological-curative model of analytic practice. I argue that research and practice suggest instead the inextricability of these conceptual domains and point to a model of analytic singularity in which they form an amalgam unique to each analyst–patient pair. This amalgam is a product of the intersubjective relationship of on-going reciprocal influence and exchange that arises from the first contacts. Viewing psychoanalysis in this way represents a paradigm shift in theory and practice that is well underway. The intersubjective perspective also underlines the importance of the analyst's presence, as opposed to verbal and affective absence, especially at the beginning of treatment. As a corollary, I propose that attention to formulation and diagnosis at the start may only reinforce and validate a fantasy of analytic knowledge and authority that is at cross-purposes to the goals of analytic work.

5

Swimming one's way up to the fundamental rule

Antonino Ferro

In the history of psychoanalytic technique "the fundamental rule" has been of immeasurable importance because it effectively establishes the mental setting within which the patient has to orient himself. "The analysand is asked to say what he thinks and feels, selecting nothing and omitting nothing from what comes into his mind, even where this seems to him unpleasant to have to communicate" (Laplanche & Pontalis, 1967).

In Freud (1913c) the injunction to "say everything that comes into one's head" is followed by the metaphor of the passenger on a train who describes the changing scenery to his fellow-travellers. Thereafter comes the request for sincerity, followed by a number of other suggestions.

I think that when psychoanalysis came into being and its method was still largely unknown it needed to have a set of regulations and simple and unambiguous rules of conduct, and for this reason these recommendations were absolutely necessary.

I remember that when I began working as an analyst I used to provide my patients with these recommendations. Then over the years I simplified them more and more. Now, however, I tend not to supply these rules—and for a number of reasons.

First of all, because I find this approach very prescriptive; on the one hand, it is superegoic and, on the other, it is very much based on focusing attention on the mental functioning of the patient (or rather on the way in which the patient "should" communicate). My position now is that I see the mental and communicative functioning of the patient as co-created by the analyst's way of being and mental attitude.

I see "free association" as the (not always immediately arrived at) endpoint of a development to which the analyst also contributes: hence the title of this paper, which borrows from the title of an Italian book on dysgraphia popular in the 1980s.

Nowadays, in the first analytic session, only if the patient is silent for a long time or there is some other kind of difficulty do I intervene with an unsaturated "so . . .?", or sometimes, "of course, you can just tell me what comes to mind", or on occasions with an interpretation of the atmosphere I feel has been created.

Some time ago, an author—I have forgotten his name—published a collection of all the opening lines or paragraphs of the major novels of world literature. A similar compilation was also made (I do not remember whether or not by the same author) of the endings of famous novels.

With the development of analysis—which has been achieved thanks to Freud and by analysts standing on the shoulders of Freud—I think we can now abandon the metaphor of the chess game in which only the opening and closing moves admit of "systematic description". One can, I think, even forget the "certainty" of these moves, as it seems to me that each analysis can open and close in its own way (this also applies to each session, and over the years I have seen that even in this respect there is an extreme variety of styles).

In narratology the term "encyclopaedia" is used to refer to the sum of knowledge we have acquired about how texts function. It follows that a highly saturated encyclopaedia deters us from co-constructing the text and traps us in prior assumptions (in its most extreme version, the murderer is always the butler), whereas an unsaturated use of "encyclopaedias" and "possible worlds" opens up unforeseen and unexpected narratives. I would rather interpret the ways we communicate (or do not communicate) as they gradually become a problem, keeping in mind a number of specific factors. Within this framework, namely, different lines of development will emerge according to the following factors:

» The analyst's ability to be "without memory and desire" (Bion, 1970), in the sense of having no expectations or making no predictions about the stories that come into being (Freud talks about this indirectly when he says that analysis is more difficult if the patient is the child of friends and acquaintances, meaning that certain lines of development have already been laid down by previous knowledge). This state of mind is not easy because we are exposed to a number of internal and external pressures that significantly affect the direction we take.

» The analyst's negative capability (Bion, 1963); in other words, his ability (as described by Bion) to tolerate being in the PS position but free of persecution as long as he can move towards a selected fact. This is like playing cat's cradle, where the figure that is formed changes according to precisely where the players pull the string. Closely related to this are the qualities of analytic listening which are open to all the possible variations that I have described as oscillations between "grasping and casting" (Ferro, 2008, 2009). "What does the analyst listen to?" Grotstein's reply (2009) is short and to the point: the analyst must "listen to the unconscious". But how are we to conceive of the unconscious? As described by Freud, by Lacan, or by Klein? Of course, this could be the starting point for a long digression about how Bion (1962, 1992) understood the Unconscious (and others, from Grotstein (2007, 2009) to Ogden (1994a, 2009)), and how this new conceptualisation can revolutionise the very way we conceive the field (this will be discussed below).

» The analyst's ability to engage in reverie; in other words, his ability to convert into images the quanta of sensoriality generated by the analytic situation and the analytic atmosphere (a topic too well covered elsewhere to require further discussion here).

» The different ways the characters who enter the session are to be considered (Ferro, 2009) from the very outset: as characters in the story, characters of the inner world, or character-holograms of the function the analytic field takes on (Ferro & Basile, 2009).

» The type of interpretive "response"—verbal, silent, acted out, countertransferential—the analyst gives to the patient's first communication. Of course, this opens up the vast problem of validating interpretations. There are two points I would like to emphasise: Bion's view of "the patient as best colleague" and then as the person who always knows what we have in mind (Bion 1983, 2005); and the idea of the patient as a navigation system that unknowingly "dreams" an answer to our interpretations and constantly gives us our bearings in the analytic situation.

In short, I am not saying that the "fundamental rule" should not be communicated, but I would stress that it is much more complex than we thought, that it has far more complex effects than we thought, and that it is much less neutral than we thought. In some ways it is even a sort of "self-disclosure" of the desires and expectations of the analyst. It is often a point of arrival; otherwise the question of being accepted and respected would represent a serious problem with regard to the criteria of analysability.

It is as if a canvas were to give information about how it should be painted. What could we then make of paintings by Fontana, or others where the canvas is torn inside the frame, or yet others where the frame itself "explodes"? Why should analysis immediately take on the feel of a confessional in which it is a "sin" to omit certain things one is not ready to share? Why should we sit at the window and pass comments, for example, in the event of a fire? What if the flames reach the train or the compartment? And what if one of the passengers were to take out a gun or a knife? And what if a Rottweiler came in? And if a thief came on the scene, or one of the passengers died?

I will stop here, but the list of questions could go on for ever: what about child analysis or patients with severe disorders (borderline, psychotic, etc.)? What is to be done with a compliant patient or a Zelig? And what should we think of the "promise of absolute sincerity" whose effect is to close off an infinite number of worlds and possible narratives?

Basically this would mean laying down over-restrictive rules that put a straitjacket, or at least a bodice, on the free expression of the patient that can only remain such as long as it is not over-codified. It would be different if, instead of being presented as a sacred rule, it came out in the freedom of the analyst's mental functioning, or through metaphors such as airport duty-free shops, or analysis as a place where dues are not paid and all games are allowed.

Of course, there is then also the problem of the model of the analytic process the analyst adopts. For example, if a patient were told the "fundamental rule" and then went on say: "I remember when I was at school and the priest used to tell us how to behave", would this be a memory that opens up an analytic scenario or would it describe the emotional state of a patient who feels as if he were attending a religious school with its own special rules of conduct?

Or if another patient said: "I remember as a child I held in my stool, I wanted to go to the toilet but I couldn't", is this to be seen as another possible opening with its origin in childhood or is the patient intimating his current difficulty in communicating what he is holding back despite himself?

Or if a patient immediately after receiving the injunction recounted a dream in which there was a wolf behind him that terrified him and that he was afraid might bite him, would this be an opening scenario (which there would be anyway) that sets off his analysis or is it the description of how he experienced the communication—as threatening, dangerous, heartbreaking?

But in what sense do I see this as a question of models?

In a model that takes its inspiration from Freud, work will have to be done on resistance, repression, memories, traumatic events, and the characters will possess a high degree of historical referentiality. Attention to historical reconstruction, collateral transference, the patient's free associations, and the analyst's evenly suspended attention will be some of the principal tools that allow access to the unconscious and in particular through sudden ideas (*Einfälle*). A model that draws on Bion, on the other hand, will see things differently: turbulence, storms of sensoriality will be transformed by the alpha function (which is always working) into sequences of pictograms (alpha elements) that will form the "dream thought of the waking state". The purpose of the analysis will be above all to develop dream-thought, and even more so the tools to generate it (alpha function and ♀♂). In other words, what will be central is the dreaming ensemble, both in the form of reverie and transformations into dreams (Ferro, 2009), both in the form of dreams and as "talking as dreaming" (Ogden, 2007).

From this latter perspective these free associations are no longer free but are forced (although the freedom to choose the narrative genre remains) as regards the formation of that particular sequence of waking dreams which in itself is unknowable but whose derivatives are knowable, albeit in distorted form (Ferro, 2002a, 2006).

Another key point is to consider whether a model is mono-personal or relational or even a field model, one in which every (not necessarily anthropomorphic) character describes the functioning that goes on between the minds of analyst and patient, in other words a fragment or rather a derivative of dream functioning.

In this sense, the session becomes a shared dream of two minds to which the analyst contributes reveries or negative reveries (–R), and enlarges or narrows the field.

In conclusion, it is my view that the "fundamental rule"—namely, that one should be in touch with and communicate one's unconscious—should be a point of arrival co-constructed and experienced *in crescendo* session after session.

Clinical reflections

Barbies and nuns

It is Roberta's first session. After a short silence she says: "I don't know what to talk about". I nod and emit one of those sounds that only long analytic practice equips analysts to produce each time with a different shade of emotional colouring (in this case confirming that I have heard her and inviting her to continue). Roberta begins to introduce into the field her first characters (as I will find out later) who will remain relatively constant during the early period of analysis. She then speaks about a colleague who attends graduate school with her, a seductive girl of the type who does everything to please men—blonde hair, blue eyes, sports car. I interrupt her to say only: "A sort of Barbie", and at this point my intervention, the product of a visual reverie, leads on to another subject: "Yes, like a Barbie doll, and just think that I was forbidden to play with Barbies as a child. Luckily at some point my grandmother bought me some and so I was able to play with them, although my mother clearly disapproved." I say: "they're something frivolous, pointless." She continues: "That's right, we must study and keep on studying, and then publish and keep on publishing." At this point another character (perhaps because of what I do) comes on the scene, who may be the true antagonist of Barbie: "Yes, at home everybody admired my aunt's sister who works as a surgeon in Africa: a degree in medicine, post-graduate specialisation in surgery, and a lifetime devoted to sick children".

It is clear from the start that the issue of femininity is introduced into the field in varying degrees of superegoism, but also embodied in the possible worlds and characters that the analysis offers—from Barbieland to Mother Teresa of Africa.

Cypresses and tigers

Arriving at her first session Claudia lies down on the couch and immediately falls silent. She had come in looking radiant, but then the atmosphere turned dark, as when a cloud covers the sun, which is what is happening for real—also meteorologically—in the room.

Faced with this prolonged silence, I say: "It seems that this new position makes you gloomy; the sun has disappeared, as we have just seen, and everything has darkened". "Yes, because I think that there are more sad things than happy things to tell" (deep sigh). Then she begins to talk about the string of boyfriends she has had, about how each of them had then also revealed a dark side, and how that led each time to the relationship breaking up. I say, "so they were all painful affairs". "Yes, but at least things are going well at work. However, what I didn't say at the preliminary consultation is that the main reason I am here is because of my psychosomatic disorders".

"Which are?"

"I am allergic to cats and cypress trees" (I wonder to myself whether it is only cats she is allergic to or possibly other felines; then I think of cypresses: an allergy to death, and this alarms me more). Claudia continues: "I have an ulcerative colitis that causes me to bleed" (I wonder silently what it is that has to be evacuated and bleeds? Tigers? Mourning? Lacerating emotions?). Then she resumes: "I also suffer from celiac disease" (so watch out with your interpretive diet, then!).

I say: "And you were afraid that if I was told about these things I would be frightened. But now that you have a residence permit that allows you to be on the couch, you are not afraid of telling me".

"That's the word," she continues, "frightened is the right word. As a child I always had nightmares about monsters, animals used to lunge at me with their claws and teeth . . ." (she continues talking about what suggests to me the relationship between evacuating and possibly containing excruciating emotions). This beginning probably needs little comment.

Luisa's turmoil

At the first session Luisa is like a frightened fawn, pretty and with a sweet look on her face.

The moment she lies down she immediately bursts out crying. She comes out with a torrent of words (which I find myself having to contain) about splitting up with two former boyfriends—even now she talks about the experiences in a very sorrowful tone of voice. Then she tells me about her holidays in a Kinderheim in Switzerland where she felt deported; then about a sister with leukaemia who is undergoing chemotherapy.

The story seems to hinge on separation and abandonment—which might be called the "main characters" and lynchpins of the story.

The narrative continues with the description of a turbulent period in her life when she had taken drugs, behaved promiscuously, taking part in orgy-like parties, a time when she frequented gambling dens and got caught up in the criminal world surrounding them.

At this point Luisa is obviously speaking about the excitatory and antidepressant defence mechanisms which she used to (and still does) deploy to save herself from the undigested, unprocessed protoemotions associated with being abandoned.

She goes on to describe how she is beginning to have a sequence of memories of "harassment" and "abuse" by her grandfather who had touched her inappropriately on several occasions.

She then recounts a nightmare she had as a child in which her mother was killed by machine gun fire.

The protoemotions associated with situations of "abandonment"—♂ ♂ ♂ ♂ hyper-contents—were not transformed or contained because they exceeded her capacity to metabolise them; they "disturb", "abuse" and "touch" her.

She goes on to describe how she had been run down by a car shortly after getting her degree and how some months later she had contracted an autoimmune disease involving an allergy to light. In a more cheerful tone of voice she then talks about her long-standing habit of having lunch with a group of girlfriends, just like the main characters in *Sex and the City*. She also describes how one of the girls tends to keep in the background, although she also steals food from the plates of others and never orders anything for herself.

At this point it is clear that there is a ghost, who could be called a tiger or a fawn, who is allergic to light, who runs her down (who runs herself down)—an extremely violent ghost who would like to machine gun them all.

The ghost survives by "nibbling" from the plates of others but now needs to come out into the open: in other words, all those protoemotional states originating from early "separations and abandonments" constitute hyper-β protocontents looking to be evacuated and in search of containers and transformation, even though the evacuation takes the form of a volley of "machine gun fire".

The first session of analysis is the moment when the "casting" of these protoemotions takes place and when an initial attempt is made to give them a name: the story becomes that of a girl in the patient's class who has had a number of tumours that have produced several metastases.

She tries to be close to this child who has been admitted to a paediatric oncology ward where she is treated by doctors who are very competent and humane.

On the one hand, the accumulated β-elements have undergone "transformation into a tumour", but at the same time there was also a transformation into dream at the moment they were narrated.

We have what we could call an "abandonoma" or a "separoma" that awaits further transformation; and the analysis is the cancer ward where perhaps it will be possible to treat these aggregates of β-elements (betalomas; Barale & Ferro, 1992).

After the first unsaturated interpretation—"It's incredible how many things you have piled up and have had to hold in"—Luisa starts talking about the older brother of the girl she looks after and about the amount of time the child spends threading coloured beads to make necklaces.

Now we have both a caring figure and the ability to connect things and develop plans, session after session.

The first manifestation of aggregates of β-elements is undifferentiated (abandonment and convex protoemotions). Later it becomes more specific in the "ghost" of anger, which instead of taking an undifferentiated path (e.g., panic attacks) becomes more and more narratable: the ghost, the machine gun, rage, etc.

But now we see a particular clinical situation, that of a girl (but it could also be an adult) with selective mutism who thus "voids" the possibility of communicating the fundamental rule. Not that we should do the same with children, but this puts us in contact with "those who cannot say and for a long time will not be able to say". One need only think of patients who for a long time hide the fact that they have hallucinations (Ferro, 2003).

Bad faith

This seems to be the right moment to bring in the problem of patients who are in bad faith—a subject Madeleine Baranger (1963) discusses in some detail.

Each patient in his own way and at various stages of the analysis is inclined to circumvent the "fundamental rule"—which is all part of the game. Baranger focuses on those situations where flouting the fundamental rule and the means used to elude the rule are more serious in nature. These are instances of bad faith—in the sense that they are planned and systematic acts that affect the authenticity and interest of the analytic process, albeit accompanied by varying degrees of awareness.

A possible example would be patients who are given an interpretation and then reply by saying that it is something they have known for a long time. However, Baranger is not satisfied with explaining the bad faith of the patient as a phenomenon of dissociation (at that time splitting mechanisms were very much the focus of attention). After discussing its most obvious feature, namely the wish to challenge and sneer at the fundamental rule, Baranger goes on to interpret the ambiguous situation represented by the inauthenticity of the material in terms of the patient's desire to radically pervert the analytic situation and to reduce the analyst to impotence. There are some exceptional insights in Baranger's work, such as her comment that the level of awareness of deception is not the distinctive feature of bad faith; it is as if the patient were exercising his right to dissociate but without actually dissociating.

In Madeleine Baranger's work, the patient's bad faith, however unpleasant it may be for the analyst, becomes a fascinating topic of study, a structure that keeps disappearing and carries forward the patient's project of deceiving both himself and the analyst, in a continuous oscillation between good faith and lies, and as part of a search for an omnipotent triumph over the analyst. Meanwhile, the patient, like Proteus, changes rapidly from one form to another primarily in an attempt to elude self-definition.

> In bad faith, the essential point seems to be an inner ego situation: a multiplicity of contemporary and contradictory identifications that have not settled down, which makes the analysand feel and stand in for various characters without knowing who he really is. (Baranger, 1963, p. 186)

I mention this issue because it stands at an important crossroads between truth and lies. It is a question we know was dear to Bion, with his distinction between K and O, and then also to Grotstein, with his notion of oscillations between Truth and varying degrees of the distortion of Truth. It was Grotstein who performed the brilliantly transgressive act of putting dreams in column 2 of the grid (Grotstein, 2007).

What then could be the antidote? I think it is the concept of tolerable truth and the act of looking it in the eye (Ferro et al., 2007). An extraordinary example of this is I think what Ogden (2007) proposes in his "On talking as dreaming". Here patients who cannot tolerate the classic style of communication are gradually led, almost without them knowing, into a situation where they are for first time (or almost the first time) able to dream together with someone. One could also mention the famous lie told by Bishop Myriel in Victor Hugo's *Les Misérables*: when the police arrest Jean Valjean, who had been given shelter by the Bishop and had then stolen all his silverware, Myriel lies: he tells the police that he had given it all to Valjean as a present. In other words, toning down the superego and avoiding the criminalisation of conduct open up new and unexpected roads. One must also be able to play with lies.

The magic filter: the contribution of Bion and field theory

There is a magic filter that can be used to enlarge the field. The idea is to precede the patient's material with the expression, "I had a dream in which . . ." This makes it possible to further develop the dream-like quality of the sessions. Any communication can serve as an example. If a patient were to say even in the first session: "I had an argument with my wife because she's always complaining about the fruit they serve her in shops but she never dares protest", clearly this could be seen from many points of view—collateral transference, negation, repressed aggression, avoidance of other hot topics. By adopting the magic filter it becomes easy to understand these as communications in the field whereby "someone receives things from someone else that are not good but lacks the courage to protest". This may lead to subsequent specifications through interpretations of transference or in transference.

It follows from this that basically we should act so as to enable the "hot-air balloon of analysis" to take off gradually on its way towards new and further points of view.

Many psychoanalysts look back on what has happened and what has been repressed or split off. In this sense analysis resembles the long-established notion of evidence-based scientific research. The paradigm is that of Sherlock Holmes and his "patient" Watson, whereby "Elementary, my dear Watson!" (a common misquotation which does not appear in any of the works by Sir Arthur Conan Doyle) is replaced with the no less famous "You told me that . . .". The effect is to distort the communication of the patient, who sees distant meanings attributed to what he says that are often taken from the Book of Meanings.

Relatively few psychoanalysts look instead to the future, in other words towards something new that can be created through analysis, or towards the possible new worlds that a patient equipped with new tools for thinking will come to inhabit. If we set aside the wagon trains of old western movies and replace them with new vehicles like the Starship Enterprise, where will the patient be able to go, what will he be able to find, what will he be able to think and desire (and we with him)?

Or if we replace the psychoanalysis of content (split off or repressed, but at any rate already given) with a psychoanalysis that develops "tools" to dream/think/hear, what will happen? In other words, if we look to the development of the patient's creativity, what will he find/invent for himself?

One way of imagining this point of view is to think of someone who is forced to see "the same movie" over and over again (the old compulsion to repeat) and then suddenly finds himself inside a "multiplex". True, he may occasionally even have heard some inter-ference, noises from rooms he suspected might be nearby, but being able to switch between them to see previously unimagined films is no small matter.

Perhaps an even better way of putting it would be to see the patient as someone who discovers his own talent as a director and who learns to dream. What he dreams is not what has been repressed or split off; he learns instead to create through the dreams he is capa-ble of dreaming—starting from the transformation into images of all present and past forms of sensoriality—a new and ever-expanding unconscious that will become a growing repository of memories, fantasies, and film clips. An analysis that looks to the future resem-bles not so much a detective story as a spy movie or a science fiction film, genres where we know what is likely to happen if nobody inter-venes in the meantime.

What will happen in the case of a psychosomatic patient? Or an obsessive patient? Or a patient with hallucinations? We are called upon to stop the "predictable" from happening and to set in motion a new and unpredictable narrative.

A step forward has been made by those authors who, standing on the shoulders of Bion, have conceptualised the development of the ability to dream as the way to gain possible access to previously unthinkable futures. A number of authors—Ogden (2007, 2009), Grotstein (2007, 2009), and the present writer (Ferro, 2008, 2009)—have developed this line of thought in various ways.

We all remember those movies about imminent catastrophes for the human race, for example, an asteroid that could have a devastat-ing impact on the earth. Here we could compare this "asteroid" to a "freeze-dried (or zipped) mass of protosensoriality", protoemotions which unless they are transformed by the patient's or the analyst's dream (or the dream of the field) will have a devastating impact on the patient's psychic life. We will have symptomatically forced stories or stories with psychiatric symptoms or stories in which the symptom will be expressed through the ankylosis of the story, which will take necessary shape, giving rise to life as a symptom. Whatever it is, the "symptom" stands for the precipitate of "dreams" that could not be dreamt.

The avoidance of disaster, civil protection, the opening up of new worlds, landing in parallel universes—these could be the new metaphors for the development of the mind. Of course there is always something upstream, something prior, but investigating it will not change fate.

Bion moves towards the subjectivism of "O". In other words, analytic work is not a matter of events, memories, repression, resistance; it consists rather in the subjective way in which each person transforms the Ultimate Reality, the Fact into alpha elements, pictograms, figurations that permit both memory and forgetfulness. And it does so thanks to the development of "tools" that perform this task: the film of the analysis consists precisely in the development of these tools that facilitate transformation, previously undreamt-of experiences. Ogden puts it very well when he says that the analysis and the analyst serve to dream the dreams that the patient was unable to dream alone and which have become symptoms.

The analytic field has shifted: from being a powerful concept referring to the explicit interpretive work of the analyst on the blind spot/bastion formed by the intersecting projective identifications of analyst and patient, it has become an ever-expanding potential space where all possible worlds activated by the analytic encounter can assume importance. What previously belonged to one person or another now belongs to the field: one can thus think in terms of the alpha function of the field, beta-elements or protoemotional turmoil in the field, the emotional characters/holograms of the field, the transformative and interpretive activity of the field.

The singularity of voice of the one or the other fades and a structure comes to life that foreshadows and enables narrative transformations.

The most significant changes will be the development (and sometimes the forging) of tools for thinking.

Recently (2009), together with Roberto Basile I wrote: The analytic field is inhabited by masses of real and virtual presences. Perhaps we could compare it to the universe as understood today.

The fact of the matter is that the analytic field coincides with that unrepeatable "universe" that comes to life at the beginning of each session, and which is then temporarily suspended at the end of each session.

The field is inhabited first by central characters, or protagonists, but then also by supporting actors and extras—and all these people are constantly changing role. But the human (or even non-anthropomorphic) character is the most highly advanced in the field. We could compare it to the constellations we make out in a starry sky. The field is a place where we find a multitude of other phenomena, most of which are unknown. A possible axiom of the field: the "big bang" and the "big crunch" are what happen at the beginning and at the end of each session. The characters are the endpoint and the outcome of prior operations.

The characters are complex and do not correspond to the people they superficially resemble. The characters in the session are the result of mental operations carried out by analyst and patient whose mental functioning (and protoemotions, emotions, unknown aspects) they depict. They are, that is, holograms of the mental functioning of the analytic couple, including however operations which in a different terminology would be called split off or not yet accessible to thought. Characters enter the session tangentially and leave tangentially; others enter tangentially and go on to become leading players; others assume key roles.

From this vertex, anything the patient speaks about describes a function of the field.

The analyst occupies a special position which can be one of maximum asymmetry (where he is responsible) or one of maximum symmetry (where the functioning of the field is determined jointly by analyst and patient).

Conclusion

I believe that the "fundamental rule" could be to dream sensoriality so as to be more in touch with the unconscious which we continually enlarge also so as to communicate it. It should be a point of arrival constructed and experienced jointly and *in crescendo* session after session using our modes of operation, those of the patient and those of the field which we only make knowable with him in *après-coup*.

Let us imagine that after the statement of the classic "fundamental rule", patient A says, "I'm always relieved when my wife gives me a shopping list", and patient B says: "I can't stand the fact that my wife always tells me how and what should I buy". Who is right?

Obviously no one—but it is a start towards the knowledge and tolerance embodied in Pirandello's "Right you are (if you think so)".

6

How Emmy silenced Freud into analytic listening

Patrick Miller

> When to the sessions of sweet silent thought,
> I summon up remembrance of things past, . . .
>
> Shakespeare, Sonnet 30, 1966

In analysis "silent thought" is the negative condition for the repetition actualised in transference of old ways of being and thinking and also for the eventual tentative emergence of new ones. But, in analysis, silent thought is rarely sweet as it summons up the sound and the fury of the repressed past, primary and oedipal love and hatred.

In his "Observations on transference love" Freud (1915a [1914]) highlights the ethical and scientific aspects of analytic technique as opposed to the common sense morality of ordinary conversation[1]. When the sound and the fury of transference love appear on the analytic stage "to urge the patient to suppress, renounce or sublimate her instincts (is) not an analytic way of dealing with them, but a senseless one." It is based on fear, which is none other than *the analyst's fear of what his own method sets in motion*: "It is just as though, after summoning up a spirit from the underworld by cunning spells, one were to send him down again without having asked him a single question" (ibid., p. 164).

This metaphor of Freud's is the kernel of analytic ethics: at the crossroads between the tendency to repeat through action in the transference and countertransference in order not to think and not to remember, and the working through capacities of the mind binding, first in silence, thought, emotion, and speech, making it possible for the analyst to question and interpret.

"Cunning spells" on the one hand, certainly a reminiscence of the hypnotic treatment, and questioning speech on the other. Along the dynamics leading from the unleashing of repetition in action to the working through of the mind, the functions of the analyst's silence are manyfold and subject to change in value.

As I shall develop further, silence is not the opposite of speech, it is the opposite of noise. And analytic speech, the analyst's or the analysand's, can silence noise.

Silence, considered as *abstinence* of speech, does not have a value in itself in promoting favourable conditions for the unfolding of an analytic process. Whether the absence of speech from the analyst is meaningful (meaning–productive) or meaningless (meaning–destructive) can only be inferred from its relation to the conscious and unconscious dynamics in the analyst's mind and their relation to the analytic context. It can be an acting out just as much as the suspension (abstinence and neutrality) of an acting out. The analyst's lack of speech can be a *compliance*, for, instance to an imaginary idealised "rule" of technique whose function is to prevent the analyst from thinking about the fundamental questions implicit in the analytic method and their relation to technique. It can also be a phobic *avoidance* protecting the analyst from addressing erotic, aggressive or non-mentalised states present in the analytic moment. Compliance can work hand in hand with avoidance as a rationalisation of it.

Therefore, one of the main issues about the relation between silence and speech in analysis seems to be the function and value of words in the analyst's mind and their use in the analytic moment with this singular patient. The fundamental rule of analysis implies the *inner action* of verbalisation, that is, the inner act of "putting into words" the silent thoughts falling into the reaches of consciousness, this action resulting in all kinds of unexpected transformations, intra-psychic and intersubjective. For Freud the pre-conscious was the psychic region where thing-presentations and word-presentations came together; where language could bind the non-verbal unconscious. The pre-conscious is a kind of go-between between two systems. There resides the matrix of transformations going on during the analytic process in both the analysand's and analyst's minds, "sheltered" from the noise of conscious will, intentions, determinations: binding and un-binding, de-organising and re-organising, evolving by itself and according to its own laws like a living organism (see below Freud's metaphors in "On beginning the treatment" (1913c) on the analytic process as pregnancy). From that first topography perspective, and bearing in mind such a notion as the "pure gold" of analysis, one could propose a model of analytic interpretation based solely on the emergence in the analyst's mind of an unintentional formula which imposes itself to his mind and of its voicing in a sort of oracular way in the session. Following on this model, the analyst could consistently remain silent except in such oracular moments, which are relatively few in the course of an analysis. Only these moments would be devoid of defensive attitudes, resistances, and the non-analytic platitudes of ordinary conversation.

Such a model is representative at a significant degree of analytic culture in France and many of its most brilliant representatives have been very much inspired by it. It would take too much space to only begin to delineate some hypotheses on the origins in the French psychoanalytic culture of such a model. The interest for psychoanalysis in France originated more in literary circles than psychiatric ones. Jacques Lacan, an eminent young psychiatrist, whose master was the great G. de Clérambault, was very much involved in literary and artistic circles, especially the surrealists in the early thirties while he was in analysis. In the next generation of analysts, some of them analysed by him, whether psychiatrists or not, many were very interested in literature, philosophy, linguistics, and the arts, and were major contributors to the French analytic culture and literature. To name a few: Michel de M'Uzan, André Green, J. B. Pontalis, Christian David, and Jean Laplanche.

Jacques Lacan's influence[2] was very important but not sufficient to explain the vivid interest, both literary and philosophical, for speech and language among French analysts, which enabled them to highlight this crucial aspect in Freud's discovery of psychoanalysis.

This interest had very diverse impacts on the conduct of analysis, technique, and the frame. Lacan's evolution is interesting because it was so paradoxical for an analyst who put so much emphasis on speech and language in analysis. It seems that his interventions and interpretations grew very sparse in time to the point of disappearance and replacement by an "act" (some would call it an acting out rationalised as technique) which he called "scansion", which came at the moment and in place of a possible interpretation and as interruption of the session. Strangely enough this passage from "the act of speech" to an acting of silence and reduction of the time of the session to virtually no-time is justified by a growing distrust towards the alienating, imaginary power of speech. In a famous metaphor Lacan compared the analyst's interpretation to the Zen master's blow on his student's head and wrote that the aim of interpretation is to make waves. A stress on the importance of the economic factor, once again interestingly paradoxical in someone who constantly denied the importance of affects in analysis, favouring as he was the mathematics of the symbolic order.

Michel de M'Uzan has a powerful way of describing, both clinically and metapsychologically, these specific analytic moments, which I described previously as "oracular", when an image and/or a sentence suddenly imposes itself in the analyst's mind, seemingly like a foreign body and demanding to be voiced in spite of its uncanniness. These emergences can only be the result of a long preconscious working-through which needs, in order to develop, a deep form of inner silence that protects them from the interference (noise) of secondary thought processes (see his seminal article "Contretransfert et système paradoxal" (M'Uzan, 1976a)). This form of inner silence is a condition for the analyst's mind to undergo the economical and topographical changes needed in order to listen with the "third ear", they are also a reflection of the absence to oneself which they imply.

Analytic silence has to do with how the analyst is going to handle words and use them, both the analysand's and his own, and how he considers (or does not consider) the transformative power of verbalisation in his explicit and implicit theories. Analytic silence is contained in the second fundamental rule of analysis, never explicated to the patient, free-floating or evenly suspended attention, which applies to the analyst. The effectiveness of this self-applied rule fluctuates a lot during the session, is subjected to a mainly pre-conscious psychic work, both sustained by the "good" psychoanalytic superego and jarred (noise) by the interferences of the "bad" super-ego, attacking and sabotaging the unbearable demands made on the analyst's ego by the scientific values of psychoanalysis. Analytic silence also means a capacity to overcome these attacks, the outcome of the battle being more in the pre-conscious dynamics than in the conscious self-righteousness of the analyst's "in good standing" morals. A more recent wording of the relationship between the rule of free-floating attention and analytic silence would be Bion's recom-mendation that an analyst should start every new session without memory or desire.

Language, words, speech, silence, and voice (tone, prosody) are presented together when the analysand or the analyst talk or remain silent during the session. Their different combinations appear in an infinite range of manifestations: from suffocating affect laden silence, to a sigh, a sob, a cry, from perfectly articulated obsessional discourse seemingly devoid of affect but conveying sometimes unbearable emotions to the analyst, to the more shifting, dreamy, polysemic open-ended free associations, seemingly very "analytic" with their expected slips, but sometimes the slips and silences are felt more like ruptures than return of the repressed or inhibitions, verging on blankness and void. Due to the demands of the fundamental rule, language and speech, during the session, are always, at one point or another, brought to their limit.

One way of naming this limit could be: resistance of the Id, the Id's refusal to be civilised, that is, somewhere at the limits between psyche and soma. This is where speech and language are silenced, this is where primitive ways of thinking manifest themselves in ways that are felt and apprehended more than thought through in secondary thought processes, even less articulated in words. This is where psychoanalysis can help gain ground, where maybe what we are confronted with, *in vivo*, are the mechanisms of what Freud called primary repression.[3] What is threatening there is not only the silencing of speech and language, but also the silencing of any capa-city to represent. This is where psyche is a frail damming against entropy. In these confines the analyst's stubborn ideological "analytic" silence works hand in hand with entropy and the death instinct. Freud said that the death instinct operates in silence. We also say that a healthy organism is a silent one. For that matter the ideological silence of the analyst can also be very talkative: words devoid of accuracy, simply trying to deny what is being experienced in those deadly confines, a chatter-box speaking its master's voice. In that respect noise coming from the analyst, interfering with and jamming the possibility to elaborate what is being experienced, has to do with what I would call the -ian syndrome: the analyst referring to himself as Kleinian, Winnicottian, Freudian, Bionian, Lacanian, etc. A sense of history and of perspective on the evolution of ideas in psychoanalysis, contributes greatly to the quality of the analyst's silence. A sense of history meaning: the history of psychoanalysis, the analyst's personal history, the history of his own personal analyses, and of his analysts, and so on. Bion's notions of saturated and unsaturated can be helpful in thinking about true psychoanalytic silence, provided they do not become -ianisms.

Talking wipes out

When a patient comes for a first interview, sits down and says: "I dreamt of you last night", how do we understand the beginning? The beginning of transference, the beginning of an analytic process, and the possibility to begin interpreting?

We can raise the same questions concerning the beginning of psychoanalysis. When did it start? When Freud began conceptualising his metapsychology and laying down the new principles of a method which claimed to be so very different from hypnosis, or when he began dreaming of a new method of treatment and understanding together with some of his attractive and seductive lady patients, during the so-called pre-analytic period when he was grappling with the enigmas of hysterical symptoms, pretending he was applying Breuer's method, but already aware that he knew better and would discover a far more interesting and efficient way of knowledge?

Only in hindsight, *après-coup*, in the light of our knowledge of Freud's later conceptualisations, can we decipher as already psychoanalytic his way of describing what he is observing and experiencing in his endeavours to apply the hypnotic treatment that was not his own invention. We can observe, in turn, that the way he is dealing with the enigmatic data he is confronted with is laying the foundations of the yet-to-come analytic method and technique.

If we want to further our understanding of the specificity of psychoanalytic silence, we can go back to the lively account of Frau Emmy von N.'s treatment and read it as paradigmatic of the emergence of a new approach of the relationship between speech, listening, understanding, and silence within the dynamics of what is not yet understood as transference and countertransference.

At the beginning of his narrative Freud describes his patient at length: her bodily features, her composure, her attitudes, her character, and, of course, her symptoms. He insists that he finds her very attractive in many respects, and he takes this as a positive indication that he can work well with her: "(her) symptoms and personality interested me so greatly that I devoted a large part of my time to her and determined to do all I could for her recovery" (Freud, 1895d, p. 48).

She is beautiful and elegant with character, she presents "an unusual degree of education and intelligence", she is sexually abstinent but sexually minded and, at times, sexually provocative, she is unhappy, neurotic, aristocratic, and wealthy. Concentrated in one person, she presents most of the traits which render a woman attractive to Freud, and which he will find embodied in different women during his lifetime, in different combinations: Martha, Minna, Lou Salomé, Marie Bonaparte.

Freud is still a young man at the time, younger by seven years than his patient, he is just turning thirty-three: attraction, desire, enigmas, are at the roots of his wish to find a cure for Emmy,[4]. His "treatment" of his own desire and attraction as he elaborates it along the process with Emmy, combined with his epistemophilia and how she pushes him to change, are at the core of the invention of the analytic method as a "joint venture". The discovery of the virtues of silence, along the way, and giving up on "noise", are central in this adventure.

Freud is using "Breuer's technique of investigation under hypnosis" for the first time,[5] not as a "Breuerian", but already as a rebellious Oedipal rival who will immediately proceed to bring some modifications to the method.[6] In the course of the clinical narration Breuer comes in and out of the picture, in and out of Emmy's room, Emmy's attention, Freud's mind. This is one of the many figures of penetration in the material that are playing in Emmy's and Freud's minds. Emmy presents a startling fear of sexual penetration, and on another more primitive level, she seems to be constantly prey to intrusion anxiety and impingements (Winnicott). Freud is struggling for and with his freedom of mind, obviously refusing to comply to penetration by Breuer's ideas which might prevent the emergence of his own. In that respect he finds in Emmy an ally when she transferentially rebels against the injunctions or intrusions; the impingements of hypnotic therapy.

From (what will later be) a psychoanalytic perspective, silencing the noise of sexuality and early traumatic excitation is exactly the contrary of "wiping out". This is one of the fruitful contradictions in Freud's narrative. What he is actually beginning to do (inventing a new method with Emmy) is the contrary of what he is supposed to be doing: applying Breuer's hypnotic therapy.

Following Breuer's method implies *talking* to the patient during her hypnotic sleep and *telling* her to erase from her mind some of the traumatic remembrances which have come back during the session. Freud uses different metaphors: to wipe out, to expunge, to extinguish.[7] Talking to the patient, from the hypnotic point of view, means erasing memories which have been summoned up, which is the exact opposite of the psychoanalytic stance.

We are confronted here with two opposite ways of dealing with the analyst's "fear factor". One is to erase, by using language in the form of some kind of "cunning spell", not the trace of the traumatic memory, but the access to remembering it, so that the fear will not be consciously felt anymore by the patient. An injunction not to think about it.

The other is to summon up the painful traumatic memory in order to keep it in mind as much as possible along with the intensity of affect it brings back, thus increasing anxiety, making the patient feel worse, and running the risk of an interruption of treatment. Analytic silence here is related to the capacity to confront psychic violence, to explore it with language, but not to dismiss it by language. In some paradoxical way psychoanalytic silence has to do with the capacity to deal with "the sound and the fury" without running away, or without trying to appease it with some kind of "*medicina*". In that sense it has more to do with the "*ferrum* and *ignis*" than with the "*medicina*".[8]

Silence, negative capability, and femininity

Psychoanalytic silence has to do with standing drive violence, not responding to it, hence suspending action, exploring it, instead of dismissing it, thinking about it and then using language to bring it to a level of understanding enabling a process of sublimation rather than of discharge (in a more recent formulation (Bion's) one would say: a containment bringing a capacity for reverie rather than an evacuation).

The capacity for silence brings the issues to another level of functioning, where the drive excitation is not suppressed but not discharged into immediate satisfaction.

When Freud is treating Emmy, he has in mind the account Breuer, his senior colleague, gave him of Anna O's treatment and its very troubling and troubled ending: Breuer running away in fear of Anna's violent erotic transference. Freud has it in his mind already in 1889 that he will not shy away from a patient's erotic seduction nor yield to it. His judgement on Breuer's attitude is very abrupt and contemptuous in a letter to Stefan Zweig (June 2, 1932) where he recalls the incident:

> On the evening of the day when all her symptoms had been disposed of, he (Breuer) was summoned to the patient again, found her confused and writhing in abdominal cramps. Asked what was wrong with her, she replied: "Now Dr B.'s child is coming!" At this moment he held in his hand the key that would have opened the "doors to the Mothers," but he let it drop. With all his intellectual gifts there was nothing Faustian in his nature. Seized by *conventional horror* he took flight and abandoned the patient to a colleague. (Freud, 1961, pp. 412–413, my italics)

The Man of Achievement (Keats) is not seized by conventional horror, his negative capability (Bion), which in this case is an equivalent of psychoanalytic silence, enables him to remain, to harbour the convulsive anxiety of not-knowing and to wait for a new idea to grow and to be born:

> . . . at once it struck me what quality went to form a Man of Achievement, especially in Literature, and which Shakespeare possessed so enormously. I mean Negative Capability, that is, when a man is capable of being in uncertainties, mysteries, doubts, without any irritable reaching after fact and reason. (Keats, 1970)

The growing child in the womb will, much later, be one of Freud's metaphors for the unfolding of the analytic process where, after a first impetus (insemination) the analyst sits back and waits for the process to go on by itself towards its natural end, like a developing organism.[9] In this instance Freud as analyst thinks of himself as active, masculine, and father, the analysand's mind being the feminine and motherly receptacle where the child of analysis will grow while the genitor remains silent. Freud is looking for the key *to* the Mothers and also to find access to the dark continent of femininity. It will take three generations of analysts to shift this representation and bring motherhood and femininity into the analyst's position. Interestingly enough this will be achieved, at least in their writings and conceptualisations, by two men[10]: Winnicott and Bion, in continuation and response to a Mother who had actively shown the way to what was difficult for Freud to conceptualise, the *sturm und drang* of hateful relationship between Mothers and infants: Melanie Klein.

Since Freud the issue of silence has been intimately linked to that of femininity and death, as it clearly appears in "The theme of the three caskets", which was written the same year, 1913, as "On beginning the treatment". Both Winnicott and Bion elaborate the capacity to construct psychic life around the infant's experience of an unthinkable and organismic *fear of dying* which is either confirmed by a deadly silence from the primary environment or addressed and transformed by the life-oriented psychic processing capacities of the primary objects' minds. The latter, although they are very active processes, are silent ones, the way a healthy organism can be said to be silent. What Winnicott describes as primary maternal preoccupation can lead to the following: the mother senses the infant's need and wakes up *before* the baby cries. "In the language of these considerations, the early building up of the ego is therefore *silent*" (Winnicott, 1956). This primary concern can be awakened in the analyst silently. There is a trajectory in the best case scenario of ego-development, and of analytic process, from successful silent adaptation to need, called primary maternal madness, to the capacity to be alone which manifests itself, in analysis, by a specific quality of silence that corresponds to a maturation and not to a resistance, and should as such be echoed by a silence from the analyst, respectful of his patient's ability to be alone:

> In almost all our psycho-analytic treatments there come times when the ability to be alone is important to the patient. Clinically

this may be represented by a silent phase or a silent session, and this silence, far from being evidence of resistance, turns out to be an achievement on the part of the patient. Perhaps it is here that the patient has been able to be alone for the first time. (Winnicott, 1958c)

Silent communication accompanies the capacity to be alone in the presence of someone.

Analytic silence together with the notion of silent communication can be brought in the vicinity of a notion elaborated by Bertram Lewin (1946): the dream screen. The analyst's silence is deeply related to the "dreamy" state induced in him by free-floating attention as a kind of self-induced hypnosis. In the analytic situation there is somehow a reversal of the hypnotic therapist's position. In that respect analytic silence could be considered as the blank screen that the analyst, in his analytic "sleep" is presenting to the patient, another way of thinking about the analyst as a mirror. In this way it is also connecting silence with the primary relation to the breast and the merging into the breast:

A dream appears to be projected on this flattened breast—the dream screen . . . the dream screen is sleep itself; it is not only the breast, but is as well that content of sleep or the dream which fulfils the wish to sleep, the wish that Freud assumes to enter into all dreaming. The dream screen is the representative of the wish to sleep. The visual contents represent its opponents, the wakers. The blank screen is the copy of primary infantile sleep. (Lewin, 1946, p. 420)

This is the most trophic aspect of silence in analysis. It is obviously not a given but the fleeting result of so many conditions determined by a specific kind of psychic work both in the analyst and the analysand. It may happen a few times, if one is lucky, in the course of a long analysis, in that virtual topographical place we call intersubjectivity, a co-creation of both protagonists of the analytic process but belonging to neither, the Topos of Neverland.

I cannot evade listening to the very end

Freud and Emmy chatted a lot together, although Emmy presented what one might call, by understatement, a speech disorder. Outside of the twice a day hypnotic sessions, "we discussed every sort of subject" notes Freud. He is in very close bodily contact with her, massaging her whole body twice a day and providing her with warm baths. He seems to be almost entirely devoted to her every need, in what looks very much indeed like a maternal preoccupation and a very active behaviour. But he is also in such intimate, sensual, and erotic contact with her that he is playing with fire while "handling explosives". He does not seem to be aware of it, which does not necessarily mean he was not aroused by it.

As a matter of fact he is doing the exact opposite of the fierce commandments repeatedly uttered, "every two or three minutes" by Emmy's changed voice as if they were spoken by someone else: "Keep still!—Don't say anything!—Don't touch me!"

Freud wonders whether she is hallucinating some kind of traumatic scene. We can wonder: when she voices this sentence, who is talking? Whom is it addressed to?

Is she addressing a man who is sexually harassing her? Is she talking to her husband on their wedding night? Is this her mother's voice forbidding her to come close both physically and emotionally? Is this the voice and the wordings of repression of her own oral cannibalistic drives toward the breast, of her own appetite for oral sex and violent desire to devour the mouse–rat–penis? Is it the voice of the Oedipal father instrumentalised by a forbidding Oedipal mother? Is it the voice of a severe superego wanting to forbid all liveliness and desire in her, or the voice of a maternal internal object constructed from aspects of her mother described by Freud from her own account: "She was brought up carefully, but under strict discipline by an over-energetic and severe mother." (Freud, 1895d, p. 49) For that matter it could also be her rebelling against her mother. "Keep still: stop being over-energetic, manically handling me instead of holding me, intruding and impinging by your constant 'doings'. Don't say anything: stop harassing me with reprimands, reproaches, scoldings, and punishments. Don't touch me, don't beat me, don't arouse me" (ibid., p. 49).

Emmy's conflicts seem very much to be focused around her mouth, tongue, and throat preventing any kind of action by the body parts involved, including speech, and partly identifying with her mother's contorted face after she died of a stroke. When speech has become impossible, Emmy becomes a bird. She vocalises a "clacking sound defying imitation". Freud asks colleagues of his who are hunters to identify the sound and they tell him that its final notes resemble the call of a capercaillie, "a ticking ending with a pop and a hiss". The capercaillie is a very big wild grouse that very likely was hunting game in the "Baltic estates" or other places in Central Europe where Emmy "possessed large estates". Could this clacking sound ending with a pop and a hiss be part of a courting song during the mating season? In which case Emmy would be identified to a male bird? If Freud becomes the courted female then who is the hunter in Emmy's fantasmatic scenarios?

Some time after Emmy's treatment Freud will link the words of the protective formula with melancholia, as he encounters later similar formulas in a "melancholic woman who endeavoured by their means to control her tormenting thoughts" (ibid., p. 49fn) Indeed Emmy's melancholic features appear in the course of the treatment, focused around the mouth and sadistic attacks on the breast and the penis, and expressed in transferential guilt of having hurt Freud, and eventually in this blunt statement: I hate myself. Biting remorse. Before hypnosis she shudders in horror: "Only think, when it's unpacked! There's a dead rat in among them—one that's been *gn-aw-aw-ed* at!" (ibid., p. 51, my italics).

Two days later in the course of what is already free associations during the massage, not under hypnosis, the teeth which have "gn-aw-aw-ed" at the rat are all being pulled out at one sitting from a cousin's mouth: "She accompanied the story with horrified looks and kept repeating her protective formula" (ibid., p. 56). Freud notes that Emmy is making use of their seemingly unconstrained and guided by chance conversation in her own way of adopting the method, which is not so aimless as it leads in a very *unexpected* way to pathogenic reminiscences "of which she unburdens herself without being asked to".

Following her own method of free-talk by using her mouth, lips, throat, and teeth randomly, Emmy is actually *unpacking* here and now in the transference the oral violence of her inner world. In the evening she expresses guilt that Freud may have been annoyed at something she said this morning during the massage. Then Freud just notes that her period has begun again today prematurely. Unable to make the link at the time, between the oral aggressivity and the vagina, he proceeds to regulate her period by hypnotic suggestion. This is one of many instances where the therapist's *talk* during hypnosis tends to undo what is being worked through in the aimless conversation before the hypnotic session. Freud by talking as hypnotic therapist obeys one of the injunctions of the protective formula: Don't say anything! and uses it to silence the patient and erase her memories.

However the same formula will be later used by Emmy to firmly ask Freud to shut up and let her talk and will therefore become the first incentive for analytic silence, thus turning around the destructive order from Emmy's superego and/or maternal internal object into an instrument of liberation, enabled by the deep confidence established within the positive transference which allows her to rebel and to use the strength of her superego in a constructive way. It becomes effective because Freud agrees to shut up. Emmy's rebellion is met by his own countertransference where it finds his rebellion against the older colleague's method, but also his own intellectual and scientific ideals. The latter tell Freud to keep still in order to observe what is going on. In order to do that he has to silence the compliance to the wiping out method. Keep still, don't say anything, and listen.

This is also made possible because Freud's intellectual values permit him to acknowledge that he was wrong. Under hypnosis he frequently interrupts his patient, stops her narration and proceeds to wipe out the memories of the "melancholy things . . . as though they had never been present in her mind" (ibid., p. 61) He observes in a note: "On this occasion my energy seems to have carried me too far". Then he writes: "I now saw that I had gained nothing by this interruption and that *I cannot evade listening* to her stories in every detail *to the very end*" (ibid., p. 61, my italics).

Still in the same session he confronts Emmy to his maddening paradoxes, asking her to talk about the stammer after he has forbidden her to think about the scenes which cause the stammer. She explodes when Freud asks her why she can't say where it comes from: " "Why not? because I *mayn't!*" (she pronounced these words violently and angrily)" (ibid., p. 61, my italics). She is so angry that she interrupts the session, Freud complies, and this could very well be one of the beginnings of psycho-analysis. The next day they, together, further the definition of the method. After she says, grudgingly, that she doesn't know why she has gastric pains, he asks her to remember by tomorrow. "She then said in a definitely grumbling tone that I was not to keep on asking her where this and that came from, but to let her tell me what she had to say. *I fell in with this . . .*" (ibid., p. 61, my italics).

The analytic pact is sealed, with its high demand on the analyst's psyche: he cannot avoid listening to the very end (Green, 1979). The protective formula has worked out positively after all. The destructive orders from Emmy's archaic and Oedipal superego have been transformed by the encounter, in the intersubjective play of forces, with the protective Oedipal superego values of Freud's, and they somehow keep on surviving in so many definitions of the analytic method and frame.

Bearing the story of Freud and Emmy's encounter in mind one cannot but think, when reading "On beginning the treatment", of Keep still!, Don't say anything!, and Don't touch me! at every page. They give meaning and substance to the specific notion of analytic silence. As your memory of Emmy and Freud's dialogue is still fresh in your mind I invite you to read this little collage of a few sentences all from "On beginning the treatment", assembled in chronological order:

> I shall endeavour to collect together the rules for the beginning of treatment. They are simply rules of the game which acquire their importance from their relation to the general plan of the game. I am well advised to call these rules "recommendations" and not to claim any unconditional acceptance of them. Let the patient do the talking and explain nothing more than what is absolutely necessary to get him to go on with what he is saying. Lengthy preliminary discussions before the beginning of the analytic treatment have special disadvantageous consequences for which one must be prepared. The patient must be left to do the talking and must be free to choose at what point he shall begin. "Before I can say anything to you I must know a great deal about you; please tell me what you know about yourself." When are we to begin making our communication to the patient? The premature communication of a solution brought the treatment to an untimely end. Our first communication should be withheld until a strong transference has been established.

In the silence of our minds, at the beginning of each first interview, of each new session, the questions and conflicts in Freud and Emmy's dialogue are revived and we learn from them. But nothing and nobody can tell us in advance how we are going to implement each of their three recommendations today with this new patient, within this new session. As Emmy often said to Freud in answer to his pressing questions: "I don't know".

Notes

1. "It would be easy for me to lay stress on the universally accepted standards of morality . . . I am able to trace the moral prescription back to its source, namely to expediency. I am in the happy position of being able to replace the moral embargo by considerations of analytic technique, without any alteration in the outcome" (Freud, 1915a [1914], pp. 163–164).

2. Here is an example, in an early (1953b) but major text by J. Lacan: "Fonction et Champ de la Parole et du Langage en Psychanalyse" of how he links the importance of speech and language with clinical issues and analytic listening (my translation): "Speech, actually, is a gift of language, and language is not immaterial. However subtle, it is a body. Words are caught in all bodily images which captivate the subject; they can impregnate the hysteric, identify to the object of the penis-neid, represent the flow of urine in urethral ambition, or the excrement held back for stingy enjoyment (*jouissance*).

Moreover words can themselves suffer symbolic lesions, accomplish imaginary acts of which the patient is subject. We remember the *Wespe* (wasp) castrated of its initial W to become S. P. the initials of the Wolfman, when he realises the symbolic punishment inflicted on him by Grouscha, the wasp." (ibid., pp. 301–302).

3. And Freud stressed that an analysis can only be considered successful when something of the primary repression has been modified.

4. "I was determined to do all I could for her recovery" (Freud, 1895d, p. 48).

5. "This was my first attempt at handling that therapeutic method" (Freud, 1895d, p. 48).

6. After her first period of treatment with Freud, Frau Emmy goes to a Sanatorium in North Germany: "At Breuer's desire I explained to the physician in charge the *modifications of hypnotic therapy which I had found effective in her case*" (Freud, 1895d, p. 78, my italics).

7. "I extinguished her plastic memory of these scenes", "My expunging from her memories", "I wiped out all these memories" (Freud, 1895d, pp. 58–59).

8. "The psycho-analyst knows that he is working with highly explosive forces and that he needs to proceed with as much caution and conscientiousness as a chemist. But when have chemists ever been forbidden, because of the danger, from handling explosive substances, which are indispensable, on

account of their effects? . . . No; in medical practice there will always be room for the *"ferrum"* and the *"ignis"* side by side with the "medicina"; and in the same way we shall never be able to do without a strictly regular, undiluted psycho-analysis which is not afraid of handling the most dangerous mental impulses and to obtain mastery over them for the benefit of the patient" (Freud, 1915a [1914], pp. 170–171).

9. "The analyst . . . sets in motion a process, that of the resolving of existing repressions. He can supervise this process, further it, remove obstacles in its way, and he can undoubtedly vitiate much of it. But on the whole, once begun, it goes its own way . . . The analyst's power over the symptoms of the disease may thus be compared to male sexual potency. A man . . ., too, only sets in motion a highly complicated process, determined by events in the remote past, which ends by the severance of the child from its mother" (Freud, 1913c, p. 130).

10. Here is an interesting passage on the same theme by Michel de M'Uzan: "To experience orgasm like a woman, it may be because he can accept this desire, after having sufficiently elaborated his castration anxiety, that a male analyst can fully use his counter-transference, and even experience himself in the analytic relationship with a female patient not only as a woman, but also as a homosexual woman" (M'Uzan, 1976b, p. 118, my translation).

7

The work that leads to interpretation

Rogelio Sosnik

The aim of this chapter is to share my reflections on the construction of interpretations. Interpretations are part of our mental activity as human beings, based on our need to make sense of the world that we inhabit, as well as the experiences that we live all along throughout our life. As psychoanalysts there is a specific activity that we need to accomplish, the building of interpretations when we have to play our role with our patients. One of my first questions was: is there something specific about an interpretation that makes it psychoanalytic? And, if it is, how can we determine its specificity? And what is the mental work that we have to do to reach it?

To explore these questions, I will first outline the issues involved, then comment on the evolution of psychoanalytic ideas on the subject in Freud and then through the contributions of Wilfred Bion. Finally, I will offer my view, following Bion, that the work of the interpretation is the result of a co-creation, and is not solely the analyst's product. I will also attempt to demonstrate why this is so.

In the introduction to his book, *Psychoanalysis from Practice to Theory* (2006), Jorge Canestri asks,

> When analysts are at work with a patient, and the question
> became even more pertinent when contemporary analysis began

to deal with more serious, borderline or para-psychotic patients, does their work faithfully reflect an official theory to which they claim adherence? Or do they integrate concepts deriving from different theories, or create new ones, usually preconsciously?

With this in mind, it is difficult to make generalisations about how analysts nowadays face their interpretative activity and the weight that they attribute to it in relation to the psychoanalytic process. I pose the question, is there any place in the analyst's mind where interpretations are born? If so, what are the theories that he holds to support them? And since a "clinical fact" is itself the result of interpretations that are made by analysts and guide their interventions, we are situated at the core of current research on present-day psychoanalytic practice (research work initiated by the European Psychoanalytic Federation and now extended by the IPA to all its regions since 2004). We hope this research will help us to recover the sense that we still speak the same language, with shared meaning.

Among the many tasks of the analyst to establish the clinical setting—organising the analytic frame within which patient and analyst interact, determining when and how to start his interpretative activity, which is one of the subjects of Freud's article around which this book is built—it is in particular the specific task of building and verbalising interpretations that is the subject of my contribution. Is there specific work that analysts have to accomplish before reaching an interpretation? Once the basic conditions of the therapeutic exchange have been established—the establishment of the psychoanalytic frame— the analyst's task will be the creation of interpretations. This constitutes the core of his contribution to the development of the psychoanalytic process.

From an epistemological point of view, interpretations are hypotheses that analysts construct in their minds, which may or may not be communicated to the patient with the intention of promoting a movement within the session with the goal to facilitate psychic change. As hypotheses, interpretations are part of the construction of a model that analysts build in their minds concerning their experience with their patients, about his/her patient's mental functioning. The analyst interprets what he feels he understands, and his understanding is not only based on the specific problem that he is facing with the patient, but includes a point of view that comes from his theory of mind. Therefore, an interpretation is a small theory about the phenomena that the analyst is observing. It reflects the need to create models that can express mental states verbally through the description of what he notices while participating in the clinical encounter.

Analysts listen to patients' messages and direct their attention to the manifold possibilities they offer. Then they intervene accordingly by producing interpretations based on their theory of technique. The latter is tied to their conception of the purpose of analysis, their conception of pathology, the process of psychic change, and of the role they play themselves in the development of such change. In this way, creating and formulating interpretations is an activity closely associated with analysts' notion of therapeutic action and of which elements contribute to this goal. Yet, producing an interpretation is in itself a work of art based on an inspiration that arises from the interaction among the various levels in which the analyst's mind works in resonance with that of the patient while absorbing the stimuli generated by their interaction.

The conditions for the production of interpretations are related to the two basic facts of the psychoanalytic frame (free association and the transference) and to the limitation of the activity of the analyst only to verbal interpretations. Transference and interpretation are products of the psychic apparatus. We attribute transference (primary process) to the patient, and interpretation (secondary process) to the analyst. We all know, however, that the opposite is also true. Patients constantly interpret analysts' responses to their messages, and analysts are always involved in their own innermost primary processes, responding to patients' conscious and unconscious messages. The analyst's mental equipment, his/her tolerance to deal with different mental states, is also part of the analyst's contribution to the psychoanalytic situation.

Following Bion, I see the analytic situation as a place where two personalities meet with the intention of relieving the suffering that the patient experiences, through learning the working of the mind in its different levels. This is achieved through an understanding of the experience of the exchanges developed in the psychoanalytic process. This understanding, which bears a transformative potential, provides the patients' personality with a new way to make sense, and with an approach to knowledge as an ongoing, endless acquisition that will help them face the uncertainties of life and of human relations.

What is the metapsychological place that defines the role of analysts in their interpretative work, and what is the connection between interpretation and the acquisition of knowledge that will facilitate mental change and evolution?

I am going to highlight what are, for me, the different ways in which Freud conceived the interpretative work of the analyst, and then I will go on to Bion's contributions on the same subject.

I will proceed then with a historical review.

Freud's conception of the interpretative work of the analyst

Freud's conceptions changed with the evolution of his notions of psychic conflict and psychic structure. As we know, psychoanalysis arose from Freud's discoveries and his description of the mind as a container split into two different spaces, the conscious and the unconscious, making the unconscious organisation and its effect on individual behaviour and on the social realm the object of study of this new discipline. The translation of the manifest into the latent content, implicit in the symptoms first and in free associations later, was the first goal of interpretations.

Manifest content is open to infinite meanings, as are infinite the interpretations that may stem from it. Nevertheless, for Freud, *Deutung* (interpretation) consists of finding a meaning that has been lost, retrieving it and, in so doing, bringing back a sense of truth that lies behind the manifest content. The assumption of the reversibility of the symptom and of the potential to restore mental coherence through this procedure places psychoanalytic interpretation from the start at the core of the psychoanalytic method and renders it the tool for psychoanalytic therapeutic action.

Analysts' activity emerged from Freud's description of the model of the mind working in unconscious, pre-conscious, and conscious levels when trying to solve the conflict between external, material reality and internal, unconscious reality. As Freud's understanding of the complexities of mental organisation that he described in the topographical and the structural models, evolved, his understanding of conflict changed. This transformation led to the redefinition of the analyst's task.

When Freud determined that the symptom was an equivalent of a forgotten memory, analysts' interpretative activity was a guide to help patients retrieve their traumatic memory by following the nature of their associations and the dynamics of repression. Analysts were very active in their interpretive task, exploring not just symptoms but also conflicts—the conflict between desire and defence. According to Freud, analysts must possess three qualities, namely, understanding of unconscious processes, conviction as to the reversibility of symptoms once the repressed memory has been found, and sympathy toward their patients. The exploration of defences and the enquiry into the content of the representation of the object of desire complement each other. The repressed representation is associated with visual memories and reappears in dream images. When the image is transformed into verbal expressions, it starts to lose its power, "like a ghost that has been laid [to rest]" (Freud and Breuer, 1895d, p. 281).

In *The Interpretation of Dreams* Freud (1900a) had asserted that the mechanisms that give rise to interpretations are the same as those that generate dreams and symptoms. Analysts' interpretations start with unconscious work. They navigate through preconscious associations toward consciousness, where the final stage of elaboration occurs. Interpretations provide conscious awareness of the memory by guiding patients' attention toward the perception of the psychic reality where the "indestructible desire" lies.

This description of the interpreting process changed after Dora's case, with Freud's discovery of the central role of the transference in the creation of the symptom and also of the cure. From now on, the symptom would be over-determined by many repressed representations, and its cause would be conflict over the fulfilment of a wish. The analytic situation awoke repressed desires, and the transference was the tool to act upon them. Analysts became the ghostly object of desire that, by offering interpretations, helped displace libidinal energy onto external, real objects. Interpretation now went beyond the image and the representation of the object to focus on the dynamics of desire. The object of research was now infantile sexuality and its partial components.

Transformations taking place during the analytic process were tied to transference movements rather than to interpretation as the main factor of change. Analysts were now in charge of preserving the process stimulated by the setting up of the analytic situation. Their work was to contribute to the development of the process—the evolution of the transference—by making clear which drives were at play in connection with the fantasy object and shedding light on resistances that contributed to patients' attachment to the symptom linked to the fantasy object represented by analysts. In his article, "On beginning the treatment", Freud warns us against making interpretations before positive transference with the person of the analyst has been established. This warning is in line with his shift toward questioning the intellectual approach to interpretation as a conscious communication. Transference brings the emotional realm to the fore as a new factor to be considered when pondering the healing process. Interpretations provide the patient with a word-presentation that, to be effective, must be linked to the thing-presentation that demands that the patient work through the resistance that manifests itself in the attempt to re-live the past in the experience with the analyst.

Analysts also must perform the internal work of attunement to patients' emotional willingness to receive the interpretation that connects affect with representation. This internal work, which takes place in analysts' preconscious while they share the experience with the patient, helps analysts to use their sense of emotional tact and of timing in their interpretative activity to help the transference to evolve. Freud describes that what is effective in addition to the verbal formulation of the interpretation is the analysts' emotional approach to the psychoanalytic situation, their silence, their approach to fees, their sense of timing in producing interpretations, the rhythm of their interactions with their patients, and the ways in which they set boundaries.

Also a new factor to take into account, is the way in which affects and verbalisation interact in the construction of interpretations.

What is clear now is that interpretation is not an addition to the existence of the transference. It is a response to a fundamental need of the nature of the transference. A dream can be interpreted by the dreamer; the transference eludes patients' awareness. Only psychoanalysts can interpret it in order to help it evolve and change. According to Freud, the transference is a manifestation of a forbidden desire that cannot be verbalised to the person who is its object.

When the transference appears, countertransference also comes into existence due to analysts' awareness of the complexities of the analytic encounter. Now, analysts' limitations linked to their unknown and unresolved conflicts affect the way in which they face the clinical situation, distorting and sometimes limiting the curative power of psychoanalysis. A new problem has emerged, namely, analysts' blind spots regarding their own personality traits. This is when personal analysis is recommended for the future analyst, for blind spots will reduce analysts' availability in the clinical situation.

Meanwhile, through research into the mechanisms at stake in the displacement from the primary object of desire to another, the theory of symbolism evolves. Freud's *Introductory Lectures on Psychoanalysis* in 1916–1917 and Jones's "The theory of symbolism" in 1923 show how the psychic apparatus builds its representations drawing from those created by the baby, that are based on its bodily sensations and on its perception of its mother's body, that will be displaced later to external objects. The symbolisation process is at the basis of this capability of displacement of interest, and at the centre of the connection between body representations and external sense impressions. In this regard, I would add that the work of analysts during the session, connecting their own bodily sensations with the images they form based on perceptions stemming from the patients' discourse and with emotional states, results from symbolic processes and helps them to formulate interpretations.

These two aspects—the discovery of the analyst's countertransference and his or her symbolic role, added to the economic aspect of the transference in the evolution of the process of the cure—thus creating a paradigm shift in the meaning of therapeutic action. The analyst's task shifted from uncovering and verbalising repressed memories by transforming them from repressed images into verbal representations that will lose their power through new associative connections, to directing patients' attention toward transference movements taking place in the analytic situation by way of their interpretations in order to detach them from the wrong connections; the goal now is expanding patients' knowledge of their fantasy life and of its evolution from infancy through childhood up to the present.

When Freud shifts from a topographical to a structural model of the mind, placing the Oedipal scene at the centre of mental organisation, that he described as comprising three agencies with their conflicts, we encounter a new role for interpretation. Two old concepts will become pivotal to analysts' task-repetition compulsion as a manifestation of the conflict between the life and death instincts, and the identification processes, from narcissistic object relations to mature, whole object relations.

The development of object relations will bring, as a result, the differentiation of the ego and superego structures, and analysts, by following and providing meaning to repetition compulsion, will trace this development to its earliest stages. Their interpretations, moreover, will help establish or re-establish the links that had been lost or that had never been created. In this way, split aspects of the personality will be reintegrated. Also, by tracing the history of patients' object relations, analysts will contribute to the reconstruction of patients' past by detaching it from current relationships. The expansion of consciousness through insight helps patients differentiate external and internal reality and create meaning out of the emotional experiences that constitute daily life.

After Freud introduced the structural model of the mind, two hypothesis contained in the model—the death instinct as part of the id and its place in the evolution of psychoanalytic treatment, and the role played by early object relations in the emergence and development of anxiety states and of the ego and superego—were at the centre of what would become a major rift in the psychoanalytic movement. The acceptance of the death instinct as a psychic principle rather than a desire, introducing *a negative* within the theory of mental functioning, and the organisation of the early ego determined by the conflict between one of the two basic tendencies around narcissistic and whole object relationships created a schism between those who endorsed and those who opposed these hypotheses. The outcome of that schism relates to the "level" of the interpretations and how far the analyst can go with it. The discussion about "deep" interpretations considering the earliest object relationships, the acceptance of aggression, and destructiveness at the bottom of anxiety states, as well as the role of the analyst as a primary object were also points of controversy.

An issue that broadened and redefined analysts' work is the progress in the understanding of countertransference that took place in the 1950s, for in itself it is an addition to the study of the clinical situation, that includes the analysts' responses to the clinical material that we must study when we examine the psychoanalytic field. The analyst's mind becomes part of the study of the analytic situation, in a way that transcends Freud's concept of how the analytic field is composed.

All of the above leads to the consideration of the complexities that analysts face when approaching our work from a contemporary perspective. The progress in our understanding of early mentation, the inclusion of psychotic anxieties and pathology as well as of borderline cases, and the reconsideration of sexual orientation and the redefinition of perversion; all these developments result from post-Freudian research into psychoanalytic practice, that expanded the field of therapeutic action. The incorporation of new pathologies triggered the need to create new models that might help analysts to accomplish their task. When these new models were accepted and appropriated by the analytic community, they became part of the "official" theory. One of these models was the notion of projective identification introduced by Melanie Klein, that nowadays is applied with different clinical and theoretical connotations.

Klein, one of the first analysts to use the notion of the "death instinct" in her clinical practice with children, started a new line of research on the workings of the mind, by exploring it in the analysis of young children. Her conjectures about how the earliest object relations are established, came after her exploration of the nature and function of unconscious phantasy. Her research on how the basic anxieties affect the earlier ego, her description of the defensive mechanisms of that early ego, that is, her theory of the schizo-paranoid and depressive positions, established a new perspective in the economy of the mind, in terms of how the life and death instincts interact.

Bion's insights into the analytic method

Thus I come to Wilfred Bion, whose ideas have transcended the Kleinian circles, which were the first to be influenced by him, and have helped to modify the approach to the session, by providing new insights into the psychoanalytic method. They have been incorporated by some American and French psychoanalysts, and have exerted a strong influence in South America.

In his epistemological approach, in which the process of "learning from the emotional experience", is central to personality development, he made the process of *knowing*, his K link, the pivot of the analytic experience.

Differentiating himself from Freud, Bion focused his attention on the way that the creation of meaning evolves out of the emotional experience, and made the analytic session the place to explore that.

In his meta-psychological extension on the working of the psychic apparatus Bion focuses on the early stages of mental organisation, and its vicissitudes in relation to the thinking process and the evolution of thoughts—from its embryonic state of basic experimental action to the mature formation of concepts, abstractions, and model making. By establishing that thinking develops out of the existence of thoughts that precede it, he described the thinking apparatus as a container where thoughts can grow from an embryonic state, alpha function, to the sophisticated level of abstract thinking. He provided a model that was born out of his work with psychotic patients, in whom he noticed the detrimental effect of the environment when the latter is not receptive to the unorganised primitive messages psychotics send by way of projective identification. From there he created a model of the earliest mother–infant relationship, in which he included "the need to know" considering it as important as the need to be fed. He postulates that if there is a correspondence between the baby's disorganised anxious messages and a mother capable of transforming them into modulated anxiety states by using intuitive knowledge (reverie), the conditions will be set for the baby's mind to become organised and to work in its two different levels—conscious and unconscious.

Freud was intrigued by the fact that mental representations were transformed into somatic impairments that, through the analytic work that revealed the repressed idea, became part of patients' thinking processes that led to the resolution of the symptom. Bion, instead, was interested in the meaning psychotic patients attribute to the experience of being analysed, since hatred and an attack on their own mental capacity and on the analysts' mind, is at the centre of their pathology. The reality principle on which the ego depends, is in constant process of "evolution" and development. The difficulties that the psychotic has in accepting realities, internal and external, that depend on the acceptance of frustration, and suffering mental pain, determined by the limits of the mental "power", based in the use of omnipotence, are demonstrations of that. Memory, desire, and understanding depend on the pleasure principle; in contrast, the need to introduce "O", the unknown, belongs to the need to introduce "reality" or "the thing in itself", beyond apprehension and comprehension, a negative that is the matrix of future developments in the thinking processes. This opens the door to intuition that plays a major role as the organ for apprehension of "realities" beyond meaning and signification.

Tolerance to mental pain and to the frustration of desire was at the core of Bion's developments regarding the ways in which thoughts grow and the thinking apparatus is organised, taking into account the dynamics between the pleasure and reality principles established by Freud, from whom he never departed. His insights into the working of projective identification in the earliest mother–infant interactions offer a model to conceptualise the analytic situation in a way that includes the back-and-forth of the different mental states that both patient and analyst traverse. In addition, his hypothesis as to the working of the mind furnishes analysts with new recommendations about how to face their task. Bion's model sees the working of the mind as analogous to the digestive system, in that the mind metabolises and transforms basic anxieties (PS-D) into emotional states (L, H, K) that, when things go well, link and connect the different levels of thought and meaning.

For me, I see the analytic situation as an encounter between two personalities that will create a metabolic organ between them, which Bion calls container–contained, in order to hold new ideas that posses disruptive qualities by disturbing the previous psychic balance, so that they can grow and expand the patients' approach to reality, both internal and external, while transforming basic anxieties into emotional states: L, H, K links.

This approach helps us to understand the mental function and the work of the analyst in the session as organiser of the inchoate experience that is evolving, and the task required to reach an interpretation of the experience into which he is immersed. To reach this place, analysts must practice their "negative capability," that is, the ability to participate in the session in a state of mental openness, free of preconceptions, so as to be receptive to the unknown. Bion's dictum to approach the session "without memory, desire, and understanding" to face the unknown that is going to emerge during the session and reach the mental state that analysed and analyst are sharing, is at the basis of psychoanalysts' work and willingness to make possible the occurrence of true psychoanalysis.

Now, I will quote Bion, in order to clarify this point: "The psycho-analyst's tool is an attitude of philosophic doubt; to preserve such 'doubt' is of first importance on which psychoanalysis can be built". (Bion, 1992, pp. 287–288). This attitude requires analysts to abandon medicine as a model, where the pursuit of cure, as any other desire, will impede his capability to face the reality of the session that lies in the unknown of the experience that is evolving, the O of the session.

In Bion's words, "physician and psychoanalyst are alike in considering that the disease should be recognized by the physician; in psychoanalysis recognition must be by the sufferer too", and

> the physician is dependent on realizations of sensuous experience, in contrast with the psychoanalyst whose dependence is on experience that is not sensuous. The physician can see and touch and smell. The realizations with which the psychoanalyst deals cannot be seen or touched; anxiety has not shape, or colour, smell or sound. For convenience I propose to use the term 'intuit' as a parallel in the psychoanalyst's domain to the physician's use of "see", "touch", "smell", and "hear". (Bion, 1970, p. 7)

Now I will quote from Bleandonu and Bion, which helped me with the description of the mental state that the analyst has to reach while in the session, in order to promote mental evolution:

> The analyst's reaction to his patient will be all the more subtle for being less bound to sensory data. The greater his wish for a precise interpretation, the greater his difficulty in describing a state of mind in terms of sensory impressions. (Bleandonu, 1994, p. 216)

> The patient's associations and the analyst's interpretations are ineffable and essential experience. (Bion, 1987, p. 122

> The psychotic's reaction to an interpretation is usually oriented more towards the ineffable aspect of the communication than towards its verbal meaning. (Bleandonu, 1994, p. 216

> In terms of the analytic practice, this means that the analyst uses his senses to know "about" what the analysand says or does, but he cannot know the O, of which words or behaviours are transformations. (ibid.)

The more he focuses on actual events, the more his activity depends on thinking, which derives from a background of sense data. Inversely, the more the analyst is real, the more he manages to engage with the analyzand's reality. He then has the opportunity to make an interpretation which facilitates the transition between knowing reality and becoming reality. (ibid., p. 221)

Bion locates the origin of memory in the process of projective identification, which he identifies as the mental mechanism that performs certain tasks before thinking can take responsibility for them. Compare this with Freud's description of memory traces as organisers of mental structure, and we can understand the difficulties that analysts face in accepting his metapsychological expansions. Projective identification creates an exchange between a container and a contained. When the pleasure principle is in motion, the contained is evacuated in order to be transformed into something pleasant or to experience the pleasure of being contained. The container absorbs evacuations for complementary reasons; it has the option of receiving or rejecting. This is a model to understand memory that retains or forgets. Also, memory retains the limitations of sensory origin. The more memory accumulates, the more it is full of saturated elements. Memory works with desire. They share a common origin—both derive from sensory experiences and from feelings of pleasure and pain. To allow oneself to be immersed in memories or desires entails utter saturation. Preconceptions are excluded, new meaning cannot be made since there is no mental space for it, and memories and desires occupy a mental space that should remain unsaturated. Analysts will find an illusory feeling of security when becoming immersed in them, but they will lose the ability to become one with "O", the ultimate reality. "Opacity of memory and desire" is the title of one of the chapters in *Attention and Interpretation*, and it is Bion's way to conceptualise "resistance" in psychoanalysis. The psychotic patient will stimulate memory and desire in the analyst. The exclusion of sensory experience displaces the pleasure principle from centre stage and reintegrates the reality principle into analytic work. Yet this exercise of excluding memory, desire, and understanding from analysts' mental activity is in itself a painful exercise, for analysts will face distressing emotions that are usually excluded or concealed by social convention. The goal to do this exercise, is to amplify the power of observation and participation in new levels of mental states, that otherwise could not have been reached. The analysts' basic attitude must be a state of philosophical doubt and an act of faith that an evolution of "O" will occur and will be captured by increased intuition. Such capture will lead to the "correct interpretation" when the experience and the theory that lies behind the experience intersect.

If we follow Bion in his description of the mental movements that must take place in the analyst's mind while following the path that leads to an interpretation, he mentions the need to traverse two mental states, one he calls "patience" and the other "security". I will quote again:

> In every session the psycho-analyst should be able if he has followed what I have said in this book, particularly with regard to memory and desire, to be aware of the aspects of the material that, however familiar they may seem to be, relate to what is unknown both to him and to the analyzand's. Any attempt to cling to what he knows must be resisted for the sake of achieving a state of mind analogous to the paranoid–schizoid position. For this state I have coined the term "patience" to distinguish it from "paranoid–schizoid position", which should be left to describe the pathological state for which Melanie Klein used it. I mean the term to retain its association with suffering and tolerance of frustration.
>
> "Patience" should be retained without "irritable reaching after fact and reason" until a pattern evolves. This state is the analogue to what Melanie Klein has called the depressive position. For this state I use the term "security". This I mean to leave with its association of safety and diminished anxiety. I consider that no analyst is entitled to believe that he has done the work required to give an interpretation unless he has passed through both phases—"patience" and "security". (Bion, 1970, p. 124)

At this point, and before arriving to the conclusion of this chapter, I want to offer Bion's description of the experience of the analyst's while being in the session, since it is so close to my subject, the work of the analyst that leads to an interpretation.

> I should explain that I regard the psycho-analyst's capacity to observe and absorb as much of the analyzand's material as possible, as important for the following reasons:
>
> 1 It will enable him to combine what he hears with what he has

already experienced from the patient to give an immediate interpretation in the circumstances of the actual session.

2 At the same time he will observe features that are not comprehensible to him but will contribute at a later stage to the comprehension of material yet to come.

3 There are still other elements of which the analyst will not even be conscious but which build up an experiential reserve that in due course will influence his conscious views about the patient's material on a specific occasion.

Reason 1, although apparently leading to the operative interpretation, is of less consequence than 2 and 3 because the interpretation is merely setting a formal seal on work that has already been done and is therefore no longer of much consequence.

Reason 2 is of great importance because it is part of the dynamic and continuing process on which the whole viability of analysis depends. The more the psycho-analyst is open to these impressions, the more he is prepared to participate in the evolution of the analysis.

Reason 3, although more remote, ensures the long-term vitality of the whole analytic process. In short, the nearer the psycho-analyst can come to observation of the kind I am desiderating here, the less likely he is to fall into the wastes of jargon, and the more the analysis will approximate to being a unique emotional experience recognizably related to an actual human being, and not a conglomerate of psychopathological mechanisms. (1992, pp. 287–88)

Here Bion is talking about the way that the analyst's mind is not only creating interpretations, but also participating in the development of the psychoanalytic process in its entirety, and how much his total personality is involved in the outcome of this process.

Conclusion

In the beginning of this chapter I raised the question of what is the specificity, and nature, and function of the psychoanalytic interpretation. I am answering this question from the prospective of Bion's metapsychology, which gives us a refined insight into therapeutic action.

The interpretation is the result of a transformational process that takes place in the mind of the analyst departing from the disconnected elements that compose the patient's message, that are part of the schizo–paranoid position. By being open to that aspect of the message, the analyst's alpha function finds a selected fact, that is, an element that provides coherence that organises an emotional pattern in the kaleidoscopic quality of the message the patient is emitting. This emotional pattern, selected fact, when verbalised, constitutes a hypothesis that the analyst formulates, the meaning of which both patient and analyst will discover, if it is close to the psychic truth that the hypotheses contains. Also the interpretation constitutes an object, a psychoanalytic object, that can be rejected or accepted, introjected, then conforming an aspect of the patient's personality, his "becoming".

Selected fact, hypotheses creation, and object to be introjected are the three mental levels in which the psychoanalytic interpretation works and contribute to expand mental functions.

In this way we can understand the interpretation in its three epistemological levels, *the informative level* that connects with the acquisition of knowledge—emotional knowledge; *the semantic level*, connected with the need to create new meaning —the formulation of a hypothesis; and the third, the *operational, instrumental level*, that as an object to be introjected will expand the ego's capability, and the personality as a whole.

In having to address the subject of the work of the analyst that leads to an interpretation, I chose to refer to the two exceptional figures that for me shared the same approach regarding the context of discovery and the transformative quality that psychoanalysis possesses in its method of research that comes together with the healing process. I started with Freud, the discoverer of psychoanalysis, the genius, according to Bion, who opened the new universe of research into the mental realm, a door to reach a new understanding of the human condition by providing us with a tool, the analytic activity. Then I referred to Bion, who following Freud's method, incorporated new insights into the early stages of mentation, using his expanded intuition on the clinical situation, and creating new theoretical tools to support his intuitions, to reach a level of description of the mental activity, that nowadays approximates the current findings of neuroscience research. Between Freud and Bion, half a century of psychoanalytic practices and theorisations went by. This is a brief period of time for a new science to become established and accepted, but enough time to give us the chance to appreciate the results of psychoanalytic research and the progress in the understanding of early mental states and of pathology connected with early difficulties.

Freud's article had warned us not to take these patients in analysis so as to preserve psychoanalysis and its promises to the public.

Bion in contrast, illuminated our further search.

I hope that my discussion may be of use to the reader and encourage him to continue the pursuit of new discoveries, a task that in the end, is the central aim of psychoanalytic activity.

8

Interpretative function:
two characters in search of meaning*

Alice Becker Lewkowicz & Sergio Lewkowicz[†]

> Phrases! Phrases! As if there was not a comfort to all,
> In face of a fact we cannot explain,
> In face of an evil that consume us,
> To find a word that doesn't mean anything
> But that calm us!
>
> Luigi Pirandello (1922)

Even though in "On beginning the treatment", of 1913, Freud's recommendations seem to be restricted to the opening of the analytic game, we consider that in that work there is an extensive and profound revision of the analytic technique used by Freud up to that moment. From issues related to the therapeutic contract and to the establishment of the setting, he goes through the study of

*A slightly modified version of this paper received the "Fábio Leite Lobo Prize" (best paper for full members of IPA) from the Brazilian Federation of Psychoanalysis during the Brazilian Congress of Psychoanalysis held in Ribeirö Preto in September 2011.
[†]Translated by Tania Mara Zalcberg.

interpretation and reaches the mechanism of cure in analysis. This is probably the work that Freud devoted most to the subject of psycho-analytic technique. The paper begins with the much praised metaphor of the chess game, describing that only the openings and end-games admit an exhaustive systematic presentation (Freud, 1913c). In his remarks on psychoanalytic technique he poses questions that still remain current.

What would be Freud's concern at that time? Why would he be so interested in the technical procedures of psychoanalysis? Peter Gay suggests that Freud's writings on technique written from 1910 to 1914 should be an answer to the abuse of the wild technique that was often occurring with premature interpretations based on hasty diagnoses that only increased the patient's resistance (Gay, 1988). Freud's major concern at that time was not only with an accurate diagnosis, but also with technical errors that were becoming increasingly serious. Thus, he decided to write a series of papers on psychoanalytic technique, based on the ethical principles that he thought fundamental, intending to delimitate the technical procedures he considered more appropriate to his model of mind and cure at that time. In this sense, we think that particularly the eroticisation of the transference–countertransference bond leading to the analyst's sexual acting out with their female patients could also have contributed to his motivation in writing those papers.

Freud at that time was essentially preoccupied in making conscious the unconscious, his technique of cure, at that moment. The aim of the treatment was to reveal the patient's unconscious hidden ideas, thus the patient would be able to recall his significant past experiences. Freud had already observed that the transference was the most important way to the recollection of past memories, but at the same time the main resistance to it (Freud, 1913c). Even in his later developments, as in his idea of the "id" giving place to the "ego" (Freud, 1923b) or in constructions in analysis (1937d), Freud describes an active, objective analyst who almost always knows what he[2] is going to find during his archaeological task.

Currently we observe a deep change on this conception, because we assume that to understand what being human is about:

> . . . it is necessary to appreciate the fragmentary, what is uncontrollable from outside. The paradigm of modernity, the time in

which psychoanalysis was born, might perhaps have decisively influenced the conception of our task as being focused on solving enigmas. This closes the gaps of inconsistencies. However, it is important to be aware that this aimed roundness; this unmistaken and unquestionable memory may be lethal to the purpose of our times. Because it is through the space "between", to the unresolved inconsistency, to the unknown, alive, open and not deciphered nor decipherable, through "this non deciphered sign" that . . . life emanates. (Moreno, 2010, p. 29)

Going back to the 1913 paper, where Freud introduces the specific issue of interpretation, he writes:

When are we to begin making our communications to the patient? When is the moment for disclosing to him the hidden meaning of the ideas that occur to him, and for initiating him into the postulates and technical procedures of analysis?

The answer to this can only be: not until an effective transference has been established in the patient, a proper *rapport* with him. It remains the first aim of the treatment to attach him to it and to the person of the doctor. To ensure this, nothing need to be done but give him time. (Freud, 1913c, p. 138)

Initially, we were stricken by the use of the word "*rapport*" in the original German version and, we confirmed that this word also was maintained in the English, French, and Portuguese versions. We think that Freud in this context equated "effective transference" to the establishment of an emotional affinity, a relationship of mutual confidence, a two-person meeting (*Robert dictionnaire*, 1988), proximity, alliance, link, and "a close relationship, in which people understand each other very well" (*Oxford English Dictionary*, 1995, p. 963).

Regarding the creation of a *rapport*, we fully agree with the postulate of the 1913 paper, but we think that it is not enough to let the time pass and have an "sympathetic understanding" (p. 138). We believe that fundamental to this process is the possibility of creating a real emotional experience with the patient and for that we have to approach the current emotional states of the pair, analyst–patient, in the session. We know that this *rapport* is established in the function of intense mental activity of the analyst and the patient, in their continuous search of meaning that occurs from the beginning of treatment.

The availability to the apprehension of emotions established when two people meet, added to the use of open, unsaturated interpretations, brings us closer to the patients and expands our ability to deal with psychic pain.

Anchored in Bion, Baranger, Ogden, and Ferro we think that our therapeutic goals are different from those proposed by Freud. Today we are more interested in grasping the emotional experience shifts in the analytic pair within the analytic field, attempting to expand the patient's ability of being more in touch with himself. Thus, we intend to help him to develop his own capacity of dreaming, thinking his own thoughts, and, whenever it is possible, to distinguish what is unconscious from what is conscious; what is real from what is phantasy, what is proper to oneself from what is another's.

In this notion of *rapport*, the emphasis is on the relationship between two people: the patient and the analyst. Therefore, a variable degree of risk to the analyst's identity will always be present, unless he is entrenched in a defensive shield that would affect his performance. When you live this kind of risk,

> this is not a price paid for neurosis (how [as] the usual discussions on counter-transference would say), but a price paid for the love of truth, the unique condition that can actually enable one's transformation. Thus, both the therapist and patient would be exposed to moments of disintegration and integration of their psychic structures which, under ideal conditions, would lead to resume [a resumption of] the desired asymmetry and to acquire an integration that did not exist until then. (Mello Franco Filho, 1994, p. 326)

In this context, in our view, how would the interpretative activity develop? It occurred to us to describe it through the expression: "Two characters in search of meaning". When we were looking for a word to describe this process, we chose the expression interpretative function (Guignard, 2010), because it covers what happens in the analytic field created by the two characters and reaches far beyond what is verbally spoken by the two participants of the scene. Thus, this includes what is thought and unsaid, what is said without being thought, the interpretative actions (Ogden, 1994b), and the narratives build up by the pair.

We think that this function is inherent to all human beings and it can be described as the *search of meaning for lived experiences* (Ferro, 2011; Guignard, 2010, Moreno, 2010) and we can also name it as Bion proposed (1962) the *analytic function of personality*.

The interpretative function is related to the constitution of the alpha function and the development of the apparatus to think the thoughts (Bion, 1962). We consider that the daydreams and the night dreams, namely, the dreamwork itself (Bion 1962, Grotstein, 2007 and Ogden, 2005) is one of the expressions of the interpretative function. In this sense, we agree with Ogden (2005) when he draws attention to the difference of conceptions about the dreamwork in Bion (1962) and Freud (1900a). According to Ogden: "in short, Freud's dreamwork *allows derivatives of the unconscious to become conscious, while Bion's work of dreaming allows conscious lived experience to become unconscious . . .*" (Ogden, 2005, p. 100, my italics)

A function with similar features can be observed, taking into account another referential, when we consider the need of a psychic work, the need of representation required by the drive, according to Freud and the developments of the French school of psychoanalysis, as in the work of Green and more recently Aisenstein (2010).

We consider that it is specific to psychoanalysis to have the creation of a space where two characters are able to get together to search for a sense of the emotional experience that is occurring between them. We think that it is essential that this *rapport*, the *capacity of containment* and the *negative capability*, as described by Bion, occurs in both participants of the process, even if initially one of them has to be the guardian for those potentialities.

Clinical illustration

The patient A[1] came for treatment because he was worried about his inability to relate to others, particularly to his parents. He was nineteen years old, attempting for the second time to attend university, but he was not satisfied and was thinking about dropping out and getting a job. He was not able to have a close relationship to his parents, avoiding speaking to them and even eating his meals with them, eating alone in the kitchen. He was even having difficulties in relating with his few friends, keeping away from them. He had never had a girlfriend or even a sexual relationship until that moment. In fact, the place where he felt better was a vacant lot next to his house, where he spent many hours during the day, sometimes sleeping, other times just laying down, but there he stayed, and no one asked him to move or make anything. He described his parents as very concerned about him. During the first sessions, the patient mentioned that he was very close to his maternal grandfather, who was a survivor of a Nazi concentration camp, but this subject was never mentioned again.

After a long evaluation period, I decided to refer him to analysis, on a four session per week basis, which he accepted with some scepticism. For about two years, he remained with an emotionally very detached behaviour. At that time, he referred to a recurrent dream, in which he just saw a castle, surrounded by deep waters, that could not be crossed over, and that the only way was via a drawbridge that was always closed. This was exactly the feeling that he elicited in me: I felt excluded. This was even more intense when I offered him an interpretation, because he listened to me very politely and continued exactly from the very point where he had been interrupted. It was as if I was there only to listen to him, he talked about many subjects, at the same time, and I had the impression of an enormous need of discharge.

By the third year of analysis, his behaviour began to change and became just the opposite. He could hardly speak and thus we went through periods of increasingly longer silence. When I asked him about what he was thinking during these moments of silence, he replied that he was listening to and singing popular songs. After some months of this silent and difficult period of time, it occurred to me asking him what was the song he was thinking of and he told me that was Pink Floyd's "The Wall". I then decided to watch the movie again and I was surprised and moved by the striking similarity between the movie plot and A's condition. Thus, gradually, all the losses, grief, family secrets, and tragedies during the Holocaust emerged. I found out that the patient's grandparents were survivors of Auschwitz, where they met and from where they departed to get married and to come to Brazil, intending to rebuild their lives after the destruction of their former families. My patient became the closest family member to his grandfather and to whom the grandfather constantly told the Holocaust histories, in a study-room, where he collected documents, photographs, letters, and memories from this terrible time. This place, according to A, was dark and dreary.

The analysis of A showed a significant change from that time on, particularly through a progressive proximity in his relationship with me, just as with other people in his life. Feelings came out to be increasingly present in the sessions that were becoming more alive and dynamic.

This patient was seen more than twenty years ago. At that time, the analyst did not have the developments about trauma, transgenerationality, and intersubjectivity that were consolidated in recent years. Neither the analyst nor the patient initially paid any attention to the situation of the Holocaust in the patient's family. This emerged in the analytic field, surprising both of them, after some years of analysis. We think that the feelings related to the "pain" suffered by the patient's grandparents, in their experience of the Holocaust, were unbearable and thus they could only be "suffered" after the establishment of a *rapport* that could support the risk of an emotional experience of extreme helplessness and despair. From there on it was possible to observe that a new melody entered the field, a melody that was gradually becoming a dream-for-two. What once seemed to be just a bizarre behaviour, like spending several hours in an abandoned lot, could now make sense: A was enacting the abandonment, despair, isolation, and neglect, and the situation of despising and being despised. From the theoretical perspective proposed in this paper, we argue that the analyst had actively contributed in the process of maintaining the castle "drawbridge" closed, because he was not yet able to share the despair that was inside it. In other words, it would be as if in this first stage, the analyst's fantasy was to remove the patient from the abandoned lot, without having to enter this "minefield", because this would mean that he also would have to face terrible feelings for himself. As the analyst is Jewish and is the son of Jewish immigrants who fled from Europe just before the Holocaust, to live these emotions would be also very difficult. Today we think that the "drawbridge" could only be downed as far as the negative capability and the interpretative function were systematically being developed.

The interpretative function

When a character is born,
he soon acquires such an independence,
even from his own author,
that it may be imagined by everyone
in many situations in which the author intended to put him,
and also acquire, sometimes,
a meaning that the author not even dreamed of giving him.

Luigi Pirandello (1922)

We think that in the analytic field the interaction between the minds of patient and analyst will expand the capacity of containment of the anxieties present in the field. The analyst's negative capability and the capacity of reverie enable him to transform raw emotions into feelings that can be lived and thought. Under favourable conditions, the patient introjects these functions and will exert them in a more autonomous way, as it possibly occurs in the individual normal development.

When the development of this function is insufficient or damaged, we think that it is necessary to have the presence of a kind of "incubator" of the interpretative function, namely, the creation of an analytic field that allows for the recovery of this function. Meltzer (1990) proposes that the analytic method includes a reappearance of the involvement of the minds of mother and baby, in such a way that two minds can cooperate again working together in order to investigate and describe themselves to one another. Nemas developing Meltzer's ideas, warns us, however, that this process is very hard on the analyst, because if he is truly available, he will have his mind invaded by the patient madness, creating emotions that are sometimes unbearable (Nemas, 2010).

In any analysis, we are constantly shifting between more integrated states (the neurotic part of the personality) and more disintegrated ones (the psychotic part of the personality). We think that the interpretative function takes place during this oscillation and is absent without it. In those moments, in which there is intense psychic pain in the field, with such feelings as despair and a sense of madness, we can lose the ability to transform this pain into suffering. There is a very high risk of concretising the interpretative function leading to the use of saturated and theoretical interventions, disregarding the interpretative function and the ambiguity of symbolic network. Then we would be in occasions of "non-dream-for-two" (Cassorla, 2009), that are essential and inevitable in any analytic process and should be used lead to the recovery of the interpretative function and thus lead to the opening of new potential meanings. At these moments, *the two characters in search of meaning* momentarily lose their features of characters of the analytic game (of characters of the dream-for-two) and become people in balance with the concrete reality, thus losing "the come and go, the trodden path, the shifts: in short, the dynamics that brings us together (Green, 2002b, p. 50, authors' translation).

The analyst's active search for the correct interpretation, be it "transferential", "mutative", or "reconstructive", among others, seem to us related to an attempt to avoid experiencing the emotions that are emerging in the analytic situation. In this way, there would be an attempt to increase the asymmetry among the participants and, thus, to ensure a safety similar to the traditional medical model, in which the knowledge belongs just to one of the participants and the pain belongs only to the other participant of the pair. Again, we agree with Ferro (1999) when he says that he does not believe "that the correct interpretation exists, but a trip made of continuing successes, trials and mistakes . . . that constitute the road . . . a journey of continuous oscillations" (p. 115).

The resistance to interpretation in one or both participants, in the analytic field, is what in Bion's (1965) and Ferro's (2002b) referential, is described as the resistance against the transformations from K to O, that is, transforming the *knowledge* of emotional experience to *living* this experience, with the emotional turbulence it causes, due to the catastrophic change it mobilises.

Therefore we consider it crucial to develop the negative capability of the analytic pair, that is, the "tolerance when one is capable of being in uncertainties, mysteries, doubts, without reaching any state irritable after fact and reason" (Bion, 1970, p. 124).

Still using Ferro's (2002b) categorisation we can consider three types of interpretation: a) *Unsaturated or weak interpretations*, located next to PS (schizo–paranoid position), therefore less integrated; b) *Saturated* interpretations, located next to PD (depressive position) related to integration and selected fact (Bion, 1962), the saturated interpretations of transference being a typical example of this, and c)

Narrative interpretations that would be intermediate on the axe PS–D, not involving a saturation of PS, but having already images of PD, and, in that case, constructions with what is happening in the session must be made. The author also raises the possibility of *evacuative interpretations or acting out by the analyst*, when his mind is not functioning properly.

In our clinical practice we see that all these forms of interpretation are always present in the analytic field with any type of patient. Thus, the more an oscillation between them occurs, more creative the interpretative function will be; on the other hand, the more there is a balance, the less creative the process will be, and a strong trend towards a homogenisation of the functioning of the pair may appear, that would lead to the stagnation of the interpretative function and the consequent loss of the necessary ambiguity.

We see the analytic process as an oscillation of creative moments when the interpretative function is preserved in the analytic field and, other moments when it is lost due to sometimes unbearable tensions, both to the patient and to the analyst. Those would be moments of intellectual or saturated "truce" in situations in which symbolisation or mentalisation is not possible.

Discussion

> The drama is in us
> the drama are we;
> and we are impatient to play it,
> feeling within us,
> increasing,
> the urgency of passion!
>
> Luigi Pirandello (1922)

The analytical field is established in the transitional space (Winnicott, 1951) and thinking about this conceptualisation of the analytic relationship we made use of the metaphor proposed by Luigi Pirandello in *Six Characters in Search of an Author* (1922). In this play the author discusses the ambiguity between reality and fiction, demystifying the seemingly sharp boundaries between them. Making use of the Pirandello's words, in the play, when the character Father says to the Director:

> . . . we have no other reality beyond illusion,
> you should also distrust your own reality,
> this reality that you breathe in and touch within yourself,
> because—just like yesterday—tomorrow,
> this reality is bound to prove itself to be an illusion."
> (Pirandello, 1922, p. 123).

By bringing to the scene characters that want, or better, need to be represented, the author decentralise the director's and actor's desires who then react to a drama that does not belong to them anymore. The permanent confrontation among character, actor, director, author, reality, and fiction will mobilise in the audience an awareness that our existence is lived much more in the "in-between" than in a definite place.

With high sensitivity Pirandello brings to the theatrical scene all of human suffering in its raw state and suggests that it may be experienced within the other's mind. In many instances, it is evident that we run the risk of detaching ourselves from the proposed emotional experience and, even the risk of not being capable of harbouring some aspects of the characters psychic pain.

We believe that, in the analytic scene, we are constantly in this struggle of attempting to bear the appearance of some characters and our desire of preventing them to have access to the field.

In our view, Pirandello put a child's death and the suicide of a youngster as conditions that, once in the scene, interrupt the staging of drama. According to our approach, this would represent what we describe as unbearable psychic pain to be transformed in a process of suffering that can be enacted and felt within the analytic field. In the analytic scene the limits of the interpretative function will depend on the *rapport* build up between analyst and patient according to the specific potentialities of each pair.

Notes

1. This clinical material was presented in further detail on the European Federation of Psychoanalysis Congress in Vienna, April 2008, with the title: "The shadow of heritage on future generation of victims and perpetrators— the breaking of the wall", and it is published in the Belgian Bulletin of Psychoanalysis, 2010.

2. The male pronoun has been use for the sake of simplicity and readability, and is not intended to reflect the actual sex of the persons referred to in that manner.

9

How to modify the unconscious:
a transformational–modular approach and its
implications for psychoanalytic psychotherapy

Hugo Bleichmar

Psychoanalytic psychotherapy has evolved since the first works of Freud, influenced by the increasing knowledge contributed by generations of analysts regarding the structure and function of the psyche, especially concerning: a) multiple sectors of the unconscious; b) complex relationships between conscious knowledge and therapeutic change; c) forces opposed to therapeutic change; and d) types of interventions capable of promoting change or the opposite—reinforcing pathology.

The discovery that conscious knowledge does not necessarily produce the desired change if unconscious resistances are not overcome is one of the themes of "On beginning the treatment" (Freud, 1913c), a subject raised again in "The unconscious" (Freud, 1915e) not as a simple technical problem but as a result of the psyche's organisation into differentiated sectors. In today's terms, we could say that Freud always conceived of the psyche as consisting of systems or modules, his first topographical model and later the structural model, each with its own origin and development, interacting and influencing each other reciprocally. Not encapsulated modules, as considered by Fodor (1983), but rather the product of a process of modularisation through interactions with other modules.

Examination of the modularity of psychic function in the light of today's knowledge and its consequences for therapeutic change is the theme of this paper. For this purpose I will review: a) modularity of the unconscious; and b) modularity of motivational systems and the mutual transformations they produce. I will also try to show how a modular–transformational approach to study of the psyche facilitates thinking in terms of differentiated and specific therapeutic interventions for what we intend to modify.

Modularity of unconscious organisation

It may be useful to examine the complexity of unconscious phenomena from the perspective of: a) their origins, forms of inscription and processing; and b) levels of activation of unconscious contents. Regarding the origins of different types of unconscious formations, we may identify:

1. An originary unconscious, not a product of repression but of interactions with significant persons that were never conscious and of automated means of self-protection from suffering. For example, those of someone in a constant state of hyperstimulation, which may be sexual, and/or cognitive, and/or affective, and/or neuro-vegetative (level of arousal); or of the persecuted and terrorised; or of the impotent and overwhelmed who are too paralysed to respond in any way; also of persons who unknowingly seek others to rid themselves of anxieties or to balance their psychic structure, etc. An originary unconscious that results from the encounter between innate dispositions and exterior ones that generates affective and action representations that are registered without ever having been conscious. These inscriptions are not only representations of the subject and the other, identities attributed or accepted, but exist in the form of procedures cathected with affect—procedural memory.

The originary unconscious, we need to emphasise even at the risk of repetition, does not result from repression but because, as many authors propose (Fonagy, 1999; Lyons-Ruth, 1999, Mitchell, 2000), it was organised in the form of automated procedures in terms of how to react neuro-vegetatively, how to relate to others, to oneself, and to the world. This level is not only representational, but also neurobiological. For this reason, below we examine the type of neuro-vegetative reactivity with which each person experiences different unconscious or conscious thematic contents, an essential aspect to take into consideration.

The term "originary unconscious" does not refer only to what is constituted in infancy; the formation of procedural memory continues throughout life. Whereas the nature of language is symbolic—something represents another thing—procedural memory is inscribed mainly, sometimes only, as affective process and action. As Clyman (1991) stated,

> This is not symbolic knowledge; procedurally encoded information does not stand for anything else. It cannot be stated in language directly, although the procedural program can be translated into declarative language. While declarative knowledge can be made conscious, procedural knowledge cannot. Declarative knowledge can be remembered; procedural knowledge can only be enacted. (p. 352).

For this reason, it is not recovered during analytic treatment as declarative memory or by decoding the patient's narrative or even by analysing the content of dreams, however important this may be, but as "enactment", that is to say, acting in the relationship.

The role of procedural memory in therapy is clearly formulated by Fonagy (1999): "Change occurs in implicit memory leading to a change in the procedure the person uses in living with himself and with others" (p. 218). He adds: "The patient's implicit memory or procedural representation of an experience of self with another is what Sandler & Joffe have called the non-experiential realm" (p. 218).

The originary unconscious does not correspond to the primal repression described by Freud (1915d): "We have reason to assume that there is a *primal repression*, a first phase of repression, which consists in the psychical (ideational) representative of the instinct being denied entrance into the conscious" (p. 148, original italics). In contrast, the originary unconscious is not rejected; it is an unconscious whose constitution and persistence in that state have nothing to do with the conscious. The originary unconscious does not refer to the representative of the drive in the psyche but instead to a very broad series of inscriptions—inscriptions of what it is like to be with others; images, affective states of the self exactly as they gradually form in the infant and develop in ulterior stages of development: sensory/affective/motor schemata where the subject's relations with others are registered.

2. An originary unconscious by identification with significant figures in terms of their characterological modes of reacting, degree of neuro-vegetative activation (arousal), intensity, and quality of their emotional states, tendency to action, fantasies, defences, etc. In relation to defences, although innate dispositions exist—all human beings are prepared to use them—the development and consolidation of some of them receive influences from identifications with those used by significant figures; for example, the tendency to projection, to affective disconnection, to denial, etc.

3. An unconscious that is an effect of defensive processes which eliminate certain representations from consciousness or prevent some representations from reaching a conscious state. It is on this unconscious that Freud centred his interest.

One consequence of therapeutic work with this organisation of the unconscious—with what is rejected from consciousness by action of defences—as if it were the only one or the main one, is that patients are always placed in the position of people resisting knowledge. Making the unconscious conscious becomes equivalent to undoing repression, overcoming different types of defences, whereas making the unconscious conscious also includes the unconscious that is not a product of defences.

Although we may differentiate unconsciouses with different origins, they undergo combinations, displacements, and transformations through which certain sectors are "sequestered" and split off from each other. This work gives rise to fantasies and representations that are not merely incorporations of the external, but also a result of the creative functioning of laws regulating unconscious processing; even of pressure exerted by the biological level on the representational by the activation of specific circuits for certain emotions. This is why unconscious phenomena are not simply effects of the external—an error of environmental conceptions—or of the internal, but instead complex, creative products of the psyche's own dynamic, where the external is articulated with the internal in reciprocal processes (Piaget's classic concepts of accommodation and assimilation are pertinent here.)

Deactivated sectors of the unconscious: the Freudian *Untergang*

In "The dissolution of the Oedipus complex" Freud (1924d) introduced a concept of the unconscious that involved a revolution of the idea of a forever active unconscious. He stated that at a certain moment the Oedipus complex suffers a vicissitude which goes beyond simple repression; due to the lack of expected satisfaction, stemming from the failure of what is desired, as a result of its internal impossibility, and because of the threat of castration, the Oedipus complex suffers a dissolution, *Der Untergang des Ödipuskomplexe*, a real demolition: "But the process we have described is more than a repression. It is equivalent, if it is ideally carried out, to a destruction and an abolition of the complex" (p. 177).

How are we to understand this? That all unconscious trace of oedipal wishes and fears is erased, that the representations, affects, and fantasies that constituted it disappear as if they had never existed, and when in a later period of life their affective constellations reappear again, they are totally new inscriptions that have nothing to do with the former ones? Clinical experience contradicts this idea: transference and the reactivation of the childhood past by day residues make it difficult to accept that something so significant could totally disappear. However, even though we may object to the emphasis or exaggeration implied by the term *Untergang* or even more so, *Zertrüm-merung* used by Freud, translated by Strachey as demolition, we cannot eliminate the issue that Freud is presenting by means of these terms: something in the unconscious may lose strength and no longer be an active presence (for a discussion about the fate of the Oedipus complex see Levy, 1995).

Freud's *Untergang* is related to the state described by Spitz (1946) when the infant, faced with its impotence to make the chosen object of desire return, finally deactivates desire itself. Or, clinically important, since these are not the great traumata but something that occurs more quietly but never fails to produce effects: children or adults faced with frustration of their wish, with internal limitations and/or the failure of significant objects to respond to what is wished of them, slowly and imperceptibly deactivate sectors of the unconscious, which thus succumb to *Untergang*.

This type of process, for which we proposed the term "deactivation" (Bleichmar, 2010, p. 81), results in decathectisation of certain sectors of wishes in the core of the unconscious due to a painful "unsatisfiable cathexis of longing" (Freud, 1926d, p. 172), produced by frustrated desire, and decathectisation of the subject's functions that generate anxiety. Sectorial deactivation of the unconscious differs from unconscious splitting or dissociation in that two nuclei remain active without influencing each other. This point is important for psychotherapy since, together with the fundamental objective of undoing the repetition compulsion of active and thriving wishes, it opens the issue as to how to reactivate something that has suffered *Untergang*. We see this in clinical work with patients whose defensive processes have gradually quenched the intensity of desire. We would say that it is easier to analyse people with intense repressed wishes than those whose desire function itself has suffered some degree of *Untergang*. For these patients the emotionally neutral analyst, however correct his interpretations may be, is impotent for certain pathologies. Certain types of interventions different from classical interpretations are needed if people in a despairing/apathetic state are to be able to feel and be interested in human relationships, in objects of the world (Alvarez, 2010). We know that this point is controversial but our experience tells us that the analyst's vitality in his exchanges with the patient, the intensity of his desire, may contribute to the undoing, though perhaps only partially, effects of *Untergang*. Even though this proposal may be questioned, the debate remains open as to what resources psychoanalytic psychotherapy could use in order to deal with these processes which lead some patients to really be "living dead".

The unconstituted

Another issue related to the former, yet different, concerns the force of unconscious desire, of the constitution of desire and its intensity. At the time when it was considered that desire sprang from drives the conclusion that seemed logical was that people have similar types of desires and that the force of their desires is also similar, the only difference was whether or not they were an object of repression. However, if desire, apart from internal conditions, is constituted in interaction with others, with the vitality of significant others, what would happen if a person had devitalised parents unable to contribute to the constitution of desirable objects in their child? In these cases it is not a question of desire weakened by anxiety due to *Untergang*—desire existed but became weak—but of a deficit in the very constitution of desire and its level of intensity. In these cases, what type of intervention is able to produce a change with something that was insufficiently constituted? Again, we believe that the contribution of the analyst's affectivity and enthusiasm is necessary. Classical technique was developed for patients with intense desires, for whom the position of an analyst with contained emotions contributes to emotional regulation and also creates an attitude that facilitates the patient's thinking instead of acting. States of lack of force of desire seem to demand something different, although there are two risks: a hyperemotional, hyperactive analyst that increases the deregulation of certain patients, and a contained analyst that reinforces pathology in others. How can we reconcile the analyst's double requirement: on the one hand, to be genuine, and on the other hand, to make instrumental use of his emotionality? Spontaneity *vs.* containment, actively influencing vs. allowing a process set by the patient to develop; these issues were examined by Friedman (1988) in a very sophisticated analysis.

The modularity of motivational systems

In former papers (Bleichmar, 1997, 2004, 2010; see also Abelin-Sas, 2008) I reworked the important idea introduced and elaborated by Stern (1985) and Lichtenberg (1989) that desires and needs driving fantasies and behaviour may be grouped into a set of motivational systems. These systems differ in their origins, development, and relative weight in each person: self-preservation, hetero-preservation (i.e., the care and preservation of others); needs and wishes for attachment, sexual needs and wishes, needs and wishes for psychobiological regulation, and narcissistic wishes.[1]

Motivational systems are organised from the beginning of life in interaction with significant others. When the needs or desires of these motivational systems are not satisfied, specific anxieties are provoked in each; for example, shame dependent on the narcissistic system, separation anxiety related to the rupture of attachment, or guilt related to the hetero-preservation system.

In cases with stable prevalence of one of these motivational systems we encounter certain types of personality structure; for example, people who present intense attachment needs, or those driven by the search for narcissistic satisfaction, or those who orient their life toward hetero-preservation, to the care of others, with complete neglect of their own needs, or those who are dominated by preoccupations with self-conservation and detection of danger (e.g., hypochondriac patients). The relative prevalence of these systems may alternate at different times and in different intersubjective contexts, an alternation that may also occur during treatment. Some possible relationships between systems are: predominance, synergy or antagonism—conflicts between motivational systems. For some people, the power of their narcissistic desires leads them to ignore self-preservation, break attachment relationships, and abandon sexuality; whereas in others deep attachment needs lead them to tolerate extreme forms of humiliation, to accept the person providing attachment as an object of sexuality, and the forms of sexuality proposed by that person. Consequently, in each particular case and at each moment of treatment, we need to evaluate which motivational system has most motivational power (Bleichmar, 2004), which one is going to oppose therapeutic change, and which one will provide support for therapeutic intervention (see below for the concept of motivational weight or motivational valency of therapeutic intervention).

In the therapeutic encounter, the patient's motivational systems also take up synergistic relations, complementary relations, or antagonism with the therapist's motivational systems, thus generating patterns in an intersubjective context of encounter/dis-encounter between the needs of one and the other. One question I ask myself with respect to my patients is how do they enter my motivational systems at each moment, from which motivational system are they grasping me; and how do I enter their motivational systems, from which of my motivational systems I am grasping the patient, and on what inner needs or wishes are we settling into each other.

Transformations produced by interaction between motivational systems

Motivational systems have interactive effects on each other. For example, the narcissistic system can trigger sexuality (activated in order to provide the subject with a grandiose self-image), so that sexuality loses its nature as purely urge-driven pleasure and becomes over-signified as an expression of the subject's potency. Sexuality is therefore activated or deactivated based on the narcissistic gratification or anxiety it produces. Attachment needs may deregulate the psychobiological regulation system when the attachment figure has the emotional instability that we see in borderline personalities.

However, interaction between motivational systems has another important consequence for therapy: the line of anxieties and defences may shift, passing from one system to another. The rupture of an attachment relationship may no longer generate separation anxiety, but narcissistic suffering when it is encoded as an indicator of the subject's lack of worth; or it may cause psychobiological deregulation with panic attacks, with self-preservation anxieties totally dominating the subject's psyche; or paranoid self-preservation anxieties may make the subject withdraw from all relationships, isolate himself, and produce intense longing for an object to satisfy attachment needs, activating this system whose fantasies, anxieties, and defences come to the fore. These transformations of emotional states require the analyst's attention on two fronts: on the one hand, the needs, anxieties, and defences of the motivational system that are active at each moment of the treatment or session; on the other hand, on the motivational system that acted as the first link in the chain of the process that led to the one that is active at this moment.

Modification of the unconscious

In an earlier paper (Bleichmar, 2004) we highlighted a paradox of analytic treatment: it considers that the unconscious is determinant, that only its modification implies structural change, and, at the same time, it uses a technique with interpretations aimed at the patient's consciousness. This did not lead us to diminish the enormous power of interpretation for therapeutic change but to ask ourselves why making the unconscious conscious is really capable of modifying the unconscious. We proposed that both the content of interpretation and the therapeutic relationship need to give the patient something with more motivational weight than the patient's habitual way of feeling, thinking, and acting. We developed the concepts of *motivational weight* or *motivational valency* to indicate that the power of change of therapeutic intervention, whether an interpretation or a type of relationship inscribed as procedural memory, depend on the dynamic interplay between this intervention and the patient's emotional needs at the time it is effected.

> Does the intervention, for instance, rely on the motivational system of attachment but come into contradiction with the narcissistic motivational system, making the subject feel inferior or humiliated, thus provoking a formal acceptance to maintain the attachment, while it is rejected at a deeper level because it damages narcissism? Or, conversely, does such an intervention buttress narcissism by promoting, for instance, the subject's feeling of autonomy, making him feel that he can follow an independent path with respect to those people to whom he so far submitted, yet creating, at the same time, anxieties of attachment, separation and loss of significant figures, and therefore generating deep resistances? (Bleichmar, 2004, p. 1387)

We consider that a conception of the transforming power of therapeutic intervention in these terms enables us to overcome the present polarisation between those who view the relationship as the factor of change *vs.* those who view interpretation as the fundamental instrument. This issue is not limited to acceptance that both have a capacity for change—clinical evidence proves it—or to an appeal to the difference between declarative memory and procedural memory, but also requires us to ask ourselves in regard to each intervention—even though we do so a posteriori, since therapeutic spontaneity is essential—which motivational system is supporting this intervention and which motivational systems, in terms of procedures, concrete fantasies, and anxieties, are opposed to change.

Why does the therapeutic relationship produce changes? Is it because procedural memory changes? It doubtless does, but this leads us to ask: why does the relationship change procedural memory in a certain direction, certain aspects of it more than others also involved in the relationship that is a complex one? And above all, why does the patient incorporate elements of this relationship and the position occupied in it? Why does the patient unconsciously accept participation in the type of interaction conditioned by the relationship with the analyst? Again, motivational valency or power for change depends on the intervention being in line with a concrete need of one of the patient's motivational systems and the absence of any powerful contradiction with the needs of other motivational systems.

The same can be said of interpretation. A patient, in order to protect his narcissism, to keep from feeling deficient or guilty, continually criticises others, projecting the identity of inadequacy onto others. We work on this defence, on the anxieties driving it, the infantile roots and fantasies present in each situation. The description is convincing for the analyst, who gathered data that for anyone except this patient would seem valid, but this is not enough, only if certain motivational components are mobilised in the patient will interpretation have any possibility of transformation. These motivational components may be diverse. Thus, if the patient has important attachment needs to maintain the relationship with the analyst, the contents of interpretation may become part of his psyche in the same way that parental messages are incorporated because this ensures the relationship with significant figures. Or if the analyst is a figure the patient needs to support his narcissism, then in order to obtain this support he will tend to change in the direction indicated by interpretation. Or, independent of the power of transference or suggestion, if the interpretation runs in a direction concordant with the patient's ego ideal and for the gratification anticipated when conforming narcissistically with it, change will become possible since defences against the narcissistic feeling that "I don't have the defect of defending myself, of denying, of ignoring . . ." may be left behind. Not infrequently, a change in narcissistic behaviour occurs because the new behaviour promotes a different modality of narcissism with the feeling that "I change and by changing I see myself as valuable for being capable of doing it". Therefore, narcissism supports giving up certain behaviours for another type of narcissistic gratification. Whether the new kind is less pathological or corresponds to criteria of mental health is not decisive, but rather the fact that it has obtained its power from the provision of narcissistic satisfaction; interplay between variants of narcissism that tip the scales in favour of change.

In other cases, when interpretation points out something that mobilises guilt feelings, hetero-conservation or caring for others, the patient may tend to change, driven by worry about the other, to escape from his egocentrism and to try to repair effects of previous aggressions or lack of attention to the other. Or, if interpretation is supported by needs of psychobiological regulation and produces, without even the patient's conscious subjectivisation of what is occurring, a state of greater calm due to decreased conflicts with external figures, what is grasped is simply this: greater psychobiological well-being, which functions as an impulse to leave aside whatever was producing tension in a process guided by the pleasure principle.

The role of the patient's state of arousal for the process of working-through

States of neuro-vegetative activation (arousal) intervene in processes of attention, fixation, and reconsolidation of memory. The pioneering study of Cahill and collaborators with subjects who were shown scenes with great affective valence found that those who received yohimbine, which activates the adrenergic system, remembered and recognised affectively significant material more than those who received metoprolol, which blocks this system (Cahill and Alkire, 2003; O'Carroll, Drysdale, Cahill, Shajahan, & Ebmeier, 1999). LeDoux and collaborators found that blockage of the adrenergic system is able to decrease reconsolidation in the memory of traumatic experiences when the blocking agent is administered at the moment of remembering (Debiec and LeDoux, 2006). McGaugh's group showed that low doses of glucocorticoids, that act through the noradrenergic system, increased consolidation of long-term memory but disturbed it in high doses (Roozendaal, Okuda, de Quervain, & McGaugh, 2006). Therefore, the neuro-vegetative/hormonal state of arousal/activation at the moment the subject experiences a certain event marks the memory, its consolidation and maintenance of affectively cathected material. This is interesting for analytic treatment because the question it presents is whether a psychoanalytic intervention has the same value/power for working through when the patient has a low level of arousal as when it is high. What is the optimal level of arousal for what is developing in the treatment to be registered and remain fixed?

Furthermore, although we tend to conflate affects and arousal, they are not only psychologically different (Hurlemann et al., 2005) but also have different cerebral locations (Kensinger & Corkin, 2004). Abundant literature leaves no doubt regarding the importance of arousal as a variable that we need to take into consideration (Roozendaal, Okuda, de Quervain, & McGaugh, 2006). This is why we think it is interesting to include this dimension when we examine exchanges between patient and analyst and their effects on working through, especially in cases in which a low level of arousal deactivates the potential emotional weight of interpretations or when the level is so high, very excited patients, that we need to regulate the patient's state of arousal before the analyst's word can have weight and lead to working through and fixation in the memory.

When we examine the state of arousal in the analytic setting, we may detect transference–countertransference resonances or dissonances in relation to it. For example, in the case of one patient, I think there was dissonance between his level of arousal and mine: the energy I put into my interventions and my rhythm was upsetting for him. For me, the slowness of his rhythm, the lack of strength in his voice, his low state of alertness, a general state that I would call phlegmatic, made me feel uncomfortable in the form of a lowering of my energy, producing sleepiness, and yawning. I felt it was my obligation to adapt to him and so I didn't say anything about this difference between us, since it would clearly have been derogatory and demanding. However, in a way that only my reconstruction of the process of our exchanges later showed me, I intuitively began to reveal my more natural way of being in terms of rhythm and general liveliness. I was helped by remembering the ideas of Winnicott (1960) regarding the mother that progressively adapts to her baby's needs, and I thought about the baby that gradually adapts to the mother's style; a process of mutual regulation, now applied to levels of arousal/activation. I think that this was what helped the patient to change his level of vitality and connection, a modification of his low level of arousal.

A female patient was characterised by the high level of agitation observable in the palpitations of the artery in her neck, stable reddening of her neck and the upper part of her chest, and a feverish tempo. It could be said that she was anxious, without doubt, but something went beyond this, and the term anxious state was insufficient to describe what was happening to her more deeply, since the same things occurred when she was happy. There was a basic state that marked her way of experiencing both what was worrying and what was not. This neuro-vegetative deregulation, once we took up this dimension as material for analysis, seemed to derive from interchanges with a borderline mother who flooded her with excitation; therefore, it was primary identification with a neuro-vegetative way of being. In her interchanges with me I had to help her to modulate her state of neuro-vegetative deregulation. Before this, my interventions concerning her fantasies and anxieties were ineffective.

This case and others led me to the conclusion that the modifying power of therapeutic intervention also depends in part on the patient's neuro-vegetative state and arousal level at the moment of the intervention. But the use of affectivity and the analyst's level of neuro-vegetative activation as components of therapeutic technique is doubtless a theme to be explored, with no clear conclusions in the present state of our knowledge, which requires conceptual and clinical investigation (Jiménez, 2007; Leuzinger—Bohleber & Fischmann, 2006).

Conclusion

In this paper I have tried to examine how a modular–transformational approach which considers the existence of multiple unconscious sectors, different motivational systems and their transformations, as well as the patient's state of arousal, enable us to think of therapeutic interventions that derive from the understanding of how the psyche is structured, the forces that mobilise it, and those opposed to therapeutic change. I have been guided by the questions: which sector or sectors of the unconscious require modification in each particular case, what type of interventions are necessary in order to reach this sector and change it; which motivational systems are supporting the intervention and which are resisting change. Our emphasis is not only on the thematic content of intervention, whether it be interpretation or what is implicit in the therapeutic relationship, the fantasies towards which it is aimed, but also on the intimate structure of what needs modification: for example, whether unconscious contents have or lack a heavy affective cathexis, the level

of symbolisation of unconscious sectors, the characterological or situ-
ational level of the patient's state of arousal, discrepancies between
states of arousal of patient and analyst, synergy or antagonism
between the emotional systems of the two participants in the therapeutic encounter. All these factors affect the *motivational weight* or
valency of interventions to produce change.

Note

1. In their recent book Lichtenberg, Lachmann, and Fossaghe (2010) say:
"To the systems previously described—physiological regulation, attachment,
exploration/assertion, aversive, and sensual/sexual—we now add affiliation
and caregiving." They are referring to caregiving behaviour that has been
extensively described in the literature (for instance by Solomon & George,
1996). With the inclusion of a caregiving motivational system, they concur
with us in what we introduced with the expression hetero-preservation system
(Bleichmar, 2004), a specific motivational system, clarifying that the term we
chose means the "care and preservation of others"; they also concur with the
term "caring" to describe the main function of this system. I chose the prefix
"hetero" not only to highlight that the system functions for taking care of
others but also because it originates as a process formed in interaction with
others ("hetero"=others); also through identification with ways in which
significant others took care of others. One of my main differences from
Lichtenberg and colleagues regarding motivational systems is that they do not
include a narcissistic motivational system which is crucial for understanding
how the psyche develops, for psychopathology, and for treatment.

10

Conflicting forces:
on the beginning of the treatment[1]

Norberto C. Marucco

Introduction

Our analytic work places us in the role of a very particular kind of researcher who must constantly reflect upon himself, his therapeutic task, the theory he supports, the cultural context in which he thinks and acts, the vicissitudes of the scientific field he belongs to, and the relation the latter has with the rest of scientific disciplines. I personally understand the psychoanalytic method as a proposal of self-knowledge implying the analyst's will to know his patient and himself, as well as the modes of psychic structuring and functioning, constantly coming and going between the theory and the clinical work. His goal is to search for the truth. This truth will be gradually revealed by patient and analyst alike in sometimes erratic approaches with no guarantees or reassurances, and does not belong to either of them. And all this will happen in the course of a dialogue of desires structured by the transference, a dialogue in which any statement is only temporarily true. I would like to quote here Maud Mannoni (1980):

> Every analyst accompanying the analysand in the latter's own journey (successively overcoming the ignorance of both of them)

is confronted, at one time or the other, by what is hidden. However, that which is hidden from him as a psychoanalyst has (readable) consequences in the patient's cure. Driven by an inner demand, the psychoanalyst will deal theoretically also with what is hidden. Just as madness destroys beliefs and thus lets the truth emerge, a "mad psychoanalytic theory" may, in moments like that, give rise to the truth. But for this to happen, the psycho-analyst must let go his control of knowledge and surrender its illusory protection.

The aim of this paper is to open the possibility of thinking about some subjects I deem essential to analytic theory and practice. I would like to stamp upon these words a colloquial tone that may stimulate the reader's desire to take part in a dialogue kindled by the warmth of the daily clinical work. This paper gives voice to the echoes gathered during those working hours, and hopes to awaken new resounding echoes.

Thus, I invite the reader to wonder, as I do now, whether the psychopathological manifestations current in the beginning of the second decade of the twenty-first century are the same that Freud described in his works. Clearly, the answer will depend on the conception each of us has of psychic structures and functioning, that in its turn will determine the analyst's approach to achieve psychic modifications and changes in his patient.

I think we, psychoanalysts, should commit ourselves to a *theory of cure*. In this paper I would like to make some theoretical considera-tions on my clinical experience, that is, my daily "encounter", within the analytic session, with the reality of the suffering of an individual, the "raw flesh" of the clinical work. That is precisely the source of the personal commitment in our everyday efforts in the intimate domain of the session, and also of the special emphasis on transference and countertransference in theorising on the clinical work.

To develop these ideas, I will start by placing myself in the beginning of the process giving rise to the action of psychoanalysis, and will ask myself why a person consults an analyst. This question will act as a kind of link among the different sub-subjects I will focus upon in this paper. Let us inquire about that particular circumstance in which someone, in a given moment of his life, decides to consult an analyst; a moment when "a feeling of strangeness" leads an in-dividual (most of the time without the clear intention to do it) to initiate an investigation on himself, his environment, and the history that constituted him as a subject. Then, taking the presenting problem and its deployment in the transference, I will try to enquire about the psychic structures and constellations staged through the transference in the course of the psychoanalytic process. Along this "journey", I will make here and there some considerations about the relevance of the spoken word and the understanding of it during the analytic process. I mean not only the word that makes possible the return of the repressed, but also the return of that which is "beyond words" (Marucco, 1986) and challenges us to find a way to represent the ineffable, the "unthought known" (Bollas, 1991), the *mute* that keeps repeating itself, that has not been recorded in a history but must become a history. Ultimately, I am speaking here of that which current pathologies demand from the psychoanalytic elucidation (Green, 2002c) and from the psychoanalyst's theoretical and clinical commitment.

Why does somebody consult an analyst?

To be open to psychoanalytic enquiry

The question made in the title of this section is the summary of old psychoanalytic interrogations and is the clinical correlate of some fundamental theoretical developments, such as those related to narcissism, the Oedipus complex, the life and death drives, and, of course, the transference. Let us ask it again: Why does somebody consult, in a specific moment of his life, an analyst? I am saying "somebody" provisionally (in the sense that he cannot be considered either a patient or an analysand yet) so as to respect the singleness of this individual in the beginning, in the same way that we will respect his personal characteristics in the course of the analysis—in case there is one. The previous meetings, the initial interviews—inasmuch as they are analytic at all (Marucco, 1998)—should, it is hoped, lead to a degree of enlightening, since this is the condition for an analysis to take place and for that individual to become an analysand. And this will only happen if the consulting person and the analyst agree on starting that enterprise which, like friendship or love, must be free and spontaneous.

I repeat: Why does anybody consult an analyst? I would rather say "consult *with*" an analyst, in the same way that the analyst does not "interview" a person but rather "has an interview *with*" a person. Why my emphasis on the preposition? Because it changes the role of the actors on the stage. To say that we "interview" a person implies that we have a degree of power or dominance over him: he is interviewed by us. On the other hand, to have an interview *with* another means that a different relation is established with the latter: it is a dialogue. Someone "consulting" an analyst takes the role of Oedipus in front of an oracle who knows his fate—while this oracle is, in fact, a mirage, a projection of that person's fate neurosis. And the analyst "interviewing" Oedipus takes perhaps the role of the Sphinx making him questions that will also decide his fate. According to Álvarez de Toledo (1996), this "magical belief" of the consulting person is the condition for the analytic situation to take place. I agree: in the beginning of an analysis, the place of knowledge is "deposited" in the analyst. That is, there is an idealisation promoting the illusion that this "other", the oracle, has the secret of one's own suffering, and that one should passively expect from him the "magical words" that, as a sort of abracadabra, will make the longed-for cure possible. That is why I think that for the analytic relationship to proceed along the ways of understanding and not of magic, it is essential that "inhibited-aim drives" (Freud, 1915c) coexist with that belief, that there is mutual trust allowing to create a bond *with* the other. Why is there the need to establish a bond *with* the other? Because the psychoanalysis is never totally exempt from the perils of suggestion (Marucco, 2007), and because idealisation always carries along a germ of persecution with it, so that this "other" who once was "totally good" will turn out to be, sooner or later, an ominous persecutor.

So, while the mythical reference reads that "In the beginning was the Word," and everything *was done* by merely stating the Word, the truth is that words only reach a truly human dimension when they are *said* by one side and the other, carrying with them both a signifier and a signified. From the very beginning of the analytic dialogue, that "magical belief" should coexist with the attempt to conjure it through the significant value of words. When, in the course of the analysis, the "magic" is gradually dismissed, the process will increasingly take on a meaningful rationality.

The symptom and the strangeness

If the concept of symptom were unequivocal, it could be said that someone consulting an analyst or with an analyst is moved by his symptoms. But what is a symptom? It is not something easy to define, less so if one takes into account the theoretical and clinical, as well as historical and social, contexts in which this question must be raised. I agree with those who think that the human subject, rather than "having" symptoms, is in himself a symptom: a compromise between Narcissus and Oedipus, between disavowal and repression, ultimately between endogamy and exogamy. To put it in the terms of physics, the subject is the resultant of forces that "push" and "pull" him and with which he "wrestles". Can we say, then, that every normal person "has" symptoms and "is" a symptom? Freud has already put the adjective "normal" between quotation marks when he wrote, in "Terminable and interminable analysis" (1937c), that "a normal 'ego' . . . is, like normality in general, an ideal fiction".

Leaving aside the economic and cultural conditionings, why does someone consult while some others do not? To use the terms "ego-syntonic" and "ego-distonic" to explain this is to remain in the level of mere description. It could be said that if a person decides to consult with an analyst it is because his symptoms are being cathected. Since psychoanalysis is still pervaded by the medical model, we could think that an "intensification of the symptom" or "the investment of the symptom" is needed for the patient to know what to expect, for him to have a "starting word", or for the consultation to be "on something", that can only be "something in particular". This starting word, predetermined by the symptom, is still very far from the words emerging through free association. Consequently, the symptom (feeling bad, having some pain, if we want to say so) is a kind of "business card" for the consulting person, as telling for what it says as for what it does not say. The symptom is the territory of sexuality, of desire, of the life drive. The patient's words are the testimony as well as the concealment of desire, the domain of the signifier and of the analyst's interpretation (Marucco, 2003).

Besides, I want to emphasise the "strangeness" of the patient; or perhaps it is the analyst who feels him "strange" and is able to put into words—whether he tells the patient or not—that *inquiétante étrangeté* evoking the feeling of "the uncanny" (Freud, 1919h). This is a clinical situation par excellence. The analyst may or may not manage a large amount of theoretical concepts, but only if he takes recourse to his floating attention, some (free) associations (Guiter and Marucco, 1984) will come out that will contribute their part so that "theories" do not close and obturate *that strange and, at the same time, familiar event being staged before him, with him.* It is the field of the transference and of the reciprocal countertransference, where the death drive is seen acting as a compulsion to repeat. We take it by surprise in some of its furtive manifestations, and soon it eludes us again. In that "someone" there is something "alien", something that we feel "strange" (Marucco, 1998), the domain of conflicts between the ego and the ideals, of the compulsion to repeat of *Beyond the Pleasure Principle* (Freud, 1920g). As in every neurosis, narcissism and death drive are always present (Marucco, 2003), and while the word employed here should be "*agieren*" rather than "content", the analyst is not relieved from his duty of reconstructing the history of the drive.

The time to consult

Let us raise again our previous question: Why does somebody consult, in a specific moment of his life, an analyst? *In a specific moment of his life,* somebody will not only have symptoms, but will feel that he is not the same person anymore, as if something familiar has uncannily turned unfamiliar and inhabited him. What is the cause? There are multiple determinants, beginning with life itself. Life confronts us with renewed situations in which a *pact* (I will soon say what kind of pact) is denounced, though perhaps everything goes on as always after that. Undoubtedly, that somebody is trying to discover something about himself, that which has turned him strange. This particular moment in his life has confronted him with the same situation of a researcher attempting to solve an enigma tumultuously dwelling within himself.

I want to emphasise that when the time to consult comes, there are not only strident manifestations of Eros (symptoms) but also more silent expressions of Narcissus' fascination and of the repetition of fate (death drive) (Freud, 1919h, 1920g). That is why the consulting person hesitates and his attitude is largely ambivalent. On the one hand, he consults the oracle having the magical illusion that the latter will save him with its answers from that almost "hypnotic" pact. On the other hand, he consults *with* (let us underline the preposition again) an analyst that will conduct the cure but does not hold all the aces and cannot pretend he does; and our consulting person knows all this but at the same time denies it. The analyst will help him struggle against that pact while *not signing any new pact with him*.

Let us turn to our first interrogation: Why does somebody consult an analyst? This person is looking for an answer to two questions that he himself could never raise. One is related to the way of denouncing that "pact"—one that he once signed without realising it or, as he obscurely glimpses, that he was obliged to sign—and be free of it. The other (also mute) question is the one both Narcissus and Oedipus make: what is my fate? As we will see later, these two terms, "pact" and "fate", converge in the analytical practice and get full meaning in my particular reading of Freudian theory.

The peculiar encounter that the analytic situation is will take place prompted by the erratic search for an answer to these questions. It is an encounter of free associations and interpretations, of which the axis, the spinal cord, is the transference. I believe that at the time of the consultation the person makes a bet involving the analyst, who also makes a bet not very different from his. The analyst must make a bet to go on denouncing his own pact though he knows he will never be completely free of it. And his bet should be a heavy one, so as to keep in force the question leading him to think that to be an analyst has been *his* own choice and life project. That permanent questioning was always a part of the Freudian endeavour. Let us briefly outline it, so as to follow then our own way with a better understanding of the distance we have already covered.

In 1920, Freud was perplexed, confused. He too had to confront a pact in order to renew or cancel his commitment. He, the discloser, the decoder, was haunted by a host of converging events that contradicted the pillars of his theory, seemingly shaking them down. In 1919 he had published "The uncanny", which he started writing in 1913. In his clinical work things did not seem to be going well. The "Wolf Man" led him to the threshold of key theoretical and clinical ideas, but the patient himself had not crossed any threshold; instead, he suffered some serious relapses. The battle for life was not fought any longer in the field of the ego confronting the sexual drives.

When Freud approaches the study of melancholy he cannot but be affected by the self-destruction the melancholic inflicts himself, and in "On narcissism: an introduction" (1914c) the conflict between the ego and the ideals turns more complex. Today, we are relatively well acquainted with that impulse to self-destruction; for Freud, in 1920, it became a serious obstacle that could make him founder. Why would someone want to self-destroy himself? The conflict between the ego and the sexual drives must be moved aside to let us see a new conflict that is beneath it, the conflict between the ego and the super-ego (Freud, 1923b), or, as Freud calls it in 1920, "the mysterious masochistic trends of the ego".

In an attempt to get a foothold in the problem, Freud reviews the development of the psychoanalytic technique and finds out that frag-ments and ramifications of the Oedipus complex are repeated in the transference, but there is now "a new and remarkable fact" that he describes in this way: "the compulsion to repeat also recalls from the past experiences which include no possibility of pleasure, and which can never, even long ago, have brought satisfaction even to instinc-tual impulses which have since been repressed" (Freud, 1920g). It is about this, too, that patients speak in analysis, sometimes without words; and those repetitions—that, as we shall see, must become a history (Green, 2002c; Marucco, 2007)—contain in them the feeling of "strangeness" I referred to above.

There are still two questions to make: who or what commands these repetitions that are not in the service of the pleasure principle? And if we accept that these never-pleasurable situations do not come from the realm of repressed drives, to what mental domain do they belong?

Naturally, it seems that what we are describing here is an "automatism". Freud calls it the "daemonic obsession to repeat". In another part of his essay, he relates it to his theory of the mnemonic traces: the repetitions might be primitive, untameable traces that cannot be bound with the secondary process, with words. He realises and communicates that the compulsion to repeat is not circum-scribed to serious pathologies only, but "is responsible for a part of the course taken by the analyses of neurotic patients" (Freud, 1919h). In my view, this compulsion is not only present in a part of the course but in the whole of it, and is a key element—as strange-ness is—of the psychoanalytic cure.

Freud emerges from his self-questioning (denunciation of the pact) theoretically enriched and postulates his last duality of drives: life drive and death drive. Both symptoms and strangeness are clinical expressions of the different degrees of merging of these two drives. Indeed, the self-destructive trend present in patients is undeniable, but why is it more noticeable in some individuals than in others? Perhaps because of a constitutional predisposition? I would rather say, to conclude this section, that the Thanatic significance of the drive is given by intersubjective determinants and by culture (Marucco, 1985).

On fate and the denunciation of the pact (maternal castration)

I return to the same subject: how is it possible that the consulting person attempts—even without realising it—to repeat his suffering in that realm which is "beyond pleasure"? Freud (1920g) called this manifestation of the compulsion to repeat "fate neurosis". Now, if the compulsion to repeat is our fate, it would be within us but would never belong to us. However, fate neuroses are as analysable as any other neurosis. When Fate is an adjective of "neurosis", it turns human. And perhaps that phrase dating from 1920 (*Beyond the Pleasure Principle*) should be understood in 2011 as "beyond" repression or "before" the Oedipus complex but "within" our analytic task; that is, as one of the analysand's problems of which the psychoanalytic therapy must give account.

I believe that symptoms, on the one side, and strangeness, on the other, confirm that in every consulting person a transference neurosis coexists with a fate neurosis. In terms of theory, what we have here is the return of the repressed (Oedipus' desires) and the compulsion to repeat of *Beyond the Pleasure Principle* (endogamic commands) (Abadi, 1980).

The idea of the splitting of the ego into an area corresponding to the Oedipus complex and a narcissistic one was the key theoretical element that led me to postulate, from 1980 on, a "third topographical scheme" as a necessary conceptual tool to understand this description of psychic structures and also, as we will see, the transference phenomenon.

If our fate is repetition, what is repeated in our fate? In other words, what, and what for, is repeated in the "daemonic obsession to repeat"? Let us remember what Freud (1920g) said on this:

[The neurotics] seek to bring about the interruption of the treatment while it is still incomplete; they contrive once more to feel themselves scorned, to oblige the physician to speak severely to them and treat them coldly; they discover appropriate objects for their jealousy; instead of the passionately desired baby of their childhood, they produce a plan or a promise of some grand present—which turns out as a rule to be no less unreal.

What is repeated, then? The need "to feel themselves scorned". Why is it repeated with a daemonic obsession? To preserve that "passionately desired baby of the primal time". Fantasy has come upon the stage; the pain caused by current repetition has forced a regression to the myth of a happy childhood and a future (fate) is projected as a promise never to be realised. This, then, is the trajectory of a fate neurosis, of the unthought known (Bollas, 1991), of that which is expressed through acts rather than words. Let us follow the trail: that "passionately desired baby of the primal time" was *unreal*, but the individual—a curious paradox—tries to preserve his existence. Why? How? For whom? Back to theory: in "On narcissism: an introduction", Freud (1914c) tells us that the love of parents (so generous and selfless that it is moving) is "a revival and reproduction of their own narcissism, which they have long since abandoned". The child must fulfil the unsatisfied wishes of his parents. If a boy, he must be the great lord his father never was; if a girl, she must marry a prince as a late reward for her mother. The boy must . . . the girl must . . . Plans for them have been already drawn up. Even while the subject may say "I want . . ." or "My wish is . . .", the ego is not the owner of his own house. The individual is structured as a human subject by the parents' intercrossed desires and by culture. In what way? As that passionately desired baby of the primal time, the child "loved" by his parents and sometimes "applauded" by culture (McDougall, 1992).

The consulting person's lack of self-love is showing that the "wonderful child" (Nasio, 1998) has begun to crack and break into pieces. His symptoms and his feeling of strangeness drive him to look for, even unknowingly, the answers to those questions about the pact and the fate. What is the role of the analyst and his word at this crossroads? Each time repetition is acted out (*agieren*), an attempt is made to preserve that child—who is real in his unreality—so that he does not age or die. To preserve him for whose pleasure? Perhaps for the pleasure of those parents (primal children in their turn) who have been incorporated to the psychic apparatus as ideal ego? "They" needed the permanent presence of this unquestioning, disavowing child who fulfils all their wishes and even is a guarantee that the wish exists and is definable. There is all that must be and none that must not be: completeness instead of incompleteness. That child (every child) risks being *hated* if he stops disavowing the parental incompleteness (Green, 2005; Marucco, 2005). In other words: each time it grows or changes, the ideal ego becomes an ambassador of death. This is what patients are telling us with their repetitions of fate in analysis. The analyst's intervention will tend again and again, in Leclaire's (1998) words, "to kill a child", that is, to put an end to the repetition of fate and let the analysis find new ways out.

I turn now to the *pact* I spoke about before in a somewhat mysterious way. In his fascinating article "Fetishism" (1927e), Freud describes something that he found astonishing: when confronted with the difference between the sexes, the subject acknowledges it and, at the same time, does not acknowledge it. His two attitudes about it cannot be more contrasting, but coexist without any difficulty. A part of the ego acknowledges that reality—the difference between the sexes—and represses its incestuous impulses for fear of castration. It "buries" (*Untergang*) its Oedipus complex and boosts up its emerging heir: the superego. The repressed unconscious is thus founded. The other part, Freud says, does not acknowledge the difference, it disavows it in order "to keep itself" in the previous situation, narcissism. What is disavowed is the lack of penis, of a particular penis that cannot be missing: the penis of the mother, who through this disavowal begins to be sacralised as a phallic mother.

As we have said, these two attitudes coexist, as if a pact was signed, a pact in which there are mutual promises and obligations. Disavowal permits the unreal child to receive unreal gifts, as Freud says, but on the condition that the real child makes the promise of not growing, not questioning neither the ideal ego nor the arbitrariness of everyday life (McDougall, 1991). The prize of that pact is a cleft, that later becomes a split, in the ego. The analytic task will be to try to make that gap shorter, that is to say, to help the patient denounce the pact. I will anticipate here the conclusion of this paper: the success of the psychoanalytic cure will depend on transforming the mythical child in no more than an agonic memory through denouncing the pact and relinquishing a fate of unreal promises.

The child reaches the Oedipus stage captured (to a greater or lesser extent) within the phallic mother way of functioning. From that primary and passive identification—identification to be in order to be (Marucco, 1998), not to be in order to have, as Freud (1921c) would have it—he progresses towards the Oedipus stage and goes through it. The degree of difficulty he will find during this transit will depend on his disavowal of his mother's castration. We could ask: why it needs to be disavowed? One hypothesis is that the goal is to preserve the idea of being complete; it would be equal to saying that Narcissus needs the water fountain to mirror his beauty. In other places (Marucco, 1986, 1998) I wondered whether it would be more proper to say that it is the fountain which needs Narcissus; now I wonder whether the child is forced to disavow for fear of the phallic mother's hate. This would explain the structuring role hate has in the transference, to which I will refer in the next section.

The role of the analyst in this particular scenario would be then, like that of the father in the individual's history, to perform the castration of the phallic mother. In the Oedipus drama, the father should be able to look at his nude wife and desire her, instead of being fascinated by that woman turned into a "Mother-Goddess". This man will hardly be able to castrate his child's mother if he could not denounce his own mother's castration first. There is always the need to be helped by one's own father . . . and starting back from here we could have an infinite history as a genealogy of a neurosis.

The analyst's words will reach their real magnitude in the re-edition of this history in the realm of transference and of the reciprocal transference.

Presences in transference

Let us see now the way in which the psychic structures I mentioned at the beginning as observational data (symptoms and strangeness) are expressed in the transference. We will deal here with the repressed and the disavowed, and consequently with ego splitting and the Oedipal and narcissistic structures.

The meaning of "transference" changed as Freud's work continued. At first it was an invariant repetition of the past, but with the

"Dora" case (Freud, 1905e) there came an important modification: transference was said to be a "revised and enlarged edition". Transference was no longer mere repetition (Neyraut, 1976), but repetition with novelty. That is, there are two histories in the transference, one that is repeated invariably and another that is revised during the transference process itself. It is a vivid history, in that it brings us the drive to the present.

What is transferred? The consequences of splitting. At one level, it is the Oedipal structure; basically, the relation between the ego and the ego ideal, a product of secondary identifications. From there, the return of the repressed, namely the symptom (different manifestations of the pact) will emerge. At another level, what is transferred is the coexistent narcissistic structure; basically, the relation between the ego and the ego ideal as structured through the identification *from* and *with* the phallic mother. In this return of the unrepressed, of the disavowed, both the strangeness and the repetition of fate will find expression.

In this way, the transference process, its work and struggle, have its start. It is a *bet* in which the analyst must be ready to really make a stake. Through the self-analysis of the reciprocal transference, he will confront his identification with the phallic mother (inherent to every subject that has passed through a passive primal identification, in the sense of "having been identified"). To free the narcissistic child from his fascination, from the spell cast on him, the analyst must first free himself from those promises that keep him bound to his own phallic mother. An important chapter of analytical practice opens here: that of self-analysis. The analysis has an end, while the self-analysis should be interminable. The analyst's floating attention will not be directed only to his patient, but also to the echoes that the patient's words have in him.

To denounce the archaic phallic mother is, then, first and foremost, to discover her in the reciprocal transference so as to penetrate the secrets of transference. Taking a further step that separates him from his own phallic mother, the analyst becomes, in the transference, the object of the drive.

We could wonder whether it is possible that the analyst ceases to be the object of the drive for his patient in that Oedipal transference, that is, whether there truly exists the "sublimated positive transference" to which Freud alluded, though only on a few occasions.

Let us stop here for a brief review. What is transferred is what Freud (1912a) called "father imago"; it will eventually be, after the Oedipus complex dissolution, the ego ideal. Then an aim-inhibited transference will take place in which the sexual impulse will be transmuted in trust, tenderness, affection, and understanding. There is only an inhibition of the aim, not a change of object. Given that sublimation implies a change both of aim and of object, it cannot be considered a sublimated transference.

Within that positive aim-inhibited transference, the erotic and the negative one may emerge. The three of them are the content of the "Oedipal structure". If there also is, as we believe, a narcissistic structure coexistent with the former, it should certainly manifest itself in the transference. And the way it chooses to do it is through an idealisation of the transference, often confused with a pseudo-sublimation. This kind of "idealisation of the transference" (which is not the same as a sublimated positive transference) is present at some time in every analysis and invokes the force of suggestion, the magic power of interpretation, the transformation of words in acts. One does not hear today about analyses going through an inevitable erotic transference as in Freud's times; however, it is the latter that dethrones suggestion and the force of the object. In other words, erotic transference, which is the drive brought to the present, challenges the idealised transference (Marucco, 1998).

As we know, transference love eventually dissolves, one way or the other. It is the twilight of an illusion and the entry into life. The infatuation, the transference idealisation, endeavours to be eternal; it unifies a dual relation and tries to make it uniform (Leclaire, 1992). Within the transference idealisation, the analyst's words have the highest degree of certainty, are like an absolute truth. We must be well-prepared for that too quick, almost automatic acceptation of our interpretations.

Is there not, perhaps, a feeling of fear between patient and analyst at those times? There might be fear, I think, in both of them. Negative transference settles in. Will it always be a kind of resistance? Both in the transference and in the reciprocal transference there is hate: hate against the phallic mother when the analysand asks himself who is he now and who was him (that "passionately desired baby of the primal time"). The moment of denunciation of the pact is also a moment of fear . . . because parental wishes, in spite of being alienating, had also been constitutive. Who am I while I question myself? There is space for strangeness. The phallic mother, who in the past has been a structuring element, now threatens not to be. The time has come for a negative therapeutic reaction: when the patient improves, he deteriorates. The analyst will have to raise the bet, tolerating the fear provoked by the denunciation of the pact. His words will give an account of the acts and contents involved in the patient's words. The analyst will transform the patient's illness in anxiety, and this anxiety then questions the narcissistic child. The analyst's words will build the unique history of his patient, the history of the constitutive wishes of his parents and of his culture, so that it may definitively become history, a remembrance of the past.

The analyst's words, similar to those indicated by Freud (1937d) in "Constructions in analysis" ("Up to your nth year you regarded yourself as the sole and unlimited possessor of your mother . . ."), will replace the repetition of the disavowed. This historical reconstruction by the analyst of that which may be even beyond words gives the individual a meaning to rewrite his own history.

Here we come, at least in theory, to the true end of the analysis, the beginning of a self-analysis that will have no end. As Freud (1940a) says, the analyst's knowledge became at last the knowledge of the analysed. A new life begins for the latter, after passing through that middle zone (transference) which was also a part of his life. But it was life for both, patient and analyst.

I ask again: was there a sublimated positive transference? Certainly there was an aim-inhibited transference making possible the search, the questioning, the wanting to know, and the coming to know. But the object of the drive, to which the questions were directed, as it were, has always been the analyst.

Now, when approaching the end of the analysis, the sublimation of the transference may indeed begin, if to the inhibition of the aim we add the unbinding of the object and the search for another exogamic sexual object, and it is also to identify with an abstraction.

We have reached the final act of the analytic drama and the curtain comes down. There are still questions to be asked, but now they are directed elsewhere: *to the place of interrogation itself*.

The time has come to bid the patient—and my reader—farewell.

Note

1. I have used the masculine pronoun throughout the text for the sake of brevity. (Translator's note.)

Acknowledgement

I thank the IPA Publications Committee for their invitation to contribute to the book "On Freud's On Beginning the Treatment" to be published by Karnac in its Contemporary Freud series.

REFERENCES

Abadi, M. (1980). ¿Deseo edípico o mandato endogámico? *Revista de Psicoanálisis, 37*: 1.

Abelin-Sas, A. (2008). Recent work by Hugo Bleichmar. *Journal of the American Psychoanalytic Association, 56*: 295–304.

Abend, S. M. (2000). Analytic technique today. *Journal of the American Psychoanalytic Association, 48*: 9–16.

Ablon, S. J. (2005). Reply to Blatt and Fonagy. *Journal of the American Psychoanalytic Assiciation, 53*: 591–594.

Ablon, S. J., & Jones, E. E. (1998). How expert clinicians' prototypes of an ideal treatment correlate with outcome in psychodynamic and cognitive behavioral therapy. *Psychotherapy Research, 8*: 71–83.

Ablon, S. J., & Jones, E. E. (1999). Psychotherapy process in the National Institute of Mental Health treatment of Depression Collaborative Research Program. *Journal of Consulting and Clinical Psychology, 67*(1): 64–75.

Ablon, S. L. (1994). "How can we know the dancer from the dance?": the analysis of a five year old girl. *Psychoanalytic Study of the Child, 49*: 315–327.

Adler, G. (1980). Transference, real relationship and alliance. *International Journal of Psycho-Analysis, 61*:547–558.

Aisenstein, M. (2010). Les exigences de la représentation. *Congrès de Psychanalyse du Langue Français*, *70*: 123.

Alvarez, A. (2010). Levels of analytic work and levels of pathology: the work of calibration. *International Journal of Psychoanalysis*, *91*: 859–878.

Álvarez de Toledo, L. G. de. (1996). The analysis of 'associating' 'interpreting' and 'words': use of this analysis to bring unconscious fantasies into the present and to achieve greater ego integration. *International Journal of Psycho-Analysis*, *77*: 291–317.

Bachrach, H. M., Weber, J. J., & Solomon, M. (1985). Factors associated with the outcome of psychoanalysis, (clinical and methodological considerations): Report of the Columbia Psychoanalytic Center Research Project. *Int. R. Psycho-Anal.*, *12*: 379–389.

Balint, M. (1960). Primary narcissism and primary love. *Psychoanalytic Quarterly*, *29*: 6–43.

Barale, F., & Ferro, A. (1992). Negative therapeutic reactions and microfractures in analytic communication. In: L. Nissim Momigliano & A. Robutti (Eds.), *Shared Experience: The Psychoanalytic Dialogue* (pp. 143–165). London: Karnac.

Baranger, M. (1963). Bad faith identity and omnipotence. In: L. Glocer Fiorini (Ed.), *The Work of Confluence. Listening and interpreting in the Psychoanalytic Field. Madeleine and Willy Baranger* (pp. 188–202). London: Karnac, 2009.

Baranger, M. (1993). The mind of the analyst: from listening to interpretation. *International Journal of Psycho-Analysis*, *74*: 15–24

Baranger, M., & Baranger, W. (2008). The analytic situation as a dynamic field. *International Journal of Psycho-Analysis*, *89*: 795–826.

Beebe, B., Rustin, J., Sorter, D., & Knoblauch, S. (2003). An expanded view of intersubjectivity. *Psychoanalytic Dialogues*, *13*: 805–841.

Bergeret, J. (1975). *La dépression et les états limites*. Paris: Payot.

Bion, W. R. (1962). *Learning From Experience*. London: Karnac.

Bion, W. R. (1963). *Elements of Psycho-analysis*. London: Karnac.

Bion, W. R. (1965). *Transformations*. London: Karnac, 1984.

Bion, W. R. (1970). *Attention and Interpretation*. London: Karnac.

Bion, W. R. (1983). *The Italian Seminars*, F. Bion (Ed.). London: Karnac.

Bion, W. R. (1987). *Second Thoughts*. London: Karnac.

Bion, W. R. (1992). *Cogitations*. London: Karnac.

Bion, W. R. (2005). *The Tavistock Seminars*, F. Bion (Ed.). London: Karnac.

Blatt, S. J. (2001). The effort to identify empirically supported psychological treatments. *Psychoanalytic Dialogues*, *11*: 635–646.

Blatt, S. J., Zuroff, D. C., Quinlan, D. M., & Pilkonis, P. A. (1996). Interpersonal factors in brief treatment of depression: Further analyses of the National Institute of Mental Health Treatment of Depression Collaborative Research Program. *Journal of Consulting and Clinical Psychology, 64*: 162–171.

Bleandonu, G. (1994). *'Wilfred Bion' His Life and Works, 1897–1979*. London: Free Association Books.

Bleichmar, H. (1997). *Avances en Psicoterapia Psicoanalitica. Hacia una Técnica de Intervenciones Específicas*. Barcelona: Paidós.

Bleichmar, H. (2004). Making conscious the unconscious in order to modify unconscious processing: some mechanisms of therapeutic change. *International Journal of Psychoanalysis, 85*: 1379–1400.

Bleichmar, H. (2010). Rethinking pathological mourning: multiple types and therapeutic approaches. *Psychoanalytic Quarterly, 1*: 71–93.

Blum, H. P. (1998). An analytic inquiry into intersubjectivity: Subjective objectivity. *Journal of Clinical Psychoanalysis, 7*: 189–208.

Bollas, C. (1991 [1987]). *The Shadow of the Object: Psychoanalysis of the Unthought Known*. New York: Columbia University Press.

Braitenberg, V., & Schüz, A. (1998). *Cortex: Statistics and Geometry of Neuronal Connectivity*. Berlin: Springer Verlag.

Brenner, C. (1979). Working alliance, therapeutic alliance, and transference. *Journal of the American Psychoanalytic Association, Supplement, 27*:137–157.

Cahill, L., & Alkire, M. T. (2003). Epinephrine enhancement of human memory consolidation interaction with arousal at encoding. *Neurobiology of Learning and Memory, 79*: 194–198.

Cahn, R. (2002). *La fin du divan?* [*The End of the Couch?*]. Paris: Odile Jacob.

Caligor, E., Hamilton, M., Schneier, H., Donovan, J., Luber, B., & Roose, S. (2003). Converted patients and clinic patients as control cases: a comparison with implications for psychoanalytic training. *Journal of the American Psychoanalytic Association, 51*: 201–220.

Caligor, E., Stern, B. L., Hamilton, M., MacCormack, V., Wininger, L., Sneed, J., & Roose, S. P. (2009). Why we recommend analytic treatment for some patients and not for others. *Journal of the American Psychoanalytic Association, 57*: 677–694.

Canestri, J. (2006). *Psycho-Analysis From Practice to Theory*. West Sussex, England: Whurr.

Cassorla, R. (2009). Reflexões sobre *não-sonho-a-dois*, *enactment* e função alfa implìcita do analista. *Revista Brasileira de Psicanálise, 43*(4): 91–120.

Castonguay, L. G., Goldfried, M. R., Wiser, S. L., Raue, P. J., & Hayes, A. M. (1996). Predicting the effect of cognitive therapy for depression: a study of unique and common factors. *Journal of Consulting and Clinical Psychology*, *64*: 497–504.

Clyman, R. B. (1991). The procedural organization of emotions: a contribution from cognitive science to the psychoanalytic theory of therapeutic action. *Journal of the American Psychoanalytic Association*, *39S*: 349–382.

Couch, A. S. (1999). Therapeutic functions of the real relationship in psychoanalysis. *Psychoanalytic Study of the Child*, *54*: 130–168.

Curtis, H. (1979). The concept of therapeutic alliance: implications for the "widening scope". *Journal of the American Psychoanalytic Association*, *27S*: 159–192.

Debiec, J., & LeDoux, J. E. (2006). Noradrenergic signalling in the amygdala contributes to the reconsolidation of fear memory: treatment implications for PTSD. *Annals of the New York Academy of Sciences*, *1071*: 521–524.

Dickes, R. (1967). Severe regressive disruptions of the therapeutic alliance. *Journal of the American Psychoanalytic Association*, *15*: 508–533.

Dispaux, M. F. (2002). Aux sources de l'interprétation [At the sources of interpretation]. In: *L'agir et les processus de transformations* [*Enactments and Transformation Processes*] (paper read to the CPLF). *Revue Française de Psychanalyse*, *XVI*(5): 1461–1496.

Donnet, J.-L. (1995a). *Surmoi I: le concept freudien et la règle fondamentale*. Paris: Presses Universitaires de France.

Donnet, J.-L. (1995b). *Le divan bien tempéré* [*The Well-Tempered Couch*]. Paris: Presses Universitaires de France.

Donnet, J.-L. (2005). *La situation analysante* [*The Analysing Situation*]. Paris: Presses Universitaires de France.

Donnet, J.-L., & Gougoulis, N. (2006). Le Centre de consultations et de traitements psychanalytiques Jean Favreau. Un entretien avec Jean-Luc Donnet [The *Jean Favreau* Consultation Centre: an interview with Jean-Luc Donnet]. *Revue Française de Psychanalyse*, *LXX*(4): 1015–1041.

Donnet, J.-L., & Minazio, N. (2005). Entretien des Carrefours psychanalytiques [An interview with the *Carrefours psychanalytiques*]. *Revue Belge de Psychanalyse*, *46*: 65–88.

Fèdida, P. (2001). *Des bienfaits de la dépression, éloge de la psychothérapie* [*On the Benefits of Depression. In Praise of Psychotherapy*]. Paris: Odile Jacob.

Ferenczi, S. (1930). The principle of relaxation and neocatharsis. *International Journal of Psycho-Analysis*, *11*: 428–443.

Ferro, A. (1999). *The Bi-Personal Field: Experiences in Child Analysis*. London/New York: Routledge.

Ferro, A. (2002a). Some implications of Bion's thought: the waking dream and narrative derivatives. *International Journal of Psychoanalysis*, *83*: 597–607.

Ferro, A. (2002b). *In the Analyst's Consulting Room*. London/New York: Routledge.

Ferro, A. (2003). Marcella from explosive sensoriality to the ability to think. *Psychoanalytic Quarterly*, *LXXII*: 183–200.

Ferro, A. (2006). Clinical implication of Bion's thought. *International Journal of Psychoanalysis*, *87*: 989–1003.

Ferro, A. (2008). *Mind Works: Technique and Creativity in Psychoanalysis*. London & New York: Routledge/New Library.

Ferro, A. (2009). Transformations in dreaming and characters in the psychoanalytic field. *International Journal of Psychoanalysis*, *90*: 2009–2030.

Ferro, A. (2011). *Avoiding Emotions, Living Emotions*. London/New York: Routledge.

Ferro, A., & Basile, R. (Eds.) (2009). *The Analytic Field*. London: Karnac.

Ferro, A., Civitarese, G., Collovà, M., Foresti, G., Mazzacane, F., Molinari, E., & Politi, P. (2007). *Sognare l'analisi. Sviluppi clinici del pensiero di Bion*. Torino: Bollati Boringhieri.

Fodor, J. A. (1983). *Modularity of Mind: An Essay on Faculty Psychology*. Cambridge, MA: MIT Press.

Fonagy, P. (1999). Memory and therapeutic action. *International Journal of Psychoanalysis*, *80*: 215–223.

Freud, A. (1954). The widening scope of indications for psychoanalysis (discussion). *Journal of the American Psychoanalytical Association*, *2*: 607–620.

Freud, S. (1891b). *ZurAuffassung der Aphasien*. [*On Aphasia. A Critical Study*]. New York: International Universities Press, 1953.

Freud, S. (1895d). *Studies on Hysteria* (with J. Breuer). *S.E.*, *2*. London: Hogarth.

Freud, S. (1900a). *The Interpretation of Dreams*. *S.E.*, *4–5*. London: Hogarth.

Freud, S. (1905a [1904]). On psychotherapy. *S.E.*, *7*: 255–268. London: Hogarth.

Freud, S. (1905e). *Fragment of an Analysis of a Case of Hysteria*. *S.E.*, *7*: 1–122. London: Hogarth.

Freud, S. (1907b). Obsessive actions and religious practices. *S.E.*, *9*: 117. London: Hogarth.

Freud, S. (1909a [1908]). Some general remarks on hysterical attacks. *S.E.*, *9*: 229. London: Hogarth.

Freud, S. (1909d). *Notes upon a Case of Obsessional Neurosis. S.E.*, *10*: 153. London: Hogarth.

Freud, S. (1912a). The dynamics of transference. *S.E.*, *12*: 97–108. London: Hogarth.

Freud, S. (1912b). The dynamics of transference. *S.E.*, *12*: 99. London: Hogarth.

Freud, S. (1912e). Recommendations to physicians practising psycho-analysis. *S.E.*, *12*: 109–120. London: Hogarth.

Freud, S. (1912–1913). *Totem and Taboo. S.E.*, *13*: ix. London: Hogarth.

Freud, S. (1913a). Letter from Freud to Ludwig Binswanger, 20 February, 1913. *The Sigmund Freud-Ludwig Binswanger Correspondence 1908–1938*, pp. 112–113.

Freud, S. (1913c). On beginning the treatment (Further recommendations on the technique of psycho-analysis I). *S.E.*, *12*: 121–144. London: Hogarth.

Freud, S. (1913j). The claims of psycho-analysis to scientific interest. *S.E.*, *13*: 165. London: Hogarth.

Freud, S. (1914c). On narcissism: an introduction. *S.E.*, *14*: 73–102. London: Hogarth.

Freud, S. (1914d). On the history of the psycho-analytic movement. *S.E.*, *14*: 3. London: Hogarth.

Freud, S. (1914g). remembering, repeating and working-through (Further recommendations on the technique of psycho-analysis, II). *S.E.*, *12*: 147. London: Hogarth.

Freud, S. (1915a [1914]). Observations on transference-love (Further Recommendations on the Technique of Psycho-Analysis, III). *S.E.*, *12*: 157–171. London: Hogarth.

Freud, S. (1915c). Instincts and their vicissitudes. *S.E.*, *14*: 109–140. London: Hogarth.

Freud, S. (1915d). Repression. *S.E.*, *14*. London: Hogarth.

Freud, S. (1915e). The unconscious. *S.E.*, *14*. London: Hogarth.

Freud, S. (1916d). Some character types met with in psychoanalytic work. *S.E.*, *14*: 311. London: Hogarth.

Freud, S. (1916–1917). *Introductory Lectures on Psycho-analysis Part III. S.E.*, *16*: 243–463. London: Hogarth.

Freud, S. (1917c). On transformations of instinct as exemplified in anal eroticism. *S.E.*, *17*: 127. London: Hogarth.

Freud, S. (1917e). Mourning and melancholia. *S.E.*, *14*: 237–258. London: Hogarth.

Freud, S. (1919a [1918]). Lines of advance in psycho-analytic therapy. *S.E.*, *17*: 159. London: Hogarth.

Freud, S. (1919h). The 'uncanny'. *S.E.*, *17*: 217–256. London: Hogarth.

Freud, S. (1920b). A note on the prehistory of the technique of analysis. *S.E.*, *18*: 263. London: Hogarth.

Freud, S. (1920g). *Beyond the Pleasure Principle*. *S.E.*, *18*. London: Hogarth.

Freud, S. (1921c). *Group Psychology and the Analysis of the Ego*. *S.E.*, *18*: 67–143. London: Hogarth.

Freud, S. (1923b). *The Ego and the Id*. *S.E.*, *19*: 12–66. London: Hogarth.

Freud, S. (1924d). The dissolution of the Oedipus complex. *S.E.*, *19*. London: Hogarth.

Freud, S. (1926d). *Inhibitions, Symptoms and Anxiety*. *S.E.*, *20*. London: Hogarth.

Freud, S. (1926e). The question of lay analysis. *S.E.*, *20*. London: Hogarth.

Freud, S. (1927e). Fetishism. *S.E.*, *21*: 149–157. London: Hogarth.

Freud, S. (1937c). Analysis terminable and interminable. *S.E.*, *23*: 209–254. London: Hogarth.

Freud, S. (1937d). Constructions in analysis. *S.E.*, *23*: 255–269. London: Hogarth.

Freud, S. (1940a [1938]). *An Outline of Psycho-Analysis*. *S.E.*, *23*: 139–208. London: Hogarth.

Freud, S. (1950a [1895]). *Project for a Scientific Psychology*. *S.E.*, *1*: 283. London: Hogarth.

Freud, S. (1961). *Letters of Sigmund Freud. 1873–1939*, E. L. Freud (Ed.), T. & J. Stern (Trans.). London: Hogarth.

Freud, S., & Breuer, J. (1895d). *Studies on Hysteria*. *S.E.*, *2*: 3–319. London: Hogarth.

Freud, S., & Breuer, J. (1940d [1892]). On the theory of hysterical attacks. *S.E.*, *1*: 151.

Friedman, L. (1988). *The Anatomy of Psychotherapy*. Hillsdale, NJ: The Analytic Press.

Gay, P. (1988). *Freud: Uma vida para nosso tempo*. São Paulo: Companhia das Letras, 1989.

Gill, M. (1982). Analysis of transference. *Psychological Issues*, *Monograph 53*. New York: International Universities Press.

Green, A. (1979). "Le silence du psychanalyste" [The analyst's silence is a laborious one, it drives his psychic apparatus to work] In: *La Folie Privée*. Paris: Gallimard, 1990.

Green, A. (1995). *Propédeutique: la métapsychologie revisitée*. Seyssel: Champ Vallon.

Green, A. (1999a). Passivité-passivation: jouissance et détresse [Passivity-passivation: ecstatic pleasure and distress]. *Revue Française de Psychanalyse*, *LXIII*(5) (Special Congress issue): 1587–1600.

Green, A. (1999b). On discriminating and not discriminating between affect and representation. *International Journal of Psycho-Analysis*, *80*: 277–231.

Green, A. (2002a). *Idées directrices pour une psychanalyse contemporaine*. Paris: Presses Universitaires de France [*Key Ideas for a Contemporary Psychoanalysis. Misrecognition and Recognition of the Unconscious*, A. Weller (Trans.). London: Routledge, 2005].

Green, A. (2002b). *Conferências Brasileiras de André Green: Metapsicologia los limites* [*Brazilian Lectures of André Green*]. Rio de Janeiro: Imago, 1990.

Green, A. (2002c). *Time in Psychoanalysis: Some Contradictory Aspects*. Michigan: Free Association Books.

Green, A. (2005). *Ideas directrices para un psicoanálisis contemporáneo*. Buenos Aires: Amorrortu editores.

Greenberg, J., & Mitchell, S. (1983). *Object Relations in Psychoanalytic Theory*. Cambridge, MA: Harvard University Press.

Greenson, R. R. (1967). *The Technique and Practice of Psychoanalysis, Volume 1*. New York: International Universities Press, Inc.

Greenson, R. R., & Wexler, M. (1969). The non-transference relationship in the psychoanalytic setting. *International Journal of Psycho-Analysis*, *50*: 27–39.

Groddeck, G. (1923). *The Book of the It*. [Das Buch vom Es]. New York: International Universities Press, 1976.

Grotstein, J. (2007). *A Beam of Intense Darkness*. London: Karnac.

Grotstein, J. (2009) ". . . *But at the Same Time and on Another Level . . .*". *Clinical Applications in the Kleinian/Bionian Mode*. London: Karnac.

Guignard, F. (2010). A interpretação através das idades da vida. *Congresso Latinoamericano de Psicanálise*, 28.

Guiter, M., & Marucco, N. (1984). Asociación libre y atención flotante. Puntualizaciones, reflexiones y comentarios. *Revista de Psicoanálisis*, *41*: 5.

Hebb, D. (1949). *The Organization of Behavior*. New York: Wiley & Sons.

Heimann, P. (1950). On countertransference. *International Journal of Psychoanalysis*, *31*: 81–84.

Hurlemann, R., Hawellek, B., Matusch, A., Kolsch, H., Wollersen, H., Madea, B., Vogeley, K., Maier, W., & Dolan, R. J. (2005). Noradrenergic modulation of emotion-induced forgetting and remembering. *Journal of Neuroscience*, *25*: 6343–6349.

Jacobs, T. (1991). *The Use of the Self: Countertransference and Communication in the Analytic Situation*. Madison, CT: International Universities Press.

Jiménez, J. P. (2007). Can research influence clinical practice? *International Journal of Psychoanalysis*, *88*: 661–679.

Jones, E. (1923). *Papers on Psycho Analysis* (3rd edn) (pp. 154–211). London: Bailliere, Tindal and Cox.

Kantrowitz, J. L. (1993). Outcome research in psychoanalysis: review and reconsiderations. *Journal of the American Psychoanalytical Association*, *41S*: 313–329.

Kantrowitz, J. L. (1995). The beneficial aspects of the patient-analyst match. *International Journal of Psycho-Analysis*, *76*: 299–313.

Kantrowitz, J. L. (1997). A different perspective on the therapeutic process: the impact of the patient on the analyst. *Journal of the American Psychoanalytical Association*, *45*: 127–153.

Kantrowitz, J. L. (2002). The external observer and the patient-analyst match. *International Journal of Psycho-analysis*, *83*: 339–350.

Keats, J. (1970). The Letters of John Keats: A Selection. R. Gittings (Ed.). Oxford: Oxford University Press.

Kensinger, E. A., & Corkin, S. (2004). Two routes to emotional memory: distinct neural processes for valence and arousal. *Proceedings of the National Academy of Sciences*, *101*: 3310–3315.

Klein, M. (1952a). The origins of the transference. In: *Envy, Gratitude and Other Works, 1946* (p. 63). London: Hogarth.

Kohut, H. (1968). The psychoanalytic treatment of narcissistic personality disorders, *Psychoanalytic Study of the Child*, *23*: 86–113.

Lacan, J. (1953a). The function and field of speech in psychoanalysis. In: B. Fink (Trans.), *Écrits* (pp. 31–106). New York: W. W. Norton & Co., 2002.

Lacan, J. (1953b). "Fonction et Champ de la Parole et du Langage en Psychanalyse". *Écrits*, pp. 301–302. Paris: Seuil, 1966.

Lacan, J. (1953–1954). *The Seminar of Jacques Lacan: Freud's Papers on Technique (Vol. Book I)*, J.-A. Miller (Ed.), J. Forrester (Trans.). New York: W. W. Norton & Co., 1988.

Laplanche, J., & Pontalis, J. B. (1967). *Vocabulaire de la psychanalyse (The Language of Psycho-Analysis)*. Paris: PUF.

Leclaire, S. (1992). Hablar en primera persona (Apuntes sobre el concepto de neurosis en la actualidad). *Revista de Psicoanálisis, 1*: 167–176.

Leclaire, S. (1998 [1975]). *A Child is Being Killed: On Primary Narcissism and the Death Drive*. California: Standford University Press.

LeDoux, J. (1996). *The Emotional Brain: The Mysterious Underpinnings of Emotional Life*. New York: Simon & Schuster.

Leuzinger-Bohleber, M., & Fischmann, T. (2006). What is conceptual research in psychoanalysis. *International Journal of Psychoanalysis, 87*:1355–1386.

Levy, I. (1995). The fate of the Oedipus complex: dissolution or waning. *International Forum of Psychoanalysis, 4*: 7–14.

Levy, S. T., & Inderbitzen, L. B. (2000). Suggestion and psychoanalytic technique. *Journal of the American Psychoanalytical Association, 48*: 739–758.

Lewin, B. (1946). Sleep, the mouth, and the dream screen. *Psychoanalytic Quarterly, 15*.

Lichtenberg, J. D. (1989). *Psychoanalysis and Motivation*. Hillsdale, NJ: The Analytic Press.

Lichtenberg, J. D., Lachmann, F. M., & Fossaghe, J. L. (2010). *Psychoanalysis and Motivational Systems. A New Look*. New York: Routledge.

Lipton, S. D. (1977). The advantages of Freud's technique as shown in his analysis of the Rat Man case. *International Journal of Psycho-Analysis, 58*: 255–273.

Little, M. (1951). Countertransference and the patient's response to it. In: *Transference Neurosis and Transference Psychosis*. New York & London: Jason Aronson.

Loewald, H. (1960). On the therapeutic action of psychoanalysis. *International Journal of Psychoanalysis, 41*: 16–35.

Lyons-Ruth, K. (1999). The two-person unconscious: intersubjective dialogue, enactive relational representation, and the emergence of new forms of relational organization. *Psychoanalytic Inquiry, 19*: 576–617.

Mannoni, M. (1980 [1979]). *La teoría como ficción. Freud, Groddeck, Winnicott, Lacan*. Barcelona: Grijalbo.

Martin, D. J., Garske, J. P, & Davis, M. K. (2000). Relation of the therapeutic alliance with outcome and other variables: a meta-analytic review. *Journal of Consulting and Clinical Psychology, 68*: 438–450.

Marucco, N. (1985). Acerca de Narciso y Edipo en la teoría y práctica analíticas. Lectura desde la inclusión de la cultura. *Revista de Psicoanálisis*, *42*: 1.

Marucco, N. (1986). Más allá del placer: la palabra y la repetición. *Revista Brasileira de Psicanálise*, *20*: 1.

Marucco, N. (1998). *Cura analÌtica y transferencia. De la represión a la desmentida*. Buenos Aires: Amorrortu editores.

Marucco, N. (2003). Algunas puntuaciones psicoanalíticas (desde mi práctica clínica). *Revista de Psicoanálisis*, *60*: 2.

Marucco, N. (2005). Current psychoanalytic practice: psychic zones and the processes of unconscientization. In: *Truth, Reality, and the Psychoanalyst: Latin American Contributions to Psychoanalysis* (Chapter 7). London: International Psychoanalytical Association.

Marucco, N. (2007). Between memory and destiny: repetition. *The International Journal of Psychoanalysis*, *88*: 309–328.

McDougall, J. (1991). *Theaters of the Mind: Illusion and Truth on the Psychoanalytic Stage*. London: Taylor & Francis Group.

McDougall, J. (1992 [1978]). *Plea For a Measure of Abnormality*. New York: Brunner/Mazel Editions.

Mello Franco Filho, O. (1994). Mudança psíquica do analista: da neutralidade à transformação. *Revista Brasileira de Psicanálise*, *28*(2): 309–328.

Meltzer, D. (1990). *The Apprehension of Beauty*. London: The Roland Harris Educational Trust Library.

Menaker, E. (1942). The masochistic factor in the psychoanalytic situation. *Psychoanalytic Quarterly*, *11*: 171–186.

Mitchell, S. A. (2000). *Relationality: From Attachment to Intersubjectivity*. Hillsdale, NJ: The Analytic Press.

Moreno, J. (2010). *Tiempo y trauma: continuidades rotas*. Buenos Aires: Lugar.

M'Uzan, M. de (1976a). Contre-transfert et système paradoxal [Counter-tranference and paradoxical system]. In: *De l'art à la mort*, Paris: Gallimard, 1977.

M'Uzan, M. de (1976b) Trajectoire de la bisexualité. In: *De l'art à la mort*, Paris: Gallimard, 1977.

Nacht, S. (1961). On technique at the beginning of psychoanalytic treatment. *Psychoanalytic Quarterly*, *30*: 155 [also in *Revue Française De Psychanalyse*, *XXIV*: 5–18, 1960].

Nasio, J. D. (1998). *Five Lessons on the Psychoanalytic Theory of Jacques Lacan*. Albany: Suny Press.

Nemas, C. (2010). Un aspecto de la contratransferencia con pacientes borderline desde la perspectiva de las ideas de Donald Meltzer:

disponibilidad como objeto de internalización. *Congresso Latino-americano de Psicanálise, 28.*

Neyraut, M. (1976). *La transferencia.* Buenos Aires: Corregidor.

Nunberg, H., & Federn, E. (Eds.) (1962). *Minutes of the Vienna Psycho-analytic Society: Volume I, 1906–1908*, M. Nunberg (Trans.). New York: International Universities Press.

O'Carroll, R. E., Drysdale, E., Cahill, L., Shajahan, P., & Ebmeier, K. P. (1999). Stimulation of the noradrenergic system enhances and blockade reduces memory for emotional material in man. *Psychological Medicine, 29*: 1083–1088.

Ogden, T. H. (1994a). The analytic third: working with intersubjective clinical facts. *International Journal of Psycho-Analysis, 75*: 3–19.

Ogden, T. H. (1994b). *Subjects of Psychoanalysis.* London: Karnac.

Ogden, T. H. (2005). *This Art of Psychoanalysis.* London: Routledge.

Ogden, T. H. (2007). On talking as dreaming. *International Journal of Psycho-Analysis, 88*: 575–589.

Ogden, T. H. (2009). *Rediscovering Psychoanalysis. Thinking and Dreaming, Learning and Forgetting.* London: Routledge.

Oxford English Dictionary (1995). Oxford: Oxford University Press.

Pirandello, L. (1922). *Six Characters in Search of an Author* (English version by E. Storer). New York: E. P. Dutton.

Racker, H. (1968). *Transference and Countertransference.* New York: International Universities Press.

Robert dictionnaire (1988). *Dictionnaire d'apprentissage de la langue française.* Paris: Le Robert.

Roozendaal, B., Okuda, S., de Quervain, D. J., & McGaugh, J. L. (2006). Glucocorticoids interact with emotion-induced noradrenergic activation in influencing different memory functions. *Neuroscience, 138*: 901–910.

Rothstein, A. (1995). *Psychoanalytic Technique and the Creation of Analytic Patients.* Madison, CT: International Universities Press.

Roussillon, R. (1991). *Paradoxes et situations limites de la psychanalyse.* Paris: Presses Universitaires de France.

Roussillon, R. (1992). *Du baquet de Mesmer au "baquet" de S. Freud* [*From Mesmer's Bucket Seat to That of Freud*]. Paris: P.U.F.

Roussillon, R. (2010). Working-through and its various models. *International Journal of Psychoanalysis, 91*:1405–1417.

Shakespeare, W. (1966). Sonnet 30. In: *The Sonnets* (p. 17). Cambridge University Press.

Shedler, J. (2010). The efficacy of psychodynamic therapy. *American Psychologist, 65*: 98–109.

Solomon, J., & George, C. (1996). Defining the caregiving system. Toward a theory of caregiving. *Infant Mental Health Journal, 17*: 183–197.

Spitz, R. C. (1946). Anaclitic depression. *Psychoanalytic Study of the Child, 2*: 313–341.

Stern, D. N. (1985). *The Interpersonal World of the Infant. A View from Psychoanalysis and Developmental Psychology*. New York: Basic Books.

Stolorow, R. D., Brandchaft, B., & Atwood, G. (1983). Intersubjectivity in psychoanalytic treatment. *Bulletin of the Menninger Clinic, 47*(2):117–128.

Stone, L. (1961). *The Psychoanalytic Situation: An Examination of Its Development and Essential Nature*. New York: International Universities Press.

Strupp, H. H. (2001). Implications of the empirically supported treatment movement for psychoanalysis. *Psychoanalytic Dialogues, 11*: 605–619.

Szecsödy, I. (2009). Sándor Ferenczi: the first intersubjectivist. *Psychoanalytic Quarterly, 78*: 1244–1244.

Viederman, M. (1991). The real person of the analyst and his role in the process of the psychoanalytic cure. *Journal of the American Psychoanalytical Association, 39*:451–489.

Viederman, M. (2000). A psychoanalytic stance. In: J. Sandler, R. Michels, R. P. Fonagy (Eds.), *Changing Ideas In A Changing World: The Revolution in Psychoanalysis. Essays in Honour of Arnold Cooper*, (pp. 57–64). London: Karnac.

Wallerstein, R. S. (2000). *Forty-Two Lives in Treatment: A Study of Psychoanalysis and Psychotherapy*. New York: The Analytic Press.

Widlöcher, D. (1996). *Les nouvelles cartes de la psychanalyse [Psychoanalysis: New Cards, New Approaches]*. Paris: Odile Jacob.

Winnicott, D. W. (1951). Objetos transicionais e fenômenos transicionais. In: *Textos selecionados da pediatria à psicanálise*. Rio de Janeiro: Francisco Alves, 1988.

Winnicott, D. W. (1956). Primary maternal preoccupation. In: *Collected Papers: Through Paediatrics to Psycho-Analysis*. London: Tavistock Publications, 1958.

Winnicott, D. W. (1958a). *Collected Papers. Through Paediatrics to Psycho-Analysis*. London: Tavistock and New York: Basic Books [reprinted as *Through Paediatrics to Psycho-Analysis*. London: Hogarth Press and The Institute of Psycho-Analysis (1975); reprinted London: Karnac, 1992].

Winnicott, D. W. (1958b). The capacity to be alone. *International Journal of Psychoanalysis, 39*: 416–420.

Winnicott, D. W. (1958c). The capacity to be alone, In: *The Maturational Processes and the Facilitating Environment*. London: Karnac, 1990.

Winnicott, D. W. (1960). The theory of the parent–infant relationship. *International Journal of Psychoanalysis, 41*: 585–595.

Winnicott, D. W. (1971). *Playing and Reality*. London: Tavistock.

INDEX

Abadi, M., 172, 181
Abelin-Sas, A., 155, 181
Abend, S. M., 80, 181
Ablon, S. J., 82–83, 181
Ablon, S. L., 83, 181
acting language, 73
acting on, 39
acting out (*agieren*), 3, 73, 90, 104,
    106, 138, 146, 173
active/passive pairing, 48
activity
    analytic, 121, 135
    interpretative, 101, 121, 123,
        125, 140
    mental, 71, 101, 132, 135, 139
    psychoanalytic, 136
    therapeutic, 82
Adler, G., 83, 181
Aesop, 14, 62
    Philosopher to the Wayfarer, 14,
        62
affect, 40, 58, 73, 82–84,
    106–107, 110, 125, 150–153,
    161–162
agieren (acting out), 169, 173

Aisenstein, M., 141, 182
Alkire, M. T., 160, 183
alliance, 80–82, 84, 86, 139
    therapeutic, 80–82, 87
    working, 41, 79–81
Alvarez, A., 154, 182
analysand, 2–5, 43, 53, 59–62, 64,
    67, 69–70, 75, 86, 88, 98,
    104–107, 112–113, 131, 164,
    166, 172, 177
anxiety, 4, 25, 45, 47, 110, 131,
    144, 150, 154–159, 161–162,
    178
    attachment, 158
    basic, 128, 130
    castration, 119
    convulsive, 111
    diminished, 133
    intrusion, 51, 110
    modulated, 129
    preservation, 157
    psychotic, 128
    separation, 51, 156–157
    state, 127, 161
    underlying, 39

aphasia, 65
après-coup, 50, 55, 102, 108
arousal, 152, 160–162
  level of, 150, 160–162
  state of, 161–163
associativity, viii, 62–65, 67,
  69–70, 74
  mental, 58, 76
  natural, 68
attachment, 25–26, 125, 139,
  155–156, 158, 163
  anxieties, 158
  figure(s), 157
  needs, 156–157, 159
  relationship(s), 156–157
  rupture of, 156
Atwood, G., 40, 193
Auschwitz, 142

Bachrach, H. M., 83, 182
bad faith, 97–98
Balint, M., 84, 182
Barale, F., 96, 182
Baranger, M., 82, 85, 97–98, 140,
  182
Baranger, W., 81–82, 182
Basile, R., 90, 185
Beebe, B., 85, 182
behaviour, 26, 131, 142, 155, 159
  active, 114
  addictive, 46
  bizarre, 143
  caregiving, 163
  detached, 142
  individual, 123
  narcissistic, 159
  nonverbal, 34, 39
  promiscuous, 95
  strange, 28
Bergeret, J., 2, 182
Bion, W. R., 4, 90–92, 98,
  100–101, 107–108, 111–112,

  120, 122–123, 128–136,
  140–141, 145, 182
  H, 130
  K, 98, 128, 130, 145
  L, 130
  O, 98, 101, 129, 131–133, 145
  PS/PS–D/PD, 90, 130,
    145–146
  –R, 93
Blatt, S. J., 81–83, 182–183
Bleandonu, G., 131, 183
Bleichmar, H., 154–158, 163, 183
Blum, H. P., 84, 183
Bollas, C., 166, 173, 183
Börne, L., 64
Braitenberg, V., 65, 183
Brandchaft, B., 40, 193
Brazilian Federation of
  Psychoanalysis, 137
Brenner, C., 80, 183
Breuer, J., 28, 72, 108–111, 118,
  124, 185, 187

Cahill, L., 160, 183, 192
Cahn, R., 43, 183
Caligor, E., 83, 183
Canestri, J., 120, 183
case studies
  Claudia, 94
  Luisa, 95–96
  Mr B, 45–47, 55
  patient A, 102, 141
  Roberta, 93
Cassorla, R., 145, 183
Castonguay, L. G., 82, 184
Civitarese, G., 98, 185
Clyman, R. B., 151, 184
Collovà, M., 98, 185
complex(es), 14, 24, 153
  father, 18, 68
  Oedipus, 68, 153, 166,
    171–172, 174, 177

conflict
  intrapsychic, 46
  narcissistic, 46
  psychic, 123
  theory, 34
  unconscious, 5
  unresolved, 126
conscious(ness), 28, 67–68, 85,
    104, 122–124, 127, 129, 134,
    138, 140–141, 150–152, 157
  awareness, 124
  communication, 125
  dynamics, 104
  ideas, 29
  knowledge, 28, 149
  pre-, 93, 105–107, 121,
    123–125
  state, 152
  subjectivisation, 160
  thought, 28
  will, 105
co-pensée, 85
coprophilic, 24
Corkin, S., 161, 189
Couch, A. S., 79, 184
countertransference, 3–4, 34,
    39–41, 70, 76, 78–79, 81–82,
    85–86, 104, 109, 116,
    125–127, 165
  reciprocal, 169
  responses, 40
  transference-, 138, 161
Curtis, H., 80, 184

David, C., 105
Davis, M. K., 82, 190
de Álvarez de Toledo, L. G., 167,
    182
death, 112
  allergy to, 94
  ambassador of, 174
  child's, 147

drive, 166, 169, 172
  instinct, 107, 127–128
Debiec, J., 160, 184
de Clérambault, G., 105
dementia praecox, 10, 74
dependence, 46–49, 131
  infantile, 47
  normal, 46
  primary, 46–47
  substance, 47
depression, 46, 51
  anti-, 95
  position, 47, 128, 133, 145
  symptoms, 54
de Quervain, D. J., 160–161, 192
development(al), 11, 35, 58, 89,
    99–101, 122, 124, 127–130,
    138, 140, 144, 149
  ego-, 112
  emotional, 47
  erotic, 48
  of a rapport, 39, 41
  of analysis, 89
  of anxiety states, 127
  of object relations, 127
  of psychoanalysis, 1, 58, 75,
    121, 134, 171
  of transference, 84
  personal, 53
  personality, 12
dialectical relationship, 70
Dickes, R., 83, 184
Dispaux, M. F., 50, 184
distress, 10, 13, 38–39, 46–49, 59
  emotional, 132
  material, 19
Dolan, R. J., 161, 189
Donnet, J.-L., 2, 49–50, 52, 184
Donovan, J., 83, 183
Doyle, A. C., 99
dream, 66, 75, 91–92, 96, 98–102,
    108, 113, 124–125, 140, 151

analyst's, 100
day, 141
Dora's, 66
-for-two, 143, 145
functioning, 93
images, 124
night, 141
patient's, 54, 100
recurrent, 142
screen, 113
shared, 93
systematic analysis of, 1
thought, 92
waking, 92
work, 141
Drysdale, E., 160, 192
dyad, 83–84
  patient, 81
  therapeutic, 81–82

Ebmeier, K. P., 160, 192
ego, 2, 5, 47–48, 57, 65, 77, 112,
    127–129, 135, 138, 169–174,
    176
  analyst's, 107
  -centric, 160
  -development, 112
  -distonic, 168
  early, 128
  function, 65
  ideal, 159, 174, 176–177
  inner, 98
  normal, 168
  splitting, 175
  super, 2, 75, 89, 94, 98, 107, 114,
    116, 127, 171, 174, 176
  Oedipal, 117
  -syntonic, 168
Einfälle, 92
Emperor Joseph II, 19
enactment, 34, 39, 46, 56, 71–72,
    151

verbal, 70
epistemophilia, 109
erotic(ism), 104, 138, 177
  auto-, 48
  contact, 114
  development, 48
  seduction, 111
  transference, 111, 177
European Psychoanalytic
    Federation, 121
excitation, 48–49, 162
  defence mechanism, 95
  drive, 111
  traumatic, 110

fantasy, 40, 72, 81, 87, 143, 173
  life, 126
  object, 125
father, 112, 173, 175
  -complex, 18, 68
  grand-, 95, 142–143
  imago, 177
  Oedipal, 114
  suggestion, 60
fear, 16, 52, 103, 110–111, 175,
    177–178
  analyst's, 103
  factor, 110
  Oedipal, 153
  of abandonment, 47
  of castration, 174
  of dependence, 46
  of dying, 112
  of sexual penetration, 110
  persistent, 80
Federn, E., 66, 192
Fèdida, P., 54, 184
Ferenczi, S., 60, 75, 79, 185
Ferro, A., 90, 92, 96–98, 100,
    140–141, 145, 182, 185
Fischmann, T., 162, 190
fixation points (idées fixes), 66

Fodor, J. A., 149, 185
Fonagy, P., vii, 150–151, 185
Foresti, G., 98, 185
Fossaghe, J. L., 163, 190
free association, viii, 4–5, 39, 64,
    67, 89, 92, 107, 115, 122–123,
    168–170
  breakdown in, 64
  patient's, 92
  potential for, 43
  process of, 39
  resistance to, 39
  rule of, 58, 63, 66, 74
Freud, A., 79, 185
Freud, S. (*passim*)
  "A note on the prehistory of the
    technique of analysis", 64
  An Outline of Psycho-Analysis, 73,
    178
  "Analysis terminable and
    interminable", 75, 168
  Anna O, 111
  Beyond the Pleasure Principle,
    169, 171–172
  "Constructions in analysis", 3,
    75, 78, 138, 178
  Dora, 1, 19, 66, 124, 176
  "Fetishism", 174
  *Fragment of an Analysis of a Case
    of Hysteria*, 19, 66, 176
  Frau Emmy von N, 109–111,
    113–118
  *Group Psychology and the Analysis
    of the Ego*, 24, 175
  Inhibitions, Symptoms and Anxiety,
    30, 154
  "Instincts and their
    vicissitudes", 167
  *Introductory Lectures on
    Psycho-analysis Part III*, 30,
    126
  Irma, 66

Letter from Freud to Ludwig
    Binswanger, 20 February,
    1913, 81
*Letters of Sigmund Freud,
    1873–1939*, 111
"Lines of advance in
    psycho-analytic therapy",
    50, 75
Monday crust, 13, 37, 49
"Mourning and melancholia",
    75
*Notes upon a Case of Obsessional
    Neurosis*, 66
"Observations on
    transference-love", 57, 59,
    103, 118–119
"Obsessive actions and religious
    practices", 72
On Aphasia. A Critical Study, 65
"On beginning the treatment",
    (*passim*)
  facsimile, 9–30
"On narcissism: an
    introduction", 43, 171, 173
"On psychotherapy", 2, 9, 44
"On the history of the
    psycho-analytic
    movement", 57
"On the theory of hysterical
    attacks", 72
"On transformations of instinct
    as exemplified in anal eroti-
    cism", 68, 76
Project for a Scientific Psychology,
    47, 65
Rat Man, 1, 66
"Recommendations to
    physicians practising
    psychoanalysis", 4, 9
"Remembering, repeating and
    working-through", 57, 60,
    63

"Repression", 151
"Some character types met with in psychoanalytic work", 75
"Some general remarks on hysterical attacks", 19, 72–73
Studies on Hysteria, 23, 28, 66–67, 70–71, 109, 114, 118, 124
"The claims of psycho-analysis to scientific interest", 71, 74
"The dissolution of the Oedipus complex", 153
"The dynamics of transference", 19, 24, 177
The Ego and the Id, 138, 171
The Interpretation of Dreams, 63, 66, 124, 141
"The question of lay analysis", 78
"The 'uncanny' ", 168–171
"The unconscious", 16, 29, 149
Totem and Taboo, 43
trial period, 2, 10, 14, 34, 43–44
Wolf Man, 118, 170
Freudian
model, 33
point, 34
Friedman, L., 155, 186
fundamental rule, viii, 2–4, 20–21, 24, 30, 63–64, 67, 69, 74, 88, 91–93, 97, 102, 104, 106–107

Garske, J. P., 82, 190
Gay, P., 138, 187
George, C., 163, 193
German Romantic Movement, 64, 65
Gill, M., 38, 40, 187
Goldfried, M. R., 82, 184
Gougoulis, N., 52, 184

Green, A., 5–6, 48, 54, 84, 105, 117, 141, 145, 166, 171, 174, 188
Greenberg, J., 40, 188
Greenson, R. R., 79–81, 188
Groddeck, G., 60, 188
Grotstein, J., 90, 98, 100, 141, 188
Guignard, F., 140–141, 188
Guiter, M., 169, 188

Hamilton, M., 83, 183
Hawellek, B., 161, 189
Hayes, A. M., 82, 184
Hebb, D., 65, 189
Heimann, P., 140, 189
helplessness (Hilflosigkeit), 47, 143
Holocaust, 142–143
Hugo, V., 98
Les Misérables, 98
Hurlemann, R., 161, 189
hypnosis, 67, 70, 108–109, 113, 115–116
hysteria, 10–11, 70–73 see also: Freud, S., Studies on Hysteria
hysterical
attacks, 19, 27, 72–73
patient, 27, 67
symptoms, 10, 108

id, 107, 127, 138
idées fixes (fixation points), 66
in crescendo, 93, 102
in vivo, 107
Inderbitzen, L. B., 82, 190
inquiétante étrangeté, 168
instinct, 103, 151
death, 107, 127–128
for looking, 20
impulse, 171
International Psychoanalytic Association (IPA), 37, 49, 121, 167

interpretation, viii, 3, 5, 20,
    38–39, 56, 58, 62, 66, 75,
    84–85, 89–91, 97, 106,
    120–127, 129, 131–135,
    138–139, 142, 145–146, 154,
    157–162, 170, 177
  analyst's, 106, 131, 168
  analytic, 105
  building of, 120
  classical, 154
  construction of, 120
  correct, 133, 145
  creation of, 121
  Deutung, 123
  early, 38
  evacuative, 146
  formulating, 122
  magic power of, 177
  mutative, 145
  narrative, 146
  operative, 134
  premature, 138
  production of, 122
  psychoanalytical, 123,
    134–135
  reconstructive, 145
  saturated, 145
  technique of, 2–3
  transference, 38, 64, 99, 146
  unsaturated, 96, 140, 145
  verbal, 122
  weak, 145

Jacobs, T., 40, 189
Janet, P., 66
Jean Favreau Centre, 52
Jiménez, J. P., 162, 189
Jones, Enrico E., 82, 181
Jones, Ernest, 126, 189
juvenile delinquencies, 28

Kantrowitz, J. L., 40, 83, 189

Keats, J., 111, 189
  The Man of Achievement, 111
Kensinger, E. A., 161, 189
Klein, M., 38, 40, 90, 108, 112,
    128, 133, 189
Knoblauch, S., 85, 182
Kohut, H., 38, 84, 189
Kolsch, H., 161, 189

Lacan, J., 59, 85, 90, 105–106,
    108, 118, 189
Lachmann, F. M., 163, 190
Laplanche, J., 88, 135, 190
lapsus calami, 70
Leclaire, S., 174, 177, 190
LeDoux, J. E., 65, 160, 184, 190
Leuzinger-Bohleber, M., 162, 190
level, 42, 122, 127, 158, 161, 168,
    176
  biological, 152
  conscious, 123, 129
  epistemological, 135
  fine-tuned, 86
  informative, 135
  instrumental, 135
  international, 37
  manifest, 73
  of abstract thinking, 129
  of activation, 150, 161–162
  of agitation, 161
  of arousal, 150, 160–161, 163
  of awareness of deception, 97
  of censorship, 63
  of functioning, 111
  of intensity, 155
  of mental state, 133, 135
  of symbolisation, 162
  of thought, 130
  of understanding, 111
  of vitality, 161
  pre-conscious, 123
  primitive, 110

representational, 151
semantic, 135
unconscious, 123, 129
university, 46
Levy, I., 153, 190
Levy, S. T., 82, 190
Lewin, B., 113, 190
Lichtenberg, J. D., 155, 163, 190
life, 18–19, 45, 51–52, 54, 65, 74,
    80, 95, 120, 139, 151, 156,
    165, 169, 177–178
active, 14
as a symptom, 100–101
battle for, 170
brought to, 3
circumstances, 37
daily, 13, 127
demands, 45
drive, 166, 168, 172
events, 65
everyday, 174
fantasy, 126
history, 20, 22–23, 54
individual's, 72
instinct, 127–128
mental, 48, 63
modern, 55
new, 178
of human beings, 68
of the unconscious, 68
ordinary, 16
-oriented, 112
person's, 74
project, 170
psychic, 100, 112
real, 13, 80
sexual, 17
social, 68
uncertainties of, 122
Lipton, S. D., 80, 190
Little, M., 40, 190
Loewald, H., 40, 190

Luber, B., 83, 183
Lyons-Ruth, K., 150, 190

MacCormack, V., 83, 183
Madea, B., 161, 189
Maier, W., 161, 189
Mannoni, M., 164, 190
Martin, D. J., 82, 190
Marucco, N., 166–169, 171–172,
    174–175, 177, 188, 191
Matusch, A., 161, 189
Mazzacane, F., 98, 185
McDougall, J., 173–174, 191
McGaugh, J. L., 160–161, 192
Mello Franco Filho, O., 140, 191
Meltzer, D., 144, 191
memory, 54–55, 71, 90, 92, 101,
    107, 117, 129, 132–133,
    160–161
accumulation, 132
agonic, 174
conscious awareness of, 124
declarative, 151, 158
excluding, 132
forgotten, 123
implicit, 151
long-term, 160
loss of, 27
of the madeleine, 54
of traumatic experiences, 160
origin of, 132
plastic, 118
procedural, 150–151, 158
reconsolidation of, 160
repressed, 124
stimulating, 132
traces, 132
traumatic, 110, 124
understanding, 132
unquestionable, 139
without, 130
Menaker, E., 79, 191

metapsychology, 29, 57, 106, 108, 123, 129, 132, 134
Minazio, N., 52, 184
Ministry of Justice, 28
Mitchell, S. A., 40, 150, 188, 191
Molinari, E., 98, 185
Monday crust, 13, 37, 49
Moreno, J., 139, 141, 191
mother, 16, 26–27, 47–48, 93, 95 111–112, 114, 119, 129, 161, 173–174, 178
  body, 126
  borderline, 162
  castration, 175
  -Goddess, 175
  grand-, 93
  hate, 175
  -hood, 112
  –infant relationship, 40–41, 129–130, 144
  phallic, 174–178
  receptacle, 142
  severe, 114
  style, 161
Mother Teresa, 94
motivational
  components, 159
  power, 156
  systems, 150, 155–159, 162–163
  valency, 156, 158–159, 163
  weight, 156, 158, 163
M'Uzan, M. de, 105–106, 119, 191

Nacht, S., 84, 191
narcissism/narcissistic, 46, 75, 158–159, 166, 169, 173–174
  anxiety, 157
  behaviour, 159
  blow, 34
  capsule, 47
  child, 176, 178

complex, 172
  conception of, 57
  conflicts, 46
  desires, 156
  gratification, 157, 159
  motivational system, 158, 163
  object relations, 127
  paradoxes of, 75
  pathology, 75
  patients, 83
  patterns, 57
  pride, 24
  problems, 50
  satisfaction, 156, 159
  structures, 175–177
  suffering, 157
  system, 156–157
  theory of, 57
  wishes, 155
Narcissus, 168–170, 175
Nasio, J. D., 173, 191
Nazi concentration camp, 142
negative capability, 90, 111, 130, 141, 143–145
Nemas, C., 144, 191
neuro-vegetative activation, 152, 160, 162
neurosis, 10, 12, 15–16, 19–20, 22–24, 27, 60, 67, 81, 140, 169, 172, 175
  fate, 167, 172–173
  obsessional, 10–11, 15
  transference, 49, 60, 172
  infantile, 80
Neyraut, M., 176, 192
nosographic factors, 46
Nunberg, H., 66, 192

object, 3, 47, 125, 135, 157, 173, 177–178
  desirable, 155

external, 47, 126
fantasy, 125
internal, 114, 116
narcissistic, 127
of analytical investigation, 12
of desire, 124, 153
of positive transference, 5
of repression, 155
of sexuality, 156
of study, 123
of the drive, 176, 178
primary, 112, 126–127
psychoanalytic, 135
real, 124
relations, 40, 85, 127–128
school, 40
sexual, 178
transference, 78
whole, 127
O'Carroll, R. E., 160, 192
Oedipal
desires, 172
father, 114
fears, 153
hatred, 103
love, 103
mother, 114
rival, 109
scene, 126
structures, 175–177
superego, 117
transference, 176
wishes, 153
Oedipus, 167–168, 170, 175
complex, 68, 153, 171–172,
174, 177
stage, 175
Ogden, T. H., 85, 90, 92, 98,
100–101, 140–141, 192
Okuda, S., 160–161, 192
Oxford English Dictionary, 139,
192

paranoid–schizoid position, 133,
135, 145
paraphrenia, 10–11, 34
phenomena, 102, 122
striking, 63
transference, 63
unconscious, 150, 152
Pilkonis, P. A., 81, 183
Pirandello, L., 102, 137, 144,
146–147, 192
Politi, P., 98, 185
Pontalis, J. B., 88, 135, 190
primal
children, 173
fantasies, 76
identification, 173
repression, 151
scene, 48
time, 173, 177
process(es)
affective, 151
analytic, 34–35, 39, 41, 61,
77–78, 91, 97, 104–105,
108, 112–113, 124, 134,
145–146, 166
psycho-, 59–60, 121–122, 134,
166
complicated, 16
conscious thought-, 28
defensive, 152, 154
healing, 125, 135
hysterical, 73
identification, 127
interpreting, 124
listening, 38
mental, 4, 9, 28, 43
normal, 46
of development, 75
of free association, 39
of knowing, 128
of modularisation, 149
of mutual regulation, 161

of projective identification,
    132
of psychic change, 122
of recovery, 17
of sublimation, 111
of suffering, 147
of the cure, 126
of thought, 28
primary, 5, 122
psychic, 112
reciprocal, 153
secondary, 5, 51, 122, 171
    thought, 106–107
symbolisation, 126
tertiary, 5
thinking, 129–130
transference, 62, 83, 176
transformational, 135
treatment, 61
unconscious, 16, 86, 124, 152
projective identification, 3, 101,
    128–130, 132
proto-
    contents, 96
    emotion(al), 95–97, 101–102
    sensoriality, 100
psychoanalytic interpretation,
    123, 134–135
psychoanalytic method, 58, 64,
    66, 68–69, 123, 128, 164
psychoanalytic therapeutic action,
    123

Quinlan, D. M., 81, 183

Racker, H., 40, 192
Raue, P. J., 82, 184
relationship, 12, 18, 46, 56, 69,
    72, 80–84, 86, 94–95, 107,
    109, 140, 143, 151, 157–159
    analytic, 41, 79, 82–83, 119,
        146, 167

attachment, 156–157
close, 139, 141
complex, 149
current, 127
dialectical, 70
everyday, 80
family, 22
hateful, 112
human, 47, 79, 154
intersubjective, 85, 87
models of, 46
mother–infant, 129
object, 127
of mutual confidence, 139
real, 79–80, 87
sexual, 142
therapeutic, 158, 162
treatment, 78
variables, 8
repression, 2–3, 16, 28, 37, 92,
    101, 114, 119, 150–153, 168,
    172
    dynamics of, 124
    object of, 155
    primal, 151
    primary, 107, 118
    simple, 153
Robert dictionnaire, 139, 192
Roose, S. P., 83, 183
Roozendaal, B., 160–161, 192
Rothstein, A., 34–35, 192
Roussillon, R., 3, 65, 75, 192
Rustin, J., 85, 182

schism, 127
schizo–paranoid, 128, 133, 135,
    145
Schneier, H., 83, 183
Schüz, A., 65, 183
scopophilia, 20
self, 48, 72–73, 151–152
    -analysis, 21, 176, 178

-appropriate, 50
-aware(ness), 40
-complacency, 26
-conservation, 156
-control, 60
-definition, 98
-destruction, 171–172
-disclosure, 85, 91
-evident, 49
-expression, 81, 84
-identity, 46
-image, 157
-induced hypnosis, 113
-knowledge, 5, 164
-less, 173
-love, 173
-preservation, 17, 155–157
-protection, 150
-psychology, 38, 83, 85
-questioning, 172
-reference, 57
-revealing, 78
-righteousness, 107
-soothing, 48
sexual, 150, 163
    abstinence, 109
    acting out, 138
    aggression, 24
    attack, 4
    de-, 68
    drives, 170–171
    factors, 17
    harassment, 114
    impulse, 177
    life, 17
    matters, 17
    needs, 155
    object, 178
    orientation, 128
    penetration, 110
    potency, 16, 119
    provocation, 109

    relationship, 142
sexuality, 48, 68, 110, 156–157,
        168
    bi-, 73
    homo-, 24, 27, 119
    tendencies, 4
    infantile, 124
Shajahan, P., 160, 192
Shakespeare, W., 103, 111, 192
Shedler, J., 82, 192
silence
    analysand's, 5
    analyst's, 104, 108, 113
    analytic, 106–107, 113, 116–117
    capacity for, 111
    idealogical, 108
    inner, 106
    of our minds, 117
    psychoanalytical, 108–111
    quality of, 112
    virtues of, 109
Sneed, J., 83, 183
Solomon, J., 163, 193
Solomon, M., 83, 182
Sorter, D., 85, 182
Spitz, R. C., 153, 193
splitting, 5, 80, 95, 97, 172, 176
    ego, 175
    unconscious, 154
statu nascendi, 2
Stern, B. L., 83, 183
Stern, D. N., 185, 193
Stolorow, R. D., 40, 193
Stone, L., 79, 83, 193
stricto sensu, 1, 45, 56
Strupp, H. H., 82–83, 193
symptoms, 37–38, 65, 71, 101,
        109, 111, 119, 123–124,
        168–169, 172–173, 175
    depressive, 54
    first, 24
    hysterical, 108

obsessional, 10
of conversion hysteria, 71
of disease, 16, 29
psychiatric, 100
relief from, 59
reversibility of, 124
translation of, 26
system
adrenergic, 160
digestive, 130
emotional, 163
hetero-preservation, 156, 163
motivational, 150, 155–159,
162–163
narcissistic, 156–157
navigation, 91
noradrenergic, 160
psychobiological regulation,
157
systematic
acts, 97
analysis, 1
description, 89
narrative, 22
presentation, 9, 138
Szecsödy, I., 79, 193

technique
analytic, 27, 40, 64, 80, 103,
109, 118, 137
artificial, 83
classical, 155
hypnotic, 24
of cure, 138
of interpretation, 2–3
of investigation, 109
psychoanalytic, 1–4, 20, 57, 66,
75, 81, 88, 138, 171
theory of, 122
therapeutic, 162
theory, 81, 87, 121, 128, 133, 164,
170–173

analytic, 165
associative, 67
conflict, 34
contemporary, 34
field, 98
Freudian, vii, 170
of cure, 165
of hysterical attacks, 72
of mental functioning, 67, 69,
127
of mind, 121
of narcissism, 57
of psychical representation, 65
of symbolism, 126
of technique, 122
psychoanalytic, vii, xiii, 75, 165
Topos of Neverland, 113
transference, viii, 1–4, 11, 17, 20,
24–25, 29–30, 35, 38–41,
58–64, 69–76, 78–79, 81–87,
99, 103–104, 108–109, 115,
117, 122, 124–126, 138, 145,
153, 159, 164–166, 169–171,
175–178
analytic, 35
arena, 61
attitude, 11
collateral, 92, 99
–countertransference, 3, 86,
138, 161
effective, 25, 139
erotic, 111, 177
idealised, 177
impulse, 79
inhibited, 177–178
interpretation, 38
lateral, 62
love, 57–59, 103, 177
material, 38
negative, 177
neurosis, 2, 5, 11, 46, 49–50,
60, 80, 172

non-, 79
object, 78
Oedipal, 176
perceptions, 38
phenomena, 76, 172
positive, 5, 38, 41, 116, 125,
    176–178
reciprocal, 175–177
-relation, 18
-resistance, 25, 30, 38
showing-, 70
sublimated, 177
unanalysable, 35
unconscious, 61
transferential, 110, 145
    counter-, 90
    guilt, 115
    non-, 79
    processes, 83

unconscious(ness), 28, 37, 41, 60,
    67, 68, 80, 90, 92–93, 100,
    102, 123, 129, 138, 140–141,
    149–154, 157–158, 162
active, 153
communication, 85–86
conception, 76
concepts, 68
conflict, 5
desire, 154
dynamics, 104
formation, 150
idea, 63
influence, 62, 71
logic, 68
messages, 122
motives, 61
networks, 67
non-verbal, 105
organisation, 150
originary, 150–152

phantasy, 128
phenomena, 150, 152
process, 16, 86, 124, 152
reality, 123
recollection, 28
repressed, 174
resistance, 149
sector, 162–163
splitting, 154
thoughts, 20
transference, 61
transmission, 40
work, 124
Untergang, 153–155, 174

Viederman, M., 83–84, 193
Vogeley, K., 161, 189

Wallerstein, R. S., vii, 82, 193
Weber, J. J., 83, 182
Wexler, M., 79, 188
Widlöcher, D., 85, 193
Wininger, L., 83, 183
Winnicott, D. W., 3, 47–48, 108,
    110, 112–113, 146, 161,
    193–194
Wiser, S. L., 82, 184
Wollersen, H., 161, 189
world
    criminal, 95
    external, 53–54
    internal, 54, 90, 115
    new, 99–100
    of language, 74
    possible, 89, 94, 99, 101
    real, 18, 53
    under-, 103

Zertrüm-merung, 153
Zuroff, D. C., 81, 183
Zweig, S., 111